Third Edition
Solutions

Advanced

Student's Book

Tim Falla **Paul A Davies**
Jane Hudson

OXFORD
UNIVERSITY PRESS

Word Skills	F Reading	G Speaking	H Writing
Phrasal verbs (1) parable/Inseparable nsitive/Intransitive ctionary work e of English	**p14 Bad beginnings** Bad beginnings **Strategy:** Locating information in a text **Vocabulary:** Nouns formed from phrasal verbs **Critical analysis:** Metaphors	**p16 Interview** **Strategy:** Using complex sentences **Key phrases:** Introducing reasons and explanations; Marking a change of topic **Use of English** 🎧 An interview	**p17 Opinion essay** **Strategy:** How to write an opinion essay **Vocabulary:** Personality **Grammar:** Linking adverbs
Writing: Opinion essay			
Compounds An internet hoax cabulary: Nouns from rasal verbs	**p26 *The Woman in White*** A strange encounter **Strategy:** Summarising a text **Critical analysis:** Formal literary language	**p28 Photo comparison** **Strategy:** Comparing photos **Grammar:** Speculating **Key phrases:** Comparing and contrasting photos; Expressing opinions 🎧 Photo descriptions	**p29 Film review** **Strategy:** Evaluating a film **Vocabulary:** Adjectives to describe films
Metaphors and similes cabulary: Metaphors and niles	**p36 Animal partnerships** Symbiosis: a mutual understanding **Strategy:** Gapped-paragraph tasks **Critical analysis:** Emphatic adjectives	**p38 Collaborative task** **Strategy 1:** Avoiding repeating words **Strategy 2:** Negotiating an agreement **Key phrases:** Talking about advantages and disadvantages; Disagreeing politely; Asking if your partner agrees; Conceding a point; Concluding the discussion 🎧 A discussion about friendships	**p39 A proposal** **Strategy:** Structuring a proposal **Key phrases:** Stating the purpose; Background information; Making recommendations and suggestions; Final recommendations
Speaking: Collaborative task • Writing: Proposal			
Binomial pairs cabulary: Binomial pairs	**p48 How language changes us** Can learning a language rewire your brain? **Strategy:** Answering multiple-choice questions **Vocabulary:** Speech verbs **Critical analysis:** Direct speech in fiction	**p50 Discussion** **Strategy:** Using rhetorical questions **Key phrases:** Acknowledging without agreeing **Vocabulary:** Adjectives to describe change 🎧 A discussion about inventions	**p51 Letter to an editor** **Strategy:** Appropriate language for a formal letter **Vocabulary:** Formal and informal equivalents
Dependent prepositions ctionary work eaking: Opinions on olence Is violent protest ever stified?	**p58 'Why?' 'Because it was there!'** **Strategy:** Gapped-text tasks **Vocabulary:** Intensifying adverbs **Critical analysis:** Techniques in fiction	**p60 Photo comparison** **Strategy:** Speaking for a minute **Speaking:** Speaking for one minute on a chosen topic **Key phrases:** Fillers and paraphrasing; Speculating 🎧 Photo comparison	**p61 For and against essay** **Strategy:** Following a logical structure (paragraphing) **Key phrases:** Introducing and listing arguments; Introducing a similar and opposing points; Putting the same idea in a different way
Speaking: Talking about photos • Writing: Letter to an editor			
Phrasal verbs (2) rasal verbs: literal and omatic meaning	**p70 I have a dream** Is Martin Luther King's 'I have a dream' the greatest speech in history? **Strategy:** Identifying similarities and differences in texts 🎧 The Lincoln Memorial **Critical analysis:** Sophisticated language	**p72 Debate** **Strategy:** Structuring arguments **Key phrases:** Discourse markers	**p73 An informal email** **Strategy:** Style and conventions of emails **Key phrases:** Showing empathy
Verb patterns	**p80 Time traveller** John Titor, Time traveller **Strategy:** Using paragraph openers to locate key information **Vocabulary:** Describing rumour and possibility **Critical analysis:** Understanding cliché	**p82 Collaborative task** **Strategy:** Asking open questions **Vocabulary:** Types of holiday; On holiday **Key phrases:** Eliciting a response; Revision advantages and disadvantages Talking about advantages and disadvantages	**p83 Letter of complaint** **Strategy:** Using more sophisticated language **Vocabulary:** Travel problems
Writing: Letter of complaint			
Prefixes and suffixes	**p92 Trade secrets** Trade Secrets **Strategy:** Multiple-matching tasks **Vocabulary:** Collocations **Critical analysis:** Avoiding repetition	**p94 Discussion** **Strategy:** Listening to other speakers **Key phrases:** Agreeing and disagreeing; Adding and justifying your opinion **Vocabulary:** Discourse markers 🎧 A discussion	**p95 Discursive essay** **Strategy:** Including all the points in the task and writing in an appropriate style **Key phrases:** Causes and consequences
Collocations with mmon verbs (*come, do, put nd take*) se of English 🎧 Four speakers talk about oilers	**p102 Grand finale** Final page vs closing scene **Strategy:** Identifying paraphrasing **Critical analysis:** Standard verbs vs phrasal verbs	**p104 Collaborative task** **Strategy:** Sharing interaction equally **Key phrases:** Dealing with, allowing and rejecting interruptions; Continuing after an interruption **Vocabulary:** Synonyms for *important*	**p105 A report** **Strategy:** Structuring a report **Key phrases:** Evaluating an experience; Comparing and contrasting different aspects
Writing: Discursive essay			

I Introduction

IA Grammar

Past simple and present perfect

I can use the past simple and present perfect tenses.

1 Read what the people say about learning English. Which experiences and opinions do you share? Which do you not share?

2 Find all the examples of the past simple, present perfect simple and present perfect continuous in the speech bubbles. When do we use the three tenses? Check your ideas in the Grammar Builder.

➤ Grammar Builder I.1 page 131

3 Complete the sentences with the verbs below. Use the past simple, present perfect simple or present perfect continuous. Say why you chose each tense.

belong bump into know leave look for not meet
move phone run see wait work out

1 Dave is at home. I know because he _____ me just a few minutes ago.
2 How long _____ you _____ that you have a half-brother?
3 Jason _____ his personal training business since he _____ to London in 2015.
4 This ring _____ to me since my grandmother _____ it to me three years ago.
5 I wish the bus would come. I _____ for it for ages!
6 He's very sweaty because he _____ at the gym.
7 If you _____ my friend Sam, I'll introduce you.
8 I must buy this jacket. It's just what I _____.
9 '_____ you _____ Darren lately?' 'Yes, I _____ him this morning in town.'

4 In your notebook, complete each sentence twice using the past simple and the present perfect simple or continuous. Use the verbs in brackets. Say how the meaning changes.

1 I (not see) Kate for three months.
2 My grandad (work) in that factory for many years.
3 Ryan (text) me three times this morning.
4 I (not visit) Greece in the summer.
5 Harry (play) the piano for years, but he (not make) much progress.
6 I (not have) any breakfast this morning.
7 Jack (spend) six years training to become a doctor.
8 I (use) the same smartphone for at least two years.

5 🎧 **1.02** Listen to five people talking about learning English. For each person, say what they have found most difficult and why.

6 🎧 **1.02** Listen again. For each person, say what they have done to overcome their problems.

Though I've been learning English since I was a little kid, I've never had the opportunity to travel to an English-speaking country.

I struggled with English at first, but I've come on in leaps and bounds in the past couple of years.

As soon as I've finished my exams, I'm hoping to spend some time abroad. I might go to Britain or Ireland.

I've already passed First Certificate – I got a B – and I've just registered for the CAE exam next summer.

7 Complete the phrases the speakers used.

1 learn words in _____ / in isolation
2 memorise _____ phrases
3 an incomprehensible _____ of sound
4 part of my _____ vocabulary
5 get my _____ round a word / sound
6 _____ pattern
7 _____ endings
8 _____ order

8 SPEAKING Work in pairs. Ask and answer. Use the ideas in the listening and the phrases in exercise 7 to help you.

1 Which of the following areas have you struggled with? Why?
   a grammar and sentence structure   e reading
   b vocabulary   f writing
   c speaking   g pronunciation
   d listening   and intonation
2 What have you done to overcome the problems? How successful have you been?
3 What is your 'top tip' for other learners of English?

➤ Vocabulary Builder Language terms: page 126

Grammar

Past tenses

I can use different past tenses correctly.

1 SPEAKING Work in pairs. Discuss the questions.

1 How long does it take to learn a language well?
2 Are there ways to speed up the process, do you think?

2 Read the text. How successful was David Bailey's attempt to learn French quickly? How do you know?

It was the summer of 2005 and British internet entrepreneur David Bailey was staying with a French friend in a tiny village in France. As a student, David had learned Spanish to a fluent standard, but since then, he'd been working so hard that he hadn't had time to study French. So he had decided to learn French – and learn quickly. In France, David set up a strict daily routine. In the mornings, he woke up and wrote out regular and irregular verb tables for about two hours. While he was writing, he listened to language-learning CDs. Then he ran for 45–60 minutes in the French countryside. He listened to catchy French music as he was running – and sang along! In the afternoons, if he wasn't playing darts or boules with his French friends, he was reading *Charlie and the Chocolate Factory* in French. He found that reading books in French that he'd read in English as a child was a great language-learning tip. After seventeen days, David left the small village but he didn't go home immediately. He went to Paris, where he met a girl in a coffee shop. They hadn't been chatting for long when she commented on his excellent French. She was sure that he had been living in France for at least a year!

3 Find one affirmative and one negative example of these tenses in the text in exercise 2.

1 past simple ✓
2 past continuous ✓
3 past perfect simple
4 past perfect continuous ✓

➡ Grammar Builder I.2 page 131

4 Complete the sentences with the correct form of the verbs in brackets. Use tenses from exercise 3. Sometimes more than one answer is possible.

1 I _____ (get) ready for bed when the phone _____ (ring).
2 They _____ (not get) married until last month although they _____ (be) engaged for years.
3 He _____ (have) paint in his hair because he _____ (decorate) his room all morning.
4 I _____ (arrive) at 9 a.m. but he _____ (leave) for work already.
5 When I _____ (open) the curtains, I knew it _____ (rain) because the pavements _____ (be) still wet.
6 This morning, while we _____ (rehearse) for the school play, one of the teachers _____ (take) photos.

LOOK OUT!

After time expressions like *after, as soon as,* and *by the time* we can use the past simple or the past perfect simple and the meaning is the same.
After I'd finished / I finished dinner, I went out.

Without a time expression, the choice of tense is important because it tells us the sequence of events.
a *My parents got home. I tidied my room.*
b *My parents got home. I'd tidied my room.*

5 Read the Look out! box. What is the sequence of events in examples a) and b)?

6 Read the pairs of sentences. Explain the difference in meaning, if there is one.

1 a I took notes while the teacher was speaking.
  b I was taking notes while the teacher was speaking.
2 a Tom had been spending all his money on apps.
  b Tom had spent all his money on apps.
3 a When we saw the man, he climbed onto the roof.
  b When we saw the man, he'd climbed onto the roof.
4 a When I walked into the room, everyone cheered.
  b When I walked into the room, everyone was cheering.
5 a Grace had been making dinner when I arrived.
  b Grace had made dinner when I arrived.

7 Complete the text with the verbs in brackets. Use the past simple, past continuous or past perfect (simple or continuous). Sometimes more than one tense is possible.

In 2004, Daniel Tammet boarded a plane to Reykjavik accompanied by a TV crew. He **1**_____ (travel) to Iceland to attempt something incredible: Daniel **2**_____ (decide) to learn Icelandic in just one week. For several years, Daniel **3**_____ (surprise) people with his amazing mental abilities. A few months earlier, he **4**_____ (astound) experts by reciting the number pi to 22,500 decimal places from memory. And four years before that, he **5**_____ (come) fourth in the World Memory Championships. But in trying to learn such a difficult language in only seven days, he **6**_____ (take) on his greatest challenge so far. Although Daniel **7**_____ (learn) languages successfully for years, after two days of Icelandic, he **8**_____ (struggle). He **9**_____ (not make) much progress, it seemed. But then everything **10**_____ (change). 'Suddenly he was like a sponge,' his teacher remembers. 'He **11**_____ (absorb) grammar and vocabulary at an amazing speed.' After seven days, to see how well he **12**_____ (learn) the language, Daniel **13**_____ (appear) on TV and **14**_____ (succeed) in giving an interview in fluent Icelandic.

8 SPEAKING Work in pairs. Discuss what you have learned from the texts about learning a language. What were some of the reasons for David's and Daniel's success, in your opinion? Are there any tips you could copy for your own studies?

Grammar

Articles

I can use articles correctly.

1 SPEAKING Work in pairs. Discuss what effect (if any) these factors have on how people in your country speak: region, age, social position, ethnic background. Think about grammar and vocabulary as well as accent.

2 🎧 **1.03** Complete the text with *a*, *an*, *the* or – (no article). Then listen and check.

Of all the accents and dialects of England, ¹ _the_ most widely known is undoubtedly Cockney. Whenever ² _a_ British or American film features ³_____ working-class Londoners, you can be sure their lines will be peppered with Cockney slang. But ⁴ _the_ truth is, today's teenagers in the capital speak ⁵ _a_ new dialect, not Cockney. ⁶ _The_ dialect is used by ⁷_____ young working-class people from all the different ethnic groups in London. Experts call it MLE (Multicultural London English). For decades, ⁸_____ young have used ⁹ _–_ slang to communicate with each other. But MLE is different because it has some words and grammar rules of its own. For example, in standard English, you might say, 'I said I was tired' but ¹⁰ _a_ speaker of MLE would say, 'This is me: man's tired'. Some schools, like the Lilian Baylis School in London, have banned MLE from the classroom; ¹¹ _the_ idea is to force students to speak 'properly'. But whether that is such ¹² _a_ good idea is open to debate.

3 SPEAKING Work in pairs. Explain what MLE is and who speaks it. Talk about age, ethnic group and location.

4 Read the Learn this! box. Complete the rules with *a*, *an*, *the* or – (no article). Which examples can you find in the text in exercise 2?

LEARN THIS! Articles

1 We use _a_ :
  a to say what somebody's job is.
  b to mean 'per' or 'every'.
  c with numbers and measurements (hundred, kilo, etc.) to mean 'one'.
  d with singular nouns after the word *such* or *what*.

2 We use _the_ :
  a when there is only one of something (e.g. moon, sun).
  b with plural countries, oceans and seas, mountain ranges and rivers (United States, Pacific, Dead Sea, Alps, Danube, etc.).
  c with adjectives like *rich* and *old* to talk about a group of people.
  d with the plural form of a surname to refer to a married couple or a family (Beckhams, Kardashians).

3 We use _–_ :
  a with plural and uncountable nouns when we are talking in general.
  b with most cities, countries and continents (France, Asia, etc.).
  c with mountains (Mount Everest, Mount Fuji).

➡ **Grammar Builder I.3** page 132

I mean the sister innit. She's about 5 times bigger than you innit, Mark?

5 Discuss the difference in meaning between these sentences.

  1 a There's a call for you. It's Stephen King.
    b There's a call for you. It's a Stephen King.
    c There's a call for you. It's the Stephen King.
  2 a Would you like a biscuit or two?
    b Would you like one biscuit or two?
  3 a The school gym is perfect for indoor football.
    b A school gym is perfect for indoor football.
  4 a What do you think of school uniform?
    b What do you think of the school uniform?
  5 a I'm a manager at the local gym.
    b I'm the manager at a local gym.

6 Complete the sentences with *a*, *an*, *one*, *the* or – (no article).

  1 Young people in _–_ Europe are too strongly influenced by their peers in _the_ USA.
  2 Most teenagers know what _the_ correct way to speak is but they often choose to speak in _a_ different way.
  3 _one_ way or another, teenagers will create _an_ identity for themselves which is different from their parents; _the_ way they speak is just part of this process.
  4 _–_ young people need to speak and write correctly because _one_ day they will have to find _a_ job, and _the_ employers expect _–_ high standards.
  5 It doesn't matter how _____ people speak or write, even at _____ work, provided _the_ meaning is clear.
  6 You can't judge _a_ person's intelligence or education by just _one_ thing, such as _the_ way they speak.

7 SPEAKING Work in pairs. Discuss the sentences in exercise 6. Do you agree or disagree with them? Give reasons.

8 SPEAKING Work in pairs. Discuss the question below.

  1 Do you speak and write differently in different situations?
  2 Give examples of contexts in which you would speak and write in the most and least formal ways.

➡ **Vocabulary Builder** Colloquial contractions: page 126

Grammar

Talking about the future

I can talk about predictions, plans, offers, routines.

Do you think English will become more or less important as an international language in the future? Why?

1 SPEAKING Work in pairs. Discuss the question above. Consider the relevance and importance of the ideas below.

1 the importance of the internet
2 the success of China and India
3 the dominance of American popular culture
4 the influence of the former British Empire
5 communicating in business, science and travel
6 how easy is it to learn English

2 🎧 **1.04** Listen to five people talking about the importance of English in their future lives. In your opinion, who has the most compelling reason to learn English? Why?

3 🎧 **1.04** Listen again. Match speakers 1–5 with the questions A–G. There are two extra questions.

Which speaker ...

A hopes to specialise in foreign languages? ___
B wants to study English abroad? ___
C will find English indispensable? ___
D will have an advantage in the labour market? ___
E would like to be an English teacher? ___
F will use English only in their leisure time? ___
G will need English for travel? ___

LEARN THIS! Future forms

We use *will*:

a to talk about facts in the future.

b for predictions based on what we know.

c for plans when we're deciding what to do as we speak.

d for offers, promises, requests and refusals (*won't*).

e in the main clause of first conditional sentences.

We use *going to*:

f for predictions based on current evidence, e.g. something we can see.

g for plans when we've already decided what to do.

We use the **present continuous**:

h for personal arrangements, especially when we mention the time and/or place.

We use the **present simple** with future meaning:

i for routines, schedules and timetables.

j in future time clauses with *after, as soon as, before, once, unless, until* and *when*. The present perfect is also possible.

k in the *if* clause in first conditional sentences.

4 Read the Learn this! box and the examples from the listening below. Match the highlighted phrases 1–10 with uses a–k.

j 1 I'm planning to go abroad – as soon as I finish university.
d 2 I've promised mum I'll get a proper job, as she calls it.
i 3 The course starts in October.
g 4 I'm going to study engineering at university.
h 5 I'm meeting my teachers tomorrow to talk about the application process.
f 6 English is everywhere nowadays and it's going to become more important for sure.
a b 7 At the university I'm planning to study at, the teaching materials and lectures will all be in English.
c 8 I hope to add another language – hopefully German. In fact, thinking about it, I definitely will.
k, e b a 9 If I am able to speak English really well, it will give me an edge when applying for a job.
b e 10 After my degree, I think I'll continue to study, for a PhD.

➡ **Grammar Builder I.4** page 133

LOOK OUT!

• Sometimes there is no difference between *will* and *going to* for predictions.
  You're going to / You'll fail your exam if you don't revise.

• Sometimes there is no difference between *going to* and the present continuous for plans and arrangements.
  I'm going to see / I'm seeing Debbie this evening.

5 Read the Look out! box. Then complete the sentences with a future form. Sometimes more than one form is possible. Give reasons for your choice(s).

1 We've booked our summer holiday. We *are going to* (visit) Cuba.
2 Our English exams *are* ___ (be) on 23 and 24 June.
3 If I'm going to be late, I *'ll* ___ (text) you.
4 I'm fed up with my car breaking down. I *am going to* (sell) it.
5 *Are you going* (you / go) into town this morning? If so, I *will* ___ (give) you a lift.
6 The car engine is making a funny noise. I'm sure it *will* ___ (break down).
7 I'm short of money. I'm afraid I *will* ___ (have to) sell my bike.
8 I *will* ___ (phone) you as soon as I ___ (know) what time the film *starts* ___ (start).

6 SPEAKING Work in pairs. Ask and answer the questions. Give reasons for your opinions.

1 Are you going to study English at university? Why? / Why not?
2 How will English be of use to you in the future?
3 For which jobs is a knowledge of English important?

1

Beginnings

Unit map

● **Vocabulary**
Remembering and forgetting
Idioms: memory
Personality

● **Word Skills**
Phrasal verbs (1)

● **Grammar**
Question forms
Habitual actions

● **Listening** Designer babies

● **Reading** Bad beginnings

● **Speaking** Interview

● **Writing** Opinion essay

● **Culture 1**
The Legend of King Arthur

● **Literature 1**
The Sword in the Stone,
TH White

● **Vocabulary Builder** page 126

● **Grammar Builder and**
Reference page 134

1A Vocabulary

Memories
I can describe childhood memories.

1 SPEAKING Work in pairs. Think back to your own childhood. Ask and answer the questions below. Then find out how many people in the class can answer all of the questions confidently.

Can you remember …
1 the name of your school teacher when you were five?
2 what you enjoyed watching on TV when you were four?
3 what types of food you really liked or disliked when you were three?
4 who you played with when you were two?
5 your favourite toy or game when you were one?

2 VOCABULARY Study the words below. Which are related to remembering and which are related to forgetting?

Remembering and forgetting
Verbs blot out evoke recall remind reminisce suppress
Nouns mind nostalgia recollections
Adjectives evocative lasting unforgettable

3 Complete the text about childhood amnesia with words from exercise 2. What three synonyms for 'remember' (two single verbs and one phrase) are there in the completed text?

THE FIRST two or three years of your life are full of new and, you would think, ¹ unforgettable experiences. But the reality is that most adults can ² recall almost nothing from those very early years, their earliest ³ recollections being, on average, from the age of about three and a half. This phenomenon is often referred to as 'childhood amnesia'. Interestingly, young children are often able to bring to ⁴ mind certain events from their first two years of life but, for reasons which are not fully understood, they generally lose this ability as they get older. (The artist Salvador Dalí claimed he could recollect being in the womb, but there is no way to prove or disprove this!) Do those earliest memories disappear or does the mind ⁵ suppress them for some reason? Nobody is sure.

As well as this tendency to lose or ⁶ _____ memories from the first three years, most people have far fewer memories up to the age of eight than for other periods in their lives and they are often quite sketchy. Sometimes a picture or a piece of music can ⁷ _____ you of something or someone from years ago, and smells can be particularly ⁸ evocative. It is also possible for a sight, smell or sound to ⁹ evoke a feeling – for example, ¹⁰ nostalgia – rather than a specific memory. We still do not know exactly how the human mind stores information, but we do know that people who frequently ¹¹ reminisce about childhood experiences are more likely to create ¹² lasting memories.

4 SPEAKING Work in pairs. Define 'childhood amnesia' in one sentence. Do your answers to exercise 1 support the theory or contradict it?

5 Choose the correct words in the sentences. Then complete them with your own ideas. Use your imagination.

1 When my grandfather is with friends, they like to sit and **evoke / reminisce** about ...

2 My aunt has **blotted / suppressed** out most of her memories of boarding school because ...

3 One thing that is particularly **evocative / unforgettable** of my uncle's childhood abroad is ...

4 The sound of fireworks has always **recalled / reminded** my grandmother of ...

5 My uncle feels a lot of **nostalgia / recollections** for the days when ...

6 One thing that made **an evocative / a lasting** impression on my grandmother in her youth was ...

6 SPEAKING Work in pairs. Compare your answers to exercise 5. How similar are your endings? Do they show you understand the meaning of the word you chose?

7 🎧 1.05 Listen to four speakers talking about something which reminded them of early childhood. For each speaker, answer the questions below.

1 Where was the speaker at the time and what was he or she doing?

2 What reminded the speaker of his or her childhood?

8 🎧 1.05 VOCABULARY What idiomatic phrases do the speakers use instead of the underlined words? Use the correct form of the idioms below. Listen and check.

Idioms: memory
a trip down memory lane   to come flooding back
to have a memory like a sieve   to jog your memory
to know sth by heart   to rack your brains   to ring a bell
to take you back to

1 The title didn't <u>remind me of anything</u>.

2 Surprisingly, the story didn't <u>cause me to remember anything</u>.

3 Some of it really <u>reminded me of</u> my childhood.

4 It was <u>an experience which brought back lots of memories</u>.

5 All the memories <u>suddenly came back to my mind</u>.

6 The amazing thing is, I still knew all the words <u>from memory</u>!

7 Mind you, she's got a <u>very bad memory</u>, so I wasn't too surprised.

8 I've been <u>trying hard to remember</u> ever since but I just can't remember.

9 SPEAKING Work in pairs. Discuss the questions below.

Can you think of ...

1 a poem or song lyric which you know by heart?

2 a particularly evocative smell which takes you back to your childhood?

3 something you do to jog your memory if you have something important to remember?

FLUENCY!

🔊 Some adjectives go naturally with certain nouns, whereas others with a similar meaning do not. Learning these collocations will help you sound more fluent. Study the adjectives from a–d which fit this example:

I have a(n) _____ memory of our first meeting.

a dim distant hazy vague

b abiding clear enduring strong vivid

c fond pleasant

d bitter painful traumatic

10 Read the Fluency! box. Then find another adjective for group a in the second paragraph of the text in exercise 3.

11 SPEAKING Work in pairs. Tell your partner some of your earliest memories. Use adjectives from the Fluency! box to describe them. How many details can you remember?

> I have a vivid memory of ... .

> I can clearly recollect ...

> I have a vague memory of ... .

> I can only bring to mind ...

Question forms

I can use a variety of high-level question forms correctly.

1 SPEAKING Work in pairs. Discuss which of these you find the easiest and most difficult to remember: people's names, people's faces, birthdays, appointments, new words in English, what you did last weekend.

2 🎧 1.06 Complete the dialogue below. Write one word in each gap. Then listen and check your answers.

Ed This reminds me of the first time we met.

Zoe But we didn't meet here.

Ed ¹_____ we? Well, it was somewhere like this. ²_____ I come over and talk to you? You were with Anna.

Zoe It was Sophie, not Anna. And no, you didn't come over and talk to me. But ³_____ worry about a few little details?

Ed So what ⁴_____ happen?

Zoe ⁵_____ you remember? You bought Sophie a coffee and asked her if she had a boyfriend.

Ed ⁶_____ I? I don't remember that! What ⁷_____ next?

Zoe When she said yes, you started talking to me! ⁸_____ not admit it? I was second choice!

3 Read the Learn this! box. Write the missing words. Then find one more example of each point in the dialogue in exercise 2.

LEARN THIS! Question forms

1 In 'subject questions', where *who* or *what* replaces the subject, we:
  a do not normally use an auxiliary (*do, did*, etc.).
  Who _____ *Hamlet*? Shakespeare wrote it.
  b can sometimes include the auxiliary for emphasis.
  'I didn't send that text.' 'Well, who _____ _____ it?'

2 A reply question is used to question another speaker's statement. A reply question can be affirmative or negative.
  a 'I was sitting in the corner.' '_____ you?'
  b 'I didn't see you.' '_____ _____?'

3 A negative question can be used:
  a to ask for confirmation. We expect the answer 'yes'.
  _____ it Jack's birthday yesterday?
  b to express surprise that something did not happen.
  I sent you an email. _____ you get it? (= I'm surprised that you didn't get it.)

4 Questions beginning *why* or *why not* can sometimes contain only a base form. The exact meaning is implied.
  a _____ _____ study abroad? It would be a great experience.
  b It isn't an important exam. So _____ bother to revise?

➡ Grammar Builder 1.1 page 134

4 In your notebook, write subject questions beginning *Who … ?* or *What … ?* in response to the statements below. Use an auxiliary verb (*does, did*, etc.) for emphasis if appropriate.

1 I didn't borrow your laptop. (borrow?)
  'Who did borrow it?'
2 I've got four tickets for a Jay Z gig in London. (pay for?)
3 We didn't order a taxi. (order?)
4 Music doesn't help me concentrate. (help?)
5 Ed Sheeran wrote the song. (perform?)
6 Chelsea have just got a goal. (score?)
7 'Believe' doesn't rhyme with 'sieve'. (rhyme?)

5 SPEAKING Work in pairs. Take turns to be A and B.

Student A: Read one of the statements (1–6) below.
Student B: Respond with a reply question. Then invent a reason to query the statement.

1 Everyone can recall the first time they met their best friend.

> Everyone can recall the first time they met their best friend.

>> Can they? Personally, I can't remember anything about it.

2 Painful memories are always more vivid than pleasant memories.
3 It's easy to blot out embarrassing memories.
4 People used to have a far wider circle of friends than they do nowadays.
5 You have to repeat somebody's name when they say it if you want to remember it.
6 Nobody knows any phone numbers by heart these days.

6 🎧 1.07 Complete the negative questions. Then listen and check your answers. Use the context to say whether each question is a) asking for confirmation or b) expressing surprise.

1 _____ you sitting next to me in our first English class?
2 _____ you with a friend?
3 _____ you find two seats together?
4 _____ I say anything to you at all?
5 _____ I listening to music?
6 _____ you talking to your brother?
7 _____ you had a big argument with him earlier that morning?

7 SPEAKING Work in pairs. Talk about the first time you met each other. Include question tags, reply questions and negative questions in your conversation. Talk about:
• where you met and what you were doing there.
• who spoke first and what he or she said.
• anything else that happened or was said.

> I've got a clear memory of meeting you in the corridor. I was …

Listening
Designer babies
I can understand a debate about gene editing.

1 SPEAKING Work in pairs. Imagine you could use genetic engineering to make one change to the human race. Which of the following would you choose and why?

create designer babies   eradicate disease
make humans live longer   make humans more intelligent

> **Listening Strategy**
> When you listen, you may need to distinguish facts from opinions and speculation. Listen out for phrases that indicate when somebody is voicing an opinion (e.g. *'The way I look at it …'*) or speculating (e.g. *'The likelihood is …'*).

2 KEY PHRASES Read the Listening Strategy. Then look at the phrases. Would they a) introduce an opinion or b) speculate about something?

Introducing and speculating
1 For me, …   4 To my mind …
2 No doubt …   5 The chances are …
3 As far as I'm concerned …   6 I dare say …

3 🎧 **1.08** Listen to four people talking about genetic engineering. For each speaker, say which option (a or b) is stated as a fact.

1 a Malaria kills millions of people every year.
   b Genetic editing is a good way to combat the disease.
2 a The laws which prohibit scientists from creating 'designer babies' are not as strict as they used to be.
   b Medical science is finding ways to tackle hereditary diseases.
3 a Glasses were the first example of humans using technology to improve their natural abilities.
   b People are already using genetic science to improve their DNA.
4 a The science of gene editing, if allowed, will make the gulf between rich and poor even wider.
   b About 90% of powerful people were born into wealthy families.

4 🎧 **1.08** Listen again. What phrases do the speakers use to indicate opinions and speculation?

5 🎧 **1.09** Listen to a debate about a gene editing technique called CRISPR and the ethics of genetic science. Which point is stated as a fact rather than speculation?

a Gene editing will be used to cure serious diseases.
b Scientists in China are trying to develop techniques for producing 'designer babies'.
c Scientists will find ways to avoid the regulations.
d Scientists do not currently have the technology to produce 'designer babies'.

6 🎧 **1.09** Listen again. Choose the best answer (a–d). Then say who you agree with more, Dr Hapgood or Ms Bennett.

1 What has changed recently in the field of gene editing?
   a It is now possible to alter very specific parts of the DNA sequence.
   b It can now be used to combat hereditary diseases.
   c New and exciting possibilities have arisen for its use.
   d Specific genes can now be edited more quickly and accurately than before.
2 Why does Dr Hapgood think changes to human DNA made through gene editing are unlikely to be reversed?
   a Because nobody will want to reverse them.
   b Because scientists won't necessarily be able to control the consequences of gene editing.
   c Because the changes made by gene editing are not being monitored closely enough.
   d Because the work is taking place in too many different laboratories around the world.
3 On which point do Dr Hapgood and Ms Bennett agree?
   a Changes to human DNA cannot be reversed.
   b The need for strict regulation in the field of genetic science.
   c Gene therapy is very different from other kinds of medical science.
   d The very real risk of genetic science being misused to produce 'designer babies'.

7 SPEAKING Work in two groups. One group is going to argue in favour of the statement below and the other group against it. Make notes. Use the phrases below to help you.

> 'It should be against the law for scientists to alter human DNA.'

designer babies   eradicate a disease
ethically unacceptable   gene therapy   genetically modified
hereditary diseases   play God

> ➡ **Vocabulary Builder** Science vocabulary: word families: page 126

8 SPEAKING Debate the statement in exercise 7. Support your group's position with as many arguments as possible.

Habitual actions

I can talk about habitual actions in the past and present.

1 Read the quotation. Do you agree with it? What do you think 'the hard way' means?

> 'Siblings are the people we practise on, the people who teach us about fairness and co-operation and kindness and caring, quite often the hard way.' Pamela Dugdale

2 🎧 **1.10** Listen to four people talking about their siblings. For each speaker, say whether over the years the relationship with their siblings has become closer, less close or stayed roughly the same.

3 🎧 **1.10** Listen again. Complete the extracts.

1 Of course we _____ occasionally, over little things.
2 We _____ our own separate books or toys even.
3 She _____ just as I'm in the middle of something!
4 We _____ for hours in the park every Saturday.
5 He _____ because he was older, but I didn't mind.
6 He _____ me about my appearance.
7 Our parents _____ me to ignore him.
8 We _____ each other once or twice a year, I guess.
9 She _____ me nasty text messages.

4 Read the Learn this! box. Then say which of the extracts in exercise 3 express annoyance.

LEARN THIS! Talking about habitual actions

1 To talk about habitual actions in the present, we can use the present simple or *will*.
   We often / We'll often go out at weekends.

2 To talk about habitual actions in the past, we can use the past simple, *would* or *used to*.
   She always got / She'd always get / She always used to get better grades than me.

   NOTE: With state verbs, we do not use *would*.
   I didn't use to like tea. ✓ NOT ~~I wouldn't like tea.~~ ✗

3 To express annoyance at habits, we use:

a the present or past continuous, often with adverbs like *always*, *forever* and *continually*.
   He's always forgetting my birthday. They were always arguing.

b *Will* or *would* for emphasis. *Will* and *would* are often stressed when spoken.
   He will phone me when I'm asleep. She would talk about me with her friends.

---

5 In your notebook, rewrite the sentences in exercise 3 using a different structure from the Learn this! box.

   Of course we used to fall out occasionally, over little things.

6 Compare the sentences. What is the difference in meaning?

1 a My sister always left her phone at home when she went out.
  b My sister was always leaving her phone at home when she went out.
2 a I used to hate swimming lessons at school.
  b I'd hate swimming lessons at school.
3 a I'll meet my sister on Sunday mornings for a coffee.
  b I'll meet my sister on Sunday morning for a coffee.
4 a My brother is always phoning me at midnight.
  b My brother is phoning me at midnight.
5 a My brother was always wearing my coat to school.
  b My brother always used to wear my coat to school.
6 a She'll spend most evenings chatting to her friends online.
  b She *will* spend most evenings chatting to her friends online.

➡ Grammar Builder 1.2 page 135

LOOK OUT!

We can also use these expressions to talk about habits:
keep doing something = *tend to do something*
have a habit of doing = *have a tendency to do something*
be apt to do something = *be prone to do something*

---

7 Read the Look out! box. Choose five sentences from exercise 6 and rewrite them using a phrase from the box.

8 **USE OF ENGLISH** Complete the second sentence so that it means the same as the first. Write no more than six words, including the word in brackets.

1 My sister kept falling out with our dad. (always)
  My sister _____ our dad.
2 Our parents would rarely get involved in our rows. (use)
  Our parents _____ in our rows very often.
3 My twin brother keeps making up stories about me. (will)
  My twin brother _____ about me.
4 My sister doesn't get in touch with me very often. (won't)
  My sister _____ with me.
5 My mum would always side with my sister. (used)
  My mum _____ with my sister.
6 My brothers will keep upsetting my sister. (continually)
  My brothers _____ my sister.
7 My dad often used to get lost when he was driving. (tendency)
  My dad _____ when he was driving.

9 **SPEAKING** Work in pairs. Use a variety of different structures from the lesson to tell your partner about:

• something you always did as a young child.
• something annoying that a friend has a habit of doing.
• something you do when you're nervous.

1E

Word Skills

Phrasal verbs (1)

I can recognise and use phrasal verbs correctly.

1 SPEAKING Work in pairs. Ask and answer the questions.

1 Does your name come from a relative? Will you <u>pass it on</u> to one of your own children? Why? / Why not?

2 How often do you <u>come across</u> people with the same name as you? *meet by chance*

3 Do you think it is better to give children names that help them <u>stand out</u> or help them <u>blend in</u>? Why?

4 If somebody is unhappy with their name, should they change it, if possible, or just <u>put up with</u> it?

2 DICTIONARY WORK Look at the dictionary entry for 'pass sth on'. How does it indicate that:

a it is a phrasal verb (i.e. a verb with one or two particles)?

b it is a transitive verb (i.e. it has a direct object)?

c it is separable (i.e. the object can come before or after the particle)?

---

pass sth <—> on (to sb) *PHR V* to give sth to sb else, especially after receiving or using it yourself.

---

3 Look at the underlined phrasal verbs in exercise 1. Which are transitive and which are intransitive? Which phrasal verb is clearly separable? Which has two particles?

4 USE OF ENGLISH Complete the text with an appropriate word in each gap. All of the missing words are particles. Use a dictionary to help you.

A GOOD START IN LIFE?

How important is the name you're given? The song *A Boy Named Sue* tells the story of a father who names his son Sue before walking ¹ _**out**_ on the family. Having a girl's name forces the boy to stand ² _**up**_ for himself – which, we learn, is why the father went ³ _**with for**_ that name in the first place. Most names do not have such a dramatic effect, but several studies have looked ⁴ _**into at**_ the link between the name you are given and the way your life turns ⁵ _**out**_. They show that:

● boys with more feminine-sounding names are more likely to play ⁶ _**out around**_ class.

● girls with more masculine-sounding names are more likely to sign ⁷ _**up**_ for maths and science at university.

● fifty years ago, the top 50 girls' names accounted ⁸ _**for**_ about half of all girls. Now that figure has gone ⁹ _**down**_ to a quarter.

● an unusual name can make it harder to fit ¹⁰ _**in**_ when you're young. When you're an adult, it may be an advantage to stand ¹¹ _**out**_.

● in many countries, the authorities turn ¹² _**down**_ requests to give children embarrassing names or names which the parents have clearly made ¹³ _**up**_. But in the UK, it really comes down ¹⁴ _**to**_ the parents' choice. In recent years, British parents have got ¹⁵ _**away**_ with naming their children Gandalf (six times) and Arsenal (36 times!).

5 SPEAKING Work in pairs. Think of another way to express each of the phrasal verbs in exercise 4.

walk out on → leave

6 Put the phrasal verbs from exercises 1 and 4 into the correct box.

	2-part phrasal verbs	3-part phrasal verbs
Transitive and separable	hand over *put on*	
Transitive and inseparable	take after	look up to *put up with*
Intransitive	catch on	

7 Complete the sentences with a transitive phrasal verb from the table in exercise 6. Include the object in brackets in the correct position.

1 I've got a book about names and their meanings. I _**came across it**_ in a second-hand bookshop. (it)

2 I sometimes get comments about my unusual name, but I just _**put up with**_ (them)

3 My unusual name comes from my great-grandfather. My father was very keen to _**pass it on**_ to me. (it)

4 A couple in New Zealand made a request to call their child Fish and Chips, but the government _**turned it down**_ (it)

5 In Iceland, parents have to choose from a list of approved names; they can't just _**make one up**_. (one)

6 I share the same name as my grandfather, but apart from that, I don't _**take after him**_ in many ways. (him)

8 USE OF ENGLISH Choose the correct options (a–d) to complete the sentences.

1 My family had a tradition of naming first-born boys Sam, but my parents didn't carry _**d**_.
   a on it   b with it   c on with   d it on

2 If somebody has a name you dislike, it can actually put _**b**_ becoming friends.
   a off from   b you off   c up with   d you back

3 Sometimes boys with feminine-sounding names behave more aggressively to make _**c**_.
   a it up   b for it   c up for it   d it up for

4 It is clearly wrong to _**b**_ down on somebody simply because of their name.
   a break   b look   c turn   d run

5 Sometimes parents choose ridiculous names because they want to _**a**_ a change in the law.
   a bring about   b come about   c turn around   d put up

9 SPEAKING Work in pairs. Discuss what name you might give to a child of yours if you wanted:

● to name him/her after somebody you look up to.

● him/her to stand out rather than blend in.

● to pass on a name from a family member.

If I wanted to name my child after somebody I looked up to, I'd probably choose …

Bad beginnings

I can understand a text about overcoming obstacles.

1 SPEAKING Work in pairs. Explain the meaning of the two expressions below.

- to be born on the wrong side of the tracks
- to be born with a silver spoon in your mouth

2 Who could you use the expressions from exercise 1 to describe? Do you think being born in either of these circumstances makes you more or less likely to succeed in life?

3 Look at the photos. What do you know about these famous people?

> **Reading Strategy**
>
> When you are looking for information in a text with several sections:
>
> **1** skim read the whole text quickly to get an overall sense of the information it contains.
>
> **2** go through the questions one by one. For each question, use your knowledge of the text to locate where the information you need is.
>
> **3** scan the relevant part of the text for the information you need. If it is not there, scan other parts of the text until you find it.

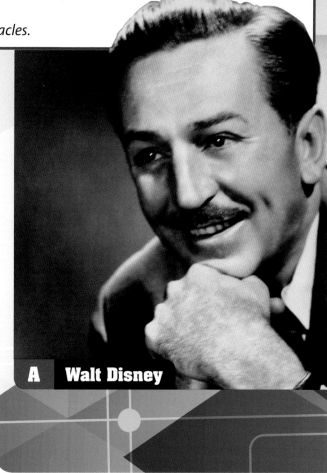

A   Walt Disney

4 Read the Reading Strategy. Then read texts A–D. In which texts are these topics mentioned?

1 education
2 family relationships
3 disability and disease
4 violence and crime
5 work and jobs

5 Match people A–D with questions 1–10. Each person can be matched with more than one question.

Which person ...
1 was given devastating news? ___
2 received a gift which helped with his/her career? ___
3 had to combine school and work at a young age? ___
4 has had roles in TV comedies? ___
5 did not live with his/her father until a teenager? ___
6 left home to escape from frequent mistreatment? ___
7 is the main source for biographical details about his/her life? ___
8 has written a best-selling book? ___
9 did not achieve a degree-level education? ___ ___
10 received support for his/her education by winning a competition? ___

6 VOCABULARY Find nouns in the texts formed from phrasal verbs and match them with the definitions.

Text A
1 somebody who does not complete their education (line 10) *drop-out*
2 a problem or obstacle (line 18) *setback*

Text B
3 the treatment received during childhood (line 29)
4 a person who has escaped (especially from their home) (line 35) *runaway*
5 a change of luck / big improvement (line 37) *turnaround*

Text C
6 a sudden collapse or crisis in your health (line 52) *break down*
7 a sudden and significant improvement (line 65)

Text D
8 a confrontation between two opponents (line 83) *standoff*

CRITICAL ANALYSIS

7 Explain the meaning of the sentence about Walt Disney below. Which word is being used metaphorically?

'But the road to this kind of success and influence wasn't easy.'

8 Explain what the underlined metaphors in the text mean. Which metaphors are related to life being a journey? What are the other metaphors related to?

9 SPEAKING Work in pairs. Which famous person from the text overcame the biggest obstacles, in your opinion? Give reasons for your choice.

There are few people who have had as enormous an impact on our culture and entertainment as Walt Disney. As the founder of Walt Disney Studios, he was an artist who changed animation and film-making for ever. But the road to this kind of success
5 and influence wasn't easy. At the age of ten, Walt had to help at his father's business before and after school; that meant getting up at 4.30 a.m. and working until the school bell rang. After school, he worked until dinner time. As a result, his school work suffered and he often fell asleep at his desk. A high-
10 school drop-out at sixteen, he attempted to join the army but they turned him down. So he focused on developing his artistic talents and learning about a new art form called animation. He moved to Hollywood and, unable to find work, decided to found his own studio. Success followed.
15 Despite, or because of, his lack of formal education, Disney never stopped learning. He showed that it's possible to be successful despite <u>following a different path</u>. He even came to regard his many setbacks in a positive light by saying: 'All the adversity I've had in my life, all my troubles and obstacles, have
20 strengthened me … You may not realise it when it happens, but <u>a kick in the teeth</u> may be the best thing in the world for you.'

C Stephen Hawking

45 Stephen Hawking was 21 years old and just embarking upon his career as a researcher in cosmology at the University of Cambridge when his father noticed he was tripping and falling frequently. After a series of tests, Hawking was diagnosed with
50 ALS (Amyotrophic Lateral Sclerosis) and doctors estimated he had two and a half years left to live. The news was, of course, devastating, but Hawking avoided an emotional breakdown by taking new interest in his studies and his research. 'In fact,' Hawking has said, 'although there was <u>a cloud hanging over my future</u>, I found, to my surprise, that I was
55 enjoying life in the present more than before.'

His disease continued to progress, however, and by the mid-1970s he needed more care and his speech was so slurred only his family could understand him. In 1985, Hawking came down with pneumonia and needed a tracheotomy, which left him without the ability to speak at
60 all. He did make a full recovery, however, allowing him to finish writing *A Brief History of Time*, which sold 10 million copies around the world.

Although it would be easy to dwell on what ALS has cost him, Hawking has chosen to focus on all that he still has in life. His brilliant mind remains unaffected by the disease and as a result Hawking has
65 made significant breakthroughs in his field and has received twelve honorary degrees, as well as multiple awards, medals and prizes. He has even appeared on a number of television shows, including *Star Trek: The Next Generation*, *The Simpsons* and *The Big Bang Theory*.

B Oprah Winfrey

Oprah Winfrey was born to a single teenage mother who was working as a housemaid in rural Mississippi. She lived in poverty and suffered abuse for years. This does not sound like the
25 beginnings of a media mogul who would go on to own a cable TV network and become one of America's most influential people and the first African-American billionaire, and yet it is.

In fact, Oprah had to overcome many obstacles before achieving the success she enjoys today. Her upbringing was on a
30 small farm in Mississippi where she was regularly beaten by her strict grandmother. At six years old, Oprah went to live with her mother in Milwaukee, Wisconsin. Since her mother worked long hours as a maid, Oprah was neglected. She suffered so much abuse at the hands of various relatives that at the age of thirteen
35 she became a runaway. By fourteen, she was pregnant; the baby died shortly after birth.

The turnaround came when she moved in with her father in Tennessee. He <u>set her on the right track</u> by making education a high priority. She began attending Nashville East High School,
40 where she took public speaking and drama classes. She received a full scholarship to Tennessee State University after winning a public-speaking contest. A few years after graduating, she took the job as host of A.M. Chicago, which became the highest-rated talk show in Chicago and was renamed *The Oprah Winfrey Show*.

D Jay Z

The American rapper Jay Z, whose real
70 name is Shawn Corey Carter, is one of the richest and most successful entrepreneurs in the entertainment industry. He and his wife, Beyoncé, are one of the world's most instantly recognisable celebrity couples.
75 But like many other hip-hop stars, he had an inauspicious start in life. Born in New York, he was raised in a publicly owned housing estate called Marcy Houses in a poor neighbourhood of Brooklyn. His
80 father walked out on the family when Jay Z was a young child.

The details of Jay Z's early life have emerged partly through his own lyrics, so they should perhaps be taken with a pinch of salt. Did he really shoot his own brother in the shoulder after a stand-off over some jewellery? Was he really involved in drug-dealing? Whether
85 or not all the details of his childhood are accurate, gun crime and drug-dealing were certainly both endemic in Marcy Houses and it would have been easy for a young man in that environment to <u>go off the rails</u>. But despite all the hardships, Jay Z's mother did her best to provide for the family, even buying Jay Z a radio-cassette player so
90 he could practise rapping.

Although Jay Z attended high school, he never graduated as it was clear by that stage that his future lay in the music business. However, he struggled at the start of his career and was unable to persuade any of the existing record labels to give him a contract.
95 So he and a couple of friends started their own label, Roc-A-Fella Records, and sold CDs from the back of a car. Soon his career took off and his small, independent record label grew into a massive business empire.

1G Speaking

Interview

I can talk about myself and my opinions in an interview.

1 SPEAKING Work in pairs. Ask your partner about:

1 a hobby that he/she does.
2 a personal ambition for the future.
3 an interesting piece of information about his/her early life.

> **Speaking Strategy**
>
> Avoid speaking in short, simple sentences. Try to use complex sentences and include explanations and examples. Use a variety of conjunctions and other expressions for extending your sentences.

2 🎧 **1.11** Read the Speaking Strategy. **Listen to two students being interviewed by an examiner. Which student:**

1 provides more complex answers than the other?
2 uses a much wider variety of vocabulary?
3 uses more complicated grammar?

3 🎧 **1.11** **KEY PHRASES** Check the meaning of the phrases below. Then listen again and tick the phrases you hear. What is being explained in each case?

> Introducing reasons and explanations
> a *given* (+ noun phrase) / *given that* (+ clause) ___
> b *what with* (+ noun phrase) ___
> c *seeing as / that* (+ clause) ___
> d *in view of* (+ noun phrase) ___
> e *owing to* (+ noun phrase) ___
> f *bearing in mind* (+ noun phrase) / *bearing in mind* (*that*) (+ clause) ___

Speaker 1 uses … when he is explaining why …

4 SPEAKING Work in pairs. Extend the sentences beginning with phrases from exercise 3.

1 I don't have a lot of free time during the week …
2 It's been a difficult year at school …
3 It was an exhausting day …
4 I probably spend too much time on my phone …
5 Skiing can be an expensive hobby …
6 It was an unforgettable party …
7 I find my new neighbour really irritating …
8 I get quite a lot of exercise …

I don't have a lot of free time during the week, given all my after-school clubs and homework.

5 Look at the sentences from the speakers in exercise 2. Then expand the sentences using the conjunction in brackets.

1 It's nice having two sets of parents! (even though)
It's nice having two sets of parents, even though I sometimes wish I could spend more time alone.
2 I'd like to play in a band one day. (if)
3 I've been doing karate for two years. (although)
4 I'd like to spend some time in the USA after university. (unless)
5 I prefer outdoor activities, like cycling and rock-climbing. (whenever)
6 A good level of English will help me to find a job. (provided that)

6 USE OF ENGLISH Choose the best conjunctions to complete the sentences.

1 I'm planning to take my exam a year earlier than I have to **even though / just in case / provided that** I have to take it again.
2 I'd like to spend a year abroad after school **although / whereas / whether** or not I get a place at medical school.
3 I often argue with my sister **even if / even though / unless** we have a lot in common.
4 I probably won't continue with my hobbies at university **as / if / in case** I'll have too much work.

7 SPEAKING Work in pairs. Choose three questions each to ask your partner. Tell your partner which ones you have chosen.

1 Can you tell me about your closest friend?
2 What's the most interesting place you have visited?
3 How do you like to relax?
4 What do you do to stay healthy?
5 How often do you use a computer and what for?
6 What are the best and worst things about school?
7 How would you describe your own personality?
8 What do you want your life to be like in ten years?

8 Prepare answers to your partner's questions. Make a note of two or three different aspects of each question that you plan to talk about.

Closest friend: personality – hobbies – style / appearance

9 KEY PHRASES Complete the phrases below. Use *as, comes, far, for* and *regarding*.

> Marking a change of topic
> As ¹_____ as (hobbies) are concerned, …
> When it ²_____ to (hobbies), …
> As ³_____ (hobbies), …
> ⁴_____ regards (hobbies), …
> ⁵_____ (hobbies), …

10 SPEAKING Work in pairs. Take turns to interview your partner. Use your questions from exercise 7 and your notes from exercise 8. Remember to follow the advice in the Strategy. Use the phrases from exercise 9 when you change to a different aspect of the question.

Opinion essay
I can write an opinion essay.

1 **SPEAKING** Work in pairs. Discuss the question below. Then compare your ideas with another pair. Are your opinions similar or very different?

> Is your personality as a teenager shaped more by your family or by your friends?

2 Read the essay. Is the writer's opinion similar to your own? Which points do you agree or disagree with?

Although your personality may be inherited to some degree, it is clearly also influenced by the people around you. But as you enter your teenage years, who plays the more significant role in this process: your family or your friends?

During the early years of your life, most of your time is spent with your family. Even though your parents take responsibility for shaping your behaviour, it is probably your siblings who have the greatest effect. For example, how you interact with your brother or sister while playing games may affect how competitive or conciliatory you become. <u>Similarly</u>, you are more likely to be thick-skinned if you grow up with an insensitive sibling!

<u>However</u>, once you enter your teenage years, you spend less time with your family and more time with your friends. <u>Moreover</u>, you start to become more aware of your own personality and how you would like to develop. <u>Consequently</u>, you may choose friends whose personality traits you admire. You may even go so far as to emulate those traits. At the same time, you may start to distance yourself from your family, even if you have a good relationship with them, since that is part of growing up and becoming more independent.

Although your family remains an important part of your life, it is clear to me that, during your teenage years, your social circle exerts a greater influence. Many personality traits will survive from childhood, but new ones will develop as you make your way towards adulthood with the help of your friends.

3 **VOCABULARY** Work in pairs. What do the adjectives below mean? Then find four more personality adjectives in the essay in exercise 2.

Personality abrasive broad-minded cynical extrovert gullible introvert narrow-minded placid punctual quick-tempered reserved self-assured self-effacing shrewd spontaneous trustworthy

4 Work in pairs. Discuss which adjectives from exercise 3:

1 best describe your own personality.
2 are more likely to describe a teenager or adult than a child.

> ➡ **Vocabulary Builder** Personality: phrases and idioms: page 126

Writing Strategy
When you write an opinion essay, remember to:

- avoid informal words and expressions.
- link your ideas together in a logical way using appropriate adverbs and conjunctions.
- divide your essay into clear paragraphs.
- state your conclusion in the final paragraph.

5 Read the Writing Strategy. How well does the writer of the essay in exercise 2 follow the advice?

6 Summarise the main idea of each paragraph.

Paragraph 1: Do friends or family have more influence on your personality as a teenager?
Paragraph 2: …

LEARN THIS! Linking adverbs

When we start a sentence with a linking adverb, it makes a logical connection with the sentence before. This is similar to the connection made between clauses by a conjunction and may express similarity or contrast, reason or result, etc.

It was raining. <u>Nonetheless,</u> we went to the beach.
<u>Even though</u> it was raining, we went to the beach.

7 Read the Learn this! box. Then study the four underlined examples of linking adverbs in the essay in exercise 2. What link do they provide: addition, contrast, result or similarity?

8 Explain how the choice of linking adverb in the sentences below would affect the meaning.

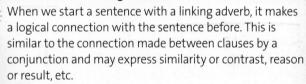

1 The party was at my grandparents' house. **Nonetheless** / **Consequently**, I invited a large number of friends.
2 Everything in the restaurant was expensive. **Indeed** / **Instead**, Jack spent €5 on an ice cream.
3 We shouldn't take the laptop to the beach. **Eventually** / **Otherwise**, it will stop working.

9 Read the task. Write a paragraph plan, summarising your main ideas for each paragraph.

> Does your personality change as you get older? Write an essay in which you discuss this question and give your own opinion.

10 Now write your essay (220–260 words) using your paragraph plan from exercise 9.

CHECK YOUR WORK

Have you …
- written 220–260 words?
- used appropriate language throughout your essay?
- checked your spelling and grammar?
- included conjunctions and linking adverbs to connect your ideas in a logical way?

Reading

1 Read the strategy above. Then read the text in exercise 2 and find phrases to match the definitions below.

  1 hear about something secret (paragraph 3)
  2 make somebody feel more cheerful (paragraph 3)
  3 give information to correct a mistaken opinion (paragraph 5)

2 Read the text and choose the correct answers (A, B, C or D).

A first for women runners

On the morning of 19 April 1966, a hooded figure was hiding in the bushes near the start line of the Boston Marathon. When the gun went off to start the race, the mysterious person allowed the faster competitors to pass before joining the main group of runners. It wasn't long before the others noticed that their new companion was a woman.

The infiltrator was 23-year-old graduate Roberta 'Bobbi' Gibb, an experienced runner who had had her application to run denied on the grounds that the Boston Marathon was a 'Men's Division race only'. Her rejection letter categorically stated: 'Women aren't allowed and furthermore are not physiologically able.' Having run up to 30 miles a day nearly every day for the two years leading up to the race, Gibb knew that this was not true. She decided it was time attitudes towards women changed, and bought a bus ticket to Boston.

Contrary to her father's fears that she would get hurt in the race, Gibb's male counterparts showed her nothing but kindness. Once reporters got wind of her participation, the radio began broadcasting news of her progress. Encouraged by adrenalin and the delighted spectators, Gibb was heading for an under three-hour time for the best part of the course, but then she began running out of steam. Starved of food and water, her legs began to falter, and her feet became almost too painful to run on. If she hadn't known that dropping out would have set women's running back 20 or 30 years, she may not have completed the course. However, the cheering crowds on the last leg of the course succeeded in lifting her spirits, and she sprinted to the finish in a very respectable time of just under three hours and 22 minutes.

On finishing the race, Gibb was treated as a hero: she was met by the governor of Massachusetts, her parents were interviewed, newspapers ran articles on her and she was invited to a TV game show. More importantly for her, she had broken the stereotype that women didn't run marathons. She began getting calls from inspired women who had taken up running themselves, and in 1967 a second female runner competed in the Boston Marathon alongside Gibb. The following year, there were five female entrants, and by 1972, the rules had been changed to allow women to compete in all US marathons. However, by then, if you had asked anyone who was the first woman to run the Boston Marathon, they would have given you a completely different name: Kathy Switzer.

Twenty-year-old journalist Kathrine Switzer shot to fame after competing against Gibb in the 1967 Boston Marathon. On discovering Switzer had entered the race by pretending to be a man, race director Jock Semple tried to physically remove her, and it was this image of Switzer being attacked while running that stuck in people's minds. Switzer continued running, finishing second in the 1975 Boston Marathon. Moreover, she became a successful media personality. It took Gibb a decade of writing letters to magazines, TV stations and book publishers to set the record straight. But in the end, she succeeded in gaining her due recognition and was retroactively awarded first-place medals for her 1966, 1967 and 1968 races.

1 The woman is hiding in the bushes
  A to cheer on the best participants.
  B so as not to be seen at the starting line.
  C in order to watch the race unfold.
  D so that she has a better view of the field.
2 Gibb was determined to compete in the Boston Marathon because she wanted to
  A prove to herself she could run the course.
  B convince the organisers to set up a Women's Division race.
  C show there was nothing stopping women from competing.
  D achieve fame as the first woman to take part.
3 What ultimately drove Gibb to finish the race?
  A She didn't want her plan to backfire.
  B She wanted her parents to be proud of her.
  C She wasn't willing to disappoint the crowd.
  D She couldn't take the shame of failure.
4 What does the writer mean when he describes Gibb's running time as 'respectable'?
  A He thinks she could have done better.
  B He considers it a benchmark to aim at.
  C He regards it as a good time.
  D He can't believe she ran so well.
5 What does the reader discover about Gibb in the fourth paragraph?
  A Her reputation grew as the years went by.
  B She was corrupted by fame.
  C She became a household name.
  D Her glory was short-lived.
6 Switzer supplanted Gibb for a time because
  A she was related to one of the race organisers.
  B she had a much higher profile than Gibb.
  C she was the first woman to compete legally.
  D she achieved a better position in a later race.

Listening

Exam Skills Trainer

3 Read the strategy above. Then read the short extract and the question below it. Choose the correct answer to fit the space. Why are the other answers wrong?

One reason for our helplessness as newborns is that human babies can't hold on to their mothers for protection and reassurance in the same way that baby chimpanzees can. Carrying their babies interferes with mothers' ability to perform daily tasks. Researchers believe that mothers in prehistory put their babies down at regular intervals to free their hands for other activities, and that they used an early form of baby talk to keep them reassured.

Baby chimps _____ their mothers whereas human babies have to be carried.

A cling   **B** cling to   **C** carry   **D** cling at

4 🎧 **1.12** You will hear a talk about the origins of music. For questions 1–8, complete the sentences with a word or short phrase.

The origins of music

The discovery of ¹_____ in Germany has led researchers to believe that music began around 40,000 years ago.

It is thought that music may have helped the first humans form ²_____ groups.

Researchers believe these instruments evolved from Neanderthal's instruments because of their ³_____ nature.

Research into Neanderthal instruments is difficult because they are very hard to ⁴_____.

Scientists have studied the shape of a bone in ⁵_____ called the hyoid to confirm that Neanderthals could sing.

1.8 million years ago an earlier human species may have been capable of a ⁶_____ form of singing.

Research into primates has shown that one species is aware of different ⁷_____.

Researcher Andrea Ravignani is currently comparing human and chimpanzees' recognition of ⁸_____.

Use of English

5 Read the strategy above. Identify the part of speech you need to fill the gaps in sentences 1–4. Complete the sentences with one word.

1 I'm _____ as tall as you. We're the same height.
2 _____ he's older than you, he isn't as mature.
3 I've only met a _____ of your relatives.
4 I'm _____ two minds whether to go out or not.

6 Complete the text with one word in each space.

Jawbone of very first human found

Archaeologists recently came ¹_____ a 2.8-million-year-old jawbone in Ethiopia. The fossil consists of ²_____ left side of the lower jaw along with five teeth. The back molar teeth are smaller than ³_____ of other hominins (human-like primates) living in the area, and are thought to be one of the features that distinguish humans from their ⁴_____ primitive ancestors. The discovery has caused great excitement ⁵_____ scientists as the fossil appears to bridge the gap between the ⁶_____ two specimens found previously in the area. The first of these is 'Lucy', a 3.2-million-year-old hominin belonging to the species *Australopithecus afarensis*. The second is an upper jaw discovered in Hadar, which dates ⁷_____ 2.35 million years and is attributed to the genus *Homo*. The Hadar fossil was previously thought to be from one of the very first humans, but the Ledi jaw disproves this theory and dates the earliest humans 400,000 years or ⁸_____ earlier.

Speaking

7 Think of complete and advanced level answers for questions 1–6 below. Then answer the questions.

1 What do you remember about your first day at school?
2 What was the first trip you went on without your parents?
3 Who was the first friend you ever had?
4 Who's the first person you tell if you're upset?
5 What's the first country you would visit if you could?
6 What's the first thing you bought with your own money?

Writing

8 Read the strategy above and the writing task below. Think about how you would write an interesting introduction to this essay.

Is it better to plan your life carefully or make spontaneous decisions? Write an essay discussing this question and giving your own opinion.

9 Write the opinion essay (220–260 words) for the task above.

2

Stories

Talking about stories
I can talk about books and stories.

Unit map

● **Vocabulary**
Aspects of stories
Literary forms
Adjectives to describe books
Adjectives to describe films
Idioms and set phrases: books
Talking about books

● **Word Skills**
Compounds

● **Grammar**
Conditionals
Inversion of subject and verb

● **Listening** Investigative
   journalism

● **Reading** *The Woman in White*

● **Speaking** Photo comparison

● **Writing** A film review

● **Culture 2** Elizabethan theatre

● **Literature 2**
   As You Like It, William
   Shakespeare

● **Vocabulary Builder** page 127

● **Grammar Builder and**
   Reference page 136

1 **SPEAKING** Do you judge a book by its cover? Look at the book covers. What kind of books are they? What kind of things might happen in the stories? Which would you like to read, based on the cover?

2 **VOCABULARY** Work in pairs. Look at the phrases to describe aspects of a story. How important are these aspects of a story to you? Give reasons for your opinions.

Aspects of stories characters you can identify with   evocative descriptions
a fast pace   a happy ending   humour   an intriguing plot   love interest
mystery and suspense   natural dialogue   realistic, believable characters

3 **SPEAKING** Do the male and female students in your class broadly agree which aspects are the most important? If not, how do their priorities differ?

4 **VOCABULARY** Complete the quiz with the correct form of some of the words below. Work in pairs and do the quiz.

Literary forms comic book   fable   fairy tale   fantasy   folk tale   graphic novel
myth   novel   play   poetry   short story

L I T E R A T U R E   QUIZ

1. Who wrote the collection of ___B short stories___ entitled *The Adventures of Sherlock Holmes*?
   A Agatha Christie   **B** Arthur Conan Doyle   **C** George Orwell
2. The moral of Aesop's ___fable___ *The Tortoise and the Hare* is:
   (A) It's better to do things slowly and steadily than act quickly and carelessly.
   B Never underestimate your opponent.
   C If you hesitate, you won't achieve your goal.
3. Which work of ___novel___ written in 2005 has become one of the most popular TV series of the century?
   (A) *Game of Thrones*   **B** *The Lord of the Rings*   **C** *Harry Potter*
4. Which ___comic book___ hero has the nickname The Caped Crusader?
   A Robin   **B** Superman   **(C)** Batman
5. Which of these ___novels___ was not written by Charles Dickens?
   A *Oliver Twist*   **(B)** *Pride and Prejudice*   **C** *A Christmas Carol*
6. In which country did the ___myth___ of Theseus and the Minotaur originate?
   A Italy   **B** Egypt   **(C)** Greece
7. In the ___fairy tale___ *Sleeping Beauty*, how long does the princess sleep before the prince wakes her with a kiss?
   A 1 year   **(B)** 100 years   **C** 1,000 years
8. Which Shakespeare ___play___ does this line come from? *'To be, or not to be, that is the question.'*
   A *Romeo and Juliet*   **(B)** *Hamlet*   **C** *Macbeth*
9. Which of the following is not a form of ___poetry___?
   A limerick   **(B)** novel   **C** sonnet

5 SPEAKING Work in pairs. Which of the works mentioned in the quiz have you read? What other examples of the literary forms in exercise 4 have you read?

> I've read a couple of Sherlock Holmes short stories. I'm currently reading a graphic novel called 'Fables'.

6 VOCABULARY Read the excerpts from book reviews. Complete the texts with the words below.

action   central   drawn   herrings   hinges   narrative
opens   point of view   portrayal   recommend   set
twists   unfolds   written

The narrative is ¹ _written_ in the third person, and is told from the ² _point of view_ of a young girl. The story ³ _opens_ in a small town in Wales but the ⁴ _action_ soon shifts to London.

⁵ _central_ to the plot is the relationship between the protagonist and his father. As the story ⁶ _unfolds_, their relationship worsens. Both characters are beautifully ⁷ _drawn_. I thoroughly ⁸ _recommend_ it.

The plot ⁹ _hinges_ on the hero's search for his missing brother. There are numerous ¹⁰ _twists_ and turns and a number of red ¹¹ _herrings_, which serve to increase the suspense.

The story is ¹² _set_ in France in the early 19th century. It is a third-person ¹³ _narrative_, fast-moving and quite exciting, but the story is let down by the unconvincing ¹⁴ _____ of the protagonist.

7 VOCABULARY Check the meaning of the adjectives below. Which adjectives have a) positive, b) negative or c) positive and negative connotations?

Adjectives to describe books breath-taking (c) chilling (c/b) compelling evocative fast-moving (c) humorous (c) light-hearted lightweight macabre nail-biting (c) poignant (c) predictable sensational sentimental shallow (b) slow-moving tedious thought-provoking touching (un)convincing (a)

FLUENCY!

Do not over-use common adjectives such as *nice, great, good, bad* and *boring*. Choose adjectives that have a more precise meaning, e.g.

nice boy: *sympathetic, caring, kind, charming, interesting*

a nice time: *pleasant, enjoyable, wonderful, relaxing*

nice weather: *beautiful, gorgeous, pleasant*

---

8 Read the Fluency! box. Then choose adjectives from exercise 7 that have a similar meaning to the adjectives below.

1 frightening, _macabre_, _chilling_
2 funny, _humorous_ _light-hearted_
3 boring, _slow-moving_, _tedious_, _shallow_
4 exciting, _breath-taking_, _fast-moving_, _nail-biting_, _compelling_, _sensational_
5 sad, _touching_, _poignant_, _sentimental_

9 🎧 1.13 Listen to someone describing two books that she has read. Answer the questions.

1 Which adjectives from exercise 7 does she use to describe
  a *Shirley*?
  b *Jane Eyre*?
2 Which of the adjectives does she use to describe the following aspects of *Jane Eyre*?
  a the characters
  b the plot
  c the ending

10 VOCABULARY Complete the idioms and set phrases from exercise 9 with the words below.

Idioms and set phrases: books
bedtime   bookworm   cover   cut   get   heavy   lines
page

1 be a bit of a _bookworm_   read a lot
2 _get_ _heavy_ going   slow, difficult to read
3 I couldn't _get_ into it   not your thing, hard to focus on
4 judge a book by its _cover_
5 a real _page_-turner
6 read between the _lines_
7 to _cut_ a long story short
8 good _bedtime_ reading

11 🎧 1.13 Listen again and check your answers.

12 Prepare to talk about a book that you have read. Try to include words and phrases and interesting adjectives from the lesson. Make notes including the following:

1 Background information (author, type of book, when it was written, etc.)
2 Brief outline of plot (but don't give away the ending!)
3 Characters (Why are they interesting? Did you identify with them?)
4 Favourite moments or scenes
5 Overall opinion and recommendation

13 SPEAKING Work in pairs. Tell your partner about your book. Try to speak for two minutes. Use the phrases below to help you.

Talking about books
First, some background information about the book, …
Turning to the story itself, …
One of the chief strengths of the book is …
My favourite moment/scene is …
Overall, I thought …

I can use a range of conditional sentences.

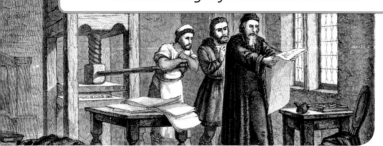

1 SPEAKING Look at the photo. Can you describe what is happening? What is the invention and how did it change the world?

2 Read the text and check your ideas.

A WORLD WITHOUT
printing

Can you imagine a world without printed books? What if printing hadn't been invented? If there weren't any printed books, how would the world be different now? *2nd conditional*

Johannes Gutenberg is often credited with the invention of printing in Germany in the middle of the fifteenth century. But Gutenberg can't take all the credit. He wouldn't have had the bright idea of creating moveable type – separate pieces of type for each letter that can be reused again and again – unless the Chinese had invented woodblock printing four hundred years earlier. *earlier*

How did the invention change the world? Firstly, prior to Gutenberg's breakthrough, few books existed and it would take weeks or months to copy them by hand. They were extremely expensive and not available to most people. If it hadn't been for Gutenberg, books and the knowledge contained in them wouldn't have spread so quickly around the world. Secondly, in the Middle Ages spelling varied greatly between different areas and dialects. For example, there were 500 different recorded spellings of the word 'through'! Printers brought consistency to spelling. Had spelling not been standardised, English spelling would be even more difficult to master! *3rd conditional*

450 years later, it's more difficult to speculate on what the world would be like today without books. But supposing there were no printing presses, would that have prevented us developing other means of communicating, such as email, texting and instant messaging? Who can say? We can say for sure, however, that the world would be a very different place.

3 Underline examples of the structures below in the text. Some sentences in the text exemplify more than one structure. Which conditional structures refer to a) the past, b) the present or c) the past and the present?

1 second conditional
2 third conditional
3 two mixed conditionals
4 a conditional clause where *if* is omitted and the subject and verb are inverted
5 a clause with *if it weren't / hadn't been for ...*
6 a question starting with *What if ... ?*

➡ **Grammar Builder 2.1** page 136

4 Rewrite the sentences using mixed conditionals.

1 I didn't remember my phone so I can't text Joel.
   If I'd remembered my phone, ...
2 You weren't on time because you don't have a watch!
3 We missed the train so we're sitting in the waiting room.
4 You're not eighteen so you couldn't get into the night club.
5 You spent all your money on apps. Now you're broke.
6 You don't know what to do because you weren't listening.
7 You don't check Facebook very often so you didn't know about Sam's party.
8 I wasn't offered the job in Rome because I don't speak Italian.

5 SPEAKING Work in pairs. Rephrase the clauses using an inversion and omitting *if*. Then complete them in your own words.

Had you phoned me, I wouldn't have been worried about you.
1 If you had phoned me, ...
2 If I had known it was going to snow, ...
3 If I were extremely rich, ...
4 If I should fail to get into university, ...
5 If it weren't for the fact that school is compulsory, ...
6 If it hadn't been for the gorgeous weather, ...

> **LEARN THIS!** Conjunctions introducing conditional clauses
> - We can introduce conditional clauses with *unless, supposing, provided that, as/so long as.*
>   *I'll lend you my mobile as long as you give it back.*
> - *In case* introduces a possibility against which a precaution is needed.
>   *Take your coat in case it rains.*

6 Read the Learn this! box. Find two clauses in the text in exercise 2 that are introduced by words other than *if*. Rephrase them using *if*.

7 USE OF ENGLISH In your notebook, rewrite the sentences using the words in brackets.

1 Revise hard and you're sure to do well. (as long as)
2 I'll take my key because you might be out when I return. (in case)
3 The match will be cancelled unless the weather improves. (provided that)
4 Even if the car was cheaper, I still wouldn't buy it. (supposing)
5 It was because of you that I passed my driving test. (if it / been)
6 I'll only apologise to him if he apologises to me first. (unless)

8 SPEAKING Work in pairs. Discuss these questions. How might the world have been different if the following things hadn't been invented?

1 the aeroplane   3 the compass   5 the internet
2 the wheel   4 the telephone   6 antibiotics

Investigative journalism

I can predict the kind of information I need to listen for.

1 SPEAKING Work in pairs. Discuss the meaning of the terms a) investigative journalist and b) undercover journalist.

➤➤ **Vocabulary Builder** Compounds: journalism: page 127

2 Read the text and check your ideas. Do you admire investigative and undercover journalists? Would you like to be one? Why? / Why not?

⚡ GOING UNDERCOVER 📷👤 🔋

Journalists are always looking for a 'scoop', a story of exceptional originality, usually involving hidden secrets or a scandal, which they can be the first to report.

Sometimes a scoop is the result of a tip-off, which merely requires the investigative journalist to dig around for more information and to conduct interviews. Frequently, though, a scoop requires more than simple research and interviews. It requires a bigger risk and greater sacrifice, like going undercover. Although the ethics and credibility of undercover tactics have been called into question, in some cases the only way to unearth the truth is to go incognito.

Fabricated identities, hidden cameras and gruesome and terrifying revelations are just a few of the aspects involved in this insider method of getting the story. And it's hard not to admire these gutsy journalists' passion and dedication to their careers, as they infiltrate everything from psychiatric hospitals and prisons to terrorist groups and soccer hooligan gangs. This is definitely not a career path for the faint-hearted.

3 VOCABULARY Match the highlighted words in the text with the definitions 1–9.

1 moral principles *ethics*
2 search hard for *dig around for*
3 surprising facts that people become aware of *revelation*
4 secretly become part of an organisation in order to discover information about it *infiltrate*
5 information about something that has happened or is about to happen
6 in disguise *incognito*
7 an informal word meaning 'brave and determined' *gutsy*
8 unpleasant and horrible, usually connected with injury or death *gruesome*
9 an event or behaviour that causes public shock or anger *scandal*

Listening Strategy

Read the task carefully and try to predict the type of information you need to listen for. This is especially important in sentence-completion tasks.

4 Read the Listening Strategy. Then look at the sentences about famous scandals. Think about what kind of information is needed to complete them.

1 The reporters discovered the truth after they had received _____.
2 The allegations have ended the _____ of two of FIFA's top officials.
3 The *News of the World* used information from Prince William's _____ to write a story about him.

5 🎧 **1.14** Listen to three extracts and complete each sentence in exercise 4 with a word or phrase. How close were your predictions?

6 You are going to listen to a journalist talking about two undercover reporters he admires. Think about what kind of information is needed to complete the sentences below.

1 MacIntyre uses _____ in order to gain entry to organisations he was investigating.
2 One of MacIntyre's investigations resulted in a _____ being shut down.
3 On another occasion, MacIntyre joined a _____ of violent football supporters.
4 A few years after the trial of the Chelsea Headhunters, MacIntyre and his wife were _____.
5 Previous experiences in _____ had a lasting influence on Griffin.
6 Griffin used drugs and _____ to change his appearance.
7 The way Griffin was treated by white people in the Deep South clearly depended on _____.
8 Griffin thought that _____ was much more widespread than he's previously believed.

7 🎧 **1.15** Listen and complete each sentence in exercise 6 with a word or short phrase.

8 SPEAKING Prepare a role-play in pairs. Read the roles below and think of two or three arguments to support your view.

Student A: Journalists should never lie to get to the truth.
Student B: Journalists should do whatever they need to get to the truth.

9 Swap your notes and think of counter-arguments to your partner's views. Make more notes.

10 SPEAKING Role-play your discussion using your notes from exercises 8 and 9. Use the phrases below to introduce your counter-arguments.

I can see what you're getting at, but ...
There may be an element of truth to that, but ...
I don't think it's fair to say that ...

Inversion of subject and verb
I can use adverbials at the start of the sentence.

Never has my friend Sherlock Holmes (the famous detective) been so intrepid as he was in the case of the Green Face. Neither have his powers of induction ever been better used. Well do I remember the night we lay in wait for the Green Face. No sooner had we hidden ourselves among the bushes than it began to rain. Seldom have I known the hours pass so slowly. Only when a cold grey dawn had begun to break in the east did the fearful spectre appear. So terrified was I that I tried to hide behind my umbrella. Silently and mysteriously and only a few yards away, there came into view a face of the most horrible appearance and ghastly colour imaginable. 'Here comes our foe, Watson,' whispered my companion, drawing his sword-stick. With these words, up sprang Holmes and lunged – and pop went the Green Face! At our feet lay the miserable rubber remnant of the terror that had haunted Abbey Grange for years. Little did I know that it was just a balloon! Had I realised of course, I would have used my umbrella!

1 SPEAKING Read the story. What was the 'Green Face'?

2 Read the Learn this! box below. Match the highlighted adverbials in the story with groups 1a–e and 2. Rewrite the sentences with normal word order.

> **LEARN THIS!** Inversion of subject and verb (1)
>
> **1** We can place some adverbials at the start of a sentence for emphasis. We then invert the subject and verb, using *do/did* if necessary.
> **a** negative or near-negative adverbials (*never, not since, rarely, in no way, no longer, only*, etc.)
> **b** the adverbs *well* and *little*
> **c** *so* or *such* with *that* to express result
> **d** some adverbs of position and movement (*in front of me, down, up, here, there*, etc.)
> **e** some words expressing noise (e.g. *bang, crash, pop*), usually with *go*
>
> **2** In conditional clauses that contain *were, had* or *should, if* can sometimes be omitted.

➤➤ Grammar Builder 2.2 page 136

3 USE OF ENGLISH In your notebook, rewrite the sentences starting with the words in brackets so that the meaning stays the same.

Never had Liam …
1 It was the first time Liam had read such a long book. (Never)
2 It's unusual for it to rain so much in June. (Seldom)
3 I'd only just arrived when she started shouting at me! (Hardly)
4 You should never drink and drive. (On no account)
5 I had no idea he would react like that. (Little … know)
6 You won't pass your exams unless you work hard. (Only if)
7 He was so terrified that he hid behind the sofa. (So)
8 The tree fell down with a tremendous crash. (Down)
9 If I'd known you were a vegetarian, I would have cooked something different. (Had)

4 Read the second Learn this! box. Find two examples of the structures in the text in exercise 1. Can you work out any rules for forming sentences like the ones in the Learn this! box?

> **LEARN THIS!** Inversion of subject and verb (2)
>
> When certain adverbials are placed at the start of the sentence, other changes are necessary in addition to inversion.
>
> **1** As soon as I got home, I went to bed.
> *No sooner had I got home than I went to bed.*
> **2** I was cold and I was tired as well.
> *Not only was I cold (but) I was also tired.*
> **3** I've never visited Paris. I've never been to Rome either.
> *Neither / Nor have I ever been to Rome.*
> **4** You can't go under any circumstances.
> *Under no circumstances can you go.*
> **5** I couldn't find a hotel anywhere.
> *Nowhere could I find a hotel.*
> **6** I didn't suspect you for one moment.
> *Not for one moment did I suspect you.*
> **7** The truth didn't come out until many years later.
> *Not until many years later did the truth come out.*

➤➤ Grammar Builder 2.3 page 137

5 USE OF ENGLISH In your notebook, rewrite the sentences using adverbials and sentence patterns from the Learn this! box.

1 She went out immediately after finishing her homework.
 No sooner had she …
2 I wouldn't doubt George's honesty for one second.
3 Books shouldn't be removed from the reference library under any circumstances.
4 It was dishonest, but it was also illegal.
5 I didn't go to sleep until I'd finished the book.
6 Josh has never tried skiing. He's never been snowboarding either.
7 I couldn't find a phone box anywhere.

6 SPEAKING Complete the sentences below in your own words. Compare your answers with a partner.

1 Not only would I like to …
2 Had I known that …
3 Seldom do teachers …
4 Never have I … . Nor have …

Don't believe everything you read!

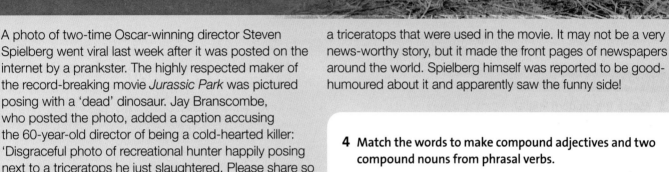

A photo of two-time Oscar-winning director Steven Spielberg went viral last week after it was posted on the internet by a prankster. The highly respected maker of the record-breaking movie *Jurassic Park* was pictured posing with a 'dead' dinosaur. Jay Branscombe, who posted the photo, added a caption accusing the 60-year-old director of being a cold-hearted killer: 'Disgraceful photo of recreational hunter happily posing next to a triceratops he just slaughtered. Please share so the world can name and shame this despicable man.' Most animal rights campaigners are used to this kind of wind-up and most saw through it. However, some fell for the scam and were outraged. 'Steven Spielberg, I'm disappointed in you. I'm not watching any of your movies again, ANIMAL KILLER,' commented one. A number of the commenters were apparently ignorant of the fact that the triceratops has been extinct for well over 60 million years. The photo is genuine, but Spielberg, one of the best-known film makers of all time, is actually sitting beside one of the full-scale models of a triceratops that were used in the movie. It may not be a very news-worthy story, but it made the front pages of newspapers around the world. Spielberg himself was reported to be good-humoured about it and apparently saw the funny side!

1 SPEAKING Work in pairs. Look at the photo. It was part of an internet hoax. What's unusual about it?

2 Read the text and check your ideas.

3 Read the Learn this! box. Find two examples of each type of compound adjective (1–5) and one example of a compound made from a phrasal verb (6) in the text.

LEARN THIS! Compounds: common patterns

1 noun, adjective or adverb + past participle
  hand-made well-dressed

2 noun, adjective or adverb + present participle
  English-speaking easy-going never-ending

3 adjective + noun with -ed
  strong-willed broad-minded many-sided

4 noun + adjective. The noun is always singular.
  tax-free lead-free worldwide

5 adjective or number + noun. The noun is always singular
  three-hour movie 800-page novel last-minute goal

6 We can sometimes make compound nouns from phrasal verbs.
  a tip-off a breakdown make-up lift off

4 Match the words to make compound adjectives and two compound nouns from phrasal verbs.

1	award	a	aged
2	best	b	down
3	crack	c	famous
4	life	d	friendly
5	middle	e	hearted
6	user	f	off
7	twenty	g	selling
8	world	h	storey
9	tip	i	threatening
10	warm	j	winning

5 🎧 1.16 Listen to another internet hoax. What was the hoax? What happened to the people who fell for the hoax?

6 🎧 1.16 Listen again and answer the questions.

1 Which compounds from exercise 4 did the speaker use?
2 What was he describing with the compounds?
3 What could you describe with the compounds from exercise 4 he didn't use?

7 VOCABULARY Make phrasal verbs from the verbs and particles below. Then use the nouns derived from them to complete the sentences.

break check make rip take warm
away down in off up up

1 They have lived apart since the _____ of their marriage.
2 Let's not cook tonight. Let's get a Chinese _____.
3 Milla never wears _____ at work.
4 That DVD player costs £900! What a _____!
5 The football team has a _____ before the match starts.
6 Go to the _____ desk at least an hour before your flight.

8 SPEAKING Work in pairs. Discuss these questions.

1 What do you think of internet hoaxes like this?
2 Do you know of any others? Describe them.

The Woman in White

I can understand and react to an extract from a 19th-century novel.

1 **SPEAKING** Work in pairs. Discuss the questions.

1 What do you think makes a good mystery story?
2 Look at the picture and read lines 1–45 of the text. How do you think the woman is involved in the story?

2 Read the text. Are the sentences true or false? Find evidence in the text for your answers.

1 Before the narrative opens, the narrator had been visiting members of his family. _____
2 The narrator did not see the woman before she touched him because she was hiding from him. _____
3 The narrator is very suspicious of the woman. _____
4 The narrator refuses to help the woman. _____

CRITICAL ANALYSIS

3 Match the modern English words and phrases below with the more formal, literary words and phrases highlighted in the text.

1 rooms	5 creep	9 feelings
2 colour	6 immediately	10 strange
3 please	7 turned towards	11 was surprised at
4 welcome	8 wish to	12 seriousness

4 Write modern English equivalents for the following words and phrases in the text.

1 determined (line 17)	5 account for (line 69)
2 high-road (line 34)	6 be of assistance (line 78)
3 garments (line 43)	7 feared (line 87)
4 grave (line 55)	8 met with (line 92)

5 Answer the questions. Find evidence in the text for your answers.

1 What are the narrator's feelings as he contemplates returning to London?
2 Which route back to London does he choose to take?
3 What effect does the landscape around him have on him as he sets off home?
4 How does the woman explain her presence on the heath so late at night?
5 In the course of the conversation, what two requests does the woman make of the narrator?
6 Where does the woman wish to go?

Reading Strategy

Being able to summarise a text will enhance your awareness of how texts are organised, of how elements of the text are related, and improve your ability to pinpoint the main ideas or events.

1 Start by dividing the text into sections. Mark the points where there is a clear change of ideas or events.
2 Underline the key points or events within each section. Ignore any insignificant facts, opinions or descriptions.
3 Rewrite the key points or events in your own words. Be brief, keeping within the word limit if there is one. Do not copy out large sections of the text.

6 Read the Reading Strategy. Then follow the instructions below.

1 Divide the text into two sections. Say why you chose the point of division.
2 Use your answers to exercises 2 and 5 to prepare a summary of the text. Make notes that include:

- the main events
- relevant descriptions of scenery and surroundings
- relevant descriptions of the characters' physical appearance
- the feelings and mood of the characters
- what was said by the characters

7 **SPEAKING** Work in pairs. Take turns to use your notes to give an oral summary of the text to your partner.

8 **SPEAKING** Work in pairs. Discuss the questions.

1 If you were the narrator, what would you have done?
2 Did you enjoy the extract? Why? / Why not?
3 Does it make you want to find out what happens? Why? / Why not?
4 How does the author create atmosphere through the extract?

➡ **Vocabulary Builder** Literary devices: page 127

A strange encounter

The heat had been painfully oppressive all day, and it was now a close and [1]sultry night. My mother and sister had spoken so many last words, and had begged me to wait another five minutes so many times, that it was nearly midnight when the servant locked the garden-gate behind me. I walked forward a few paces on the shortest way back to London, then stopped and hesitated.

The moon was full and broad in the dark blue starless sky, and the [2]heath looked wild enough in the mysterious light to be hundreds of miles away from the great city that lay beneath it. The idea of descending any sooner than I could help into the heat and [3]gloom of London repelled me. The prospect of going to bed in my airless chambers, and the prospect of gradual suffocation, seemed, in my present restless frame of mind and body, to be one and the same thing. I determined to stroll home in the purer air by the most [4]roundabout way I could take; to follow the white winding paths across the lonely heath. I wound my way slowly down, enjoying the divine stillness of the scene, and admiring the soft alternations of light and shade as they followed each other over the ground on every side of me. So long as I was proceeding through this first and prettiest part of my night walk, my mind remained passively open to the impressions produced by the view; and I thought but little on any subject – indeed, so far as my own sensations were concerned, I can hardly say that I thought at all.

I had now arrived at that particular point of my walk where four roads met – the road to Hampstead, along which I had returned, the road to Finchley, the road to West End, and the road back to London. I had [5]mechanically turned in this latter direction, and was strolling along the lonely high-road when, in one moment, every drop of blood in my body was brought to a stop by the touch of a hand laid lightly and suddenly on my shoulder from behind me.

I turned on the instant, with my fingers tightening round the handle of my stick. There, in the middle of the broad bright high-road – there, as if it had that moment sprung out of the earth or dropped from the heaven – stood the figure of a [6]solitary Woman, dressed from head to foot in white garments, her face bent in grave inquiry on mine, her hand pointing to the dark cloud over London, as I faced her.

I was far too seriously startled by the suddenness with which this extraordinary apparition stood before me, in the [7]dead of night and in that lonely place, to ask what she wanted. The strange woman spoke first.

'Is that the road to London?' she said.

I looked attentively at her, as she put that singular question to me. It was then nearly one o'clock. All I could [8]discern distinctly by the moonlight was a colourless, youthful face, [9]meagre and sharp about the cheeks and chin; large, grave, [10]wistfully attentive eyes; nervous, uncertain lips; and light hair of a pale, brownish-yellow hue. There was nothing wild, nothing immodest in her manner: it was quiet and self-controlled, a little melancholy and a little [11]touched by suspicion. What sort of a woman she was, and how she came to be out alone in the high-road, an hour after midnight, I altogether failed to guess.

'Did you hear me?' she said, still quietly and rapidly, and without the least [12]fretfulness or impatience. 'I asked if that was the way to London.'

'Yes,' I replied, 'that is the way. You must excuse my not answering you before. I was rather startled by your sudden appearance in the road; and I am, even now, quite unable to account for it.'

'You don't suspect me of doing anything wrong, do you? I have done nothing wrong. I have met with an accident – I am very unfortunate in being here alone so late. Why do you suspect me of doing wrong?'

She spoke with unnecessary earnestness and agitation, and [13]shrank back from me several paces. I did my best to reassure her.

'Pray don't suppose that I have any idea of suspecting you,' I said, 'or any other wish than to be of assistance to you, if I can. I only wondered at your appearance in the road, because it seemed to me to be empty the instant before I saw you.'

She turned, and pointed back to a place at the junction of the road to London and the road to Hampstead, where there was a gap in the hedge.

'I heard you coming,' she said, 'and hid there to see what sort of man you were, before I risked speaking. I doubted and feared about it till you passed; and then I was obliged to steal after you, and touch you.' Steal after me and touch me? Why not call to me? Strange, to say the least of it.

'May I trust you?' she asked. 'You don't think the worse of me because I have met with an accident?' She stopped in confusion; [14]shifted her bag from one hand to the other; and sighed bitterly. The loneliness and helplessness of the woman touched me.

'If it troubles you to explain your strange situation to me, don't think of returning to the subject again. I have no right to ask you for any explanations. Tell me how I can help you; and if I can, I will.'

'You are very kind, and I am very, very thankful to have met you. I have only been in London once before,' she went on, more and more rapidly, 'Can I get a carriage of any kind? Is it too late? I don't know. If you could show me where to get a carriage, and if you will only promise to let me leave you, when and how I please – I have a friend in London who will be glad to receive me – I want nothing else – will you promise?'

She looked anxiously up and down the road; shifted her bag again from one hand to the other; repeated the words, 'Will you promise?' and looked hard in my face, with a [15]pleading fear and confusion that it troubled me to see.

'Are you sure that your friend in London will receive you at such a late hour as this?' I said.

'Quite sure. Only say you will let me leave you when and how I please. Will you promise?'

'Yes.'

GLOSSARY

1 sultry = hot and uncomfortable
2 heath = large area of land with rough grass
3 gloom = darkness
4 roundabout = indirect
5 mechanically = automatically

6 solitary = completely alone
7 the dead of night = the middle of the night
8 discern = recognise; see
9 meagre = (here) thin
10 wistfully = sadly

11 touched by = affected by
12 fretfulness = discomfort; unhappiness
13 shrank back = step back in fear
14 shifted = moved
15 pleading = begging; asking in an emotional way

Photo comparison

I can compare and contrast photos.

1 SPEAKING Work in pairs. How many reasons can you think of for why people read? Brainstorm ideas. Then compare your ideas with the class.

2 Read the exam task. Make notes for your answer.

Compare photos A and B and say what and why the people might be reading, and how they might be feeling.

3 🎧 1.17 Listen to a student doing the task in exercise 2. Which of her ideas are similar to yours? Which ideas are different?

4 Read the Learn this! box. Think of examples of speculation about the photos to illustrate each of the points 1–3.

LEARN THIS! Speculating
1 We can use *must* (*have*), *can't* (*have*), *might* (*have*).
2 We use *look, seem, appears,* etc. with an adjective.
3 We use *look like* + noun and *look as if* + a clause.

5 🎧 1.17 Listen again. Which structures from the Learn this! box does the student use. Can you quote her exact words?

6 KEY PHRASES Do the task in exercise 2 using photos C and D and phrases below. Try to speak for about one minute.

Comparing and contrasting photos
The most obvious similarity between the photos is …
The photos are similar in that …
What the photos have in common is …
The clearest difference between the photos is …
In contrast to photo 1, photo 2 depicts …
Photo 1 shows … . On the other hand, photo 2 shows …
In photo 1 … , while / whereas in photo 2 …

Speaking Strategy
The examiner might ask you a question about the photos which the other student has just compared. Listen carefully while the other student is speaking, and at the same time think about the photos and what you might say about them.

7 SPEAKING Read the Speaking Strategy. Work in pairs. Discuss the examiner's follow-up question below. Agree on two ways in which technology is having an effect on the way we read.

How do you think technology is affecting the way we read?

8 🎧 1.18 Listen to a student answering the question. Are her ideas similar to yours? Which of her opinions do you agree with, and which do you disagree with?

9 🎧 1.18 KEY PHRASES Read the phrases below. Then listen again and tick the phrases you hear.

Expressing opinions
a Off the top of my head, I'd say … ☐
b I tend to think that, … ☐
c There's a part of me that thinks … ☐
d All things considered, … ☐
e It would seem to me that … ☐
f I'm of the opinion that … ☐
g I think it's true to say that … ☐
h It would be wrong to argue that … ☐
i As I see it, … ☐

10 SPEAKING Work in pairs. Turn to page 151 and do the picture comparison task. Use the phrases in exercises 4, 6 and 9 to help you.

2H Writing
A film review
I can write a film review.

1 SPEAKING Work in pairs. Discuss the quotation. Do you agree? Why? / Why not?

> People who like movies have a favourite. People who love movies couldn't possibly choose.

Writing Strategy

When you write a film review, you aren't being asked to write a straightforward description but to evaluate the film from a particular point of view, e.g. its suitability for a particular audience, how it affected you, or how it exceeded or failed to meet your expectations.

2 Read the Writing Strategy and the model review. From what point of view does the writer review the film?

A I recently went to see *Boyhood* at the cinema. Made in 2015 by director Richard Linklater, it received rave reviews, was short-listed for an Oscar, and my friends all loved it. I was therefore expecting to be similarly impressed but I have to say that I was disappointed.

B The film was shot over a twelve-year period and tells the story, in 'real time', of a child named Mason who literally grows up before our eyes, from a young boy in first grade to his first day in college. We see him and his family on holiday, on road trips, at birthday parties, anniversary celebrations and other family get-togethers.

C The concept is certainly ground-breaking, and my friends found the storyline gripping, but I'm afraid I thought the film was too slow-moving, and I found all the hum-drum details of their everyday lives very tedious. It's also too long – nearly three hours!

D Ellar Coltrane is superbly cast in the role of Mason, but the supporting cast give only adequate performances, which detracts from the film. What is more, unlike my friends, I didn't find many of the characters very likeable, and so I wasn't particularly curious to know how the film would end.

E To sum up, thought-provoking and well-filmed it certainly is, but the only really clever and unique aspect of the film is that it was filmed over twelve years. If, like me, you're into fast-paced action films with breath-taking digital effects, this film is not for you.

3 VOCABULARY Read the review again. Match the paragraphs (A–E) with the descriptions (1–5) below.

1 what my friends liked, but I didn't like about the plot
2 overall impressions
3 give background and establish the writer's 'point of view'
4 what my friends liked, but I didn't like about the characters
5 brief description of the plot

Adjectives to describe films big-budget breath-taking chilling clichéd complex disappointing far-fetched fast-paced gripping ground-breaking low-budget mediocre nail-biting powerful slow-moving spectacular tedious thought-provoking two-dimensional well-rounded

4 Look at the adjectives above and answer the questions.

1 How many can you find in the review in exercise 2? What are they used to describe?
2 Which aspects of films below can they be used to describe? Some can describe more than one aspect.
   a characters   b plot
   c digital effects   d the film in general

5 Find sentences or phrases in the review in exercise 2 which have the opposite meaning to:

1 it was panned by the critics
2 it failed to make the short-list for
3 I was pleasantly surprised
4 was miscast in the role of
5 enhances the film
6 this film will appeal to you

6 Read the task below. Make notes and a paragraph plan.

> Write a review of a film which your friends didn't enjoy, but which you really liked. What aspects of the film did you disagree on?

7 Write your review (220–260 words). Use your notes from exercise 6.

CHECK YOUR WORK

 Have you ...
• written 220–260 words?
• written from the point of view specified in the task?
• checked your spelling and grammar?

3

Partners

3A Vocabulary

Friendships
I can talk about different kinds of relationships.

1 SPEAKING Work in pairs. Answer the questions.

1 What does it mean to know someone?
2 How many people do you think it is possible for a person to be friends with?

2 Read the article. How many friends does Dunbar think we can have? Why?

If you're a Facebook user, no doubt you have hundreds – if not thousands – of 'friends'. But how well do you actually know the people on your list? Are the majority classmates you see a lot of or people you got talking to once and haven't seen since? According to Robin Dunbar, a professor of evolutionary anthropology at Oxford University, there's a limit to the number of people we can know. Dunbar has done extensive research into primates and has found a correlation between the size of a primate's brain – specifically the part that controls memory – and the size of its social group. In the case of humans, Dunbar estimates that the average number of people we can maintain a stable social relationship with at any one time is around 150. Not only is Dunbar's number relevant to real-life friendships, but a study at Indiana University has shown that it may also apply to online society. Researchers analysed the complete history of three million Twitter users, and found that they maintained actual relationships with a maximum of 100 to 200 friends. These findings suggest that social media users with contact lists exceeding Dunbar's number have friended more people than they can keep track of. One way of making the list more manageable is to spring-clean it at least once a year and unfriend all the people you don't wish to stay in touch with. Just be careful not to delete anyone you're likely to run into as they won't be pleased they've been dropped.

3 VOCABULARY Complete the table with the highlighted words and phrases in the text.

Stages of friendship		
making friends	**being friends**	**losing friends**
bond with sb over sth	be inseparable	drift apart
get acquainted with sb	keep a friendship going	fall out with sb
strike up a friendship with sb		wreck a friendship

4 Read the sentences and choose the correct answer.

1 When Kim first met Meg, they **bonded over** / **ran into** / **dropped** their mutual interest in music.

2 Mia has **got acquainted** / **stayed in touch** / **fallen out** with Oscar as he accused her of being stingy. — selfish with money

3 Sharing a room can **bond** / **run into** / **wreck** a friendship.

4 My two sisters spend all of their time together – they **got talking** / **are inseparable** / **drifted apart**.

5 I **got acquainted with** / **kept track of** / **unfriended** Allie on the first day of my summer job and now we're getting to know each other.

6 It isn't easy to **strike up a friendship** / **keep a friendship going** / **wreck a friendship** when a classmate changes school.

7 As kids, my brother and I used to be very close, but now we're older, we've **run into each other** / **seen a lot of each other** / **drifted apart**.

8 My grandparents quickly settled into their new home as they **struck up a friendship** / **were inseparable** / **fell out** with their neighbours.

> **spring-clean** (verb) to clean a house, room, etc. thoroughly, including the parts you do not normally clean

5 Read the definition of 'spring-clean' from the *Oxford Advanced Learner's Dictionary* and find the word in the text. What does 'spring-clean' mean in the context of social media?

6 🎧 1.19 Listen to five speakers who have been affected by spring-cleaning on social media. Why did their 'friends' unfriend them?

7 🎧 1.19 Listen again. Match speakers 1–5 to how they feel (A–H) about being unfriended.

Speaker 1 _____
Speaker 2 _____
Speaker 3 _____
Speaker 4 _____
Speaker 5 _____

A confused
B delighted
C disappointed
D indifferent
E offended
F proud and pleased
G surprised
H worried

8 VOCABULARY Work in pairs. Check the meaning of the adjectives below. Match two adjectives with each of the adjectives A–H in exercise 7.

Feelings aggrieved baffled devastated ecstatic elated gobsmacked gutted honoured impervious outraged perplexed perturbed privileged stunned troubled unconcerned

> **FLUENCY!**
> An idiom is a phrase whose meaning is different from the meanings of the individual words.
> *Jess and I go back a long way.*
> When you come across a new idiom, make a note of the context it is used in. For example, the idiom above is used in the context of relationships.

9 🎧 1.19 VOCABULARY Read the Fluency! box. Complete the relationship idioms from the recording with the words below. Then listen again and check your answers.

Idioms: relationships back behind inside like off on same through to ups

1 go back a long way
2 have (your) _____ups_____ and downs
3 hit it _____off_____
4 know somebody _inside_ out
5 be on the _____same_____ wavelength
6 get on like a house _____on_____ fire
7 be _like_ chalk and cheese
8 not see eye _____to_____ eye
9 stick together _____through_____ thick and thin
10 talk about sb _____behind_____ (their) back

10 Replace the underlined words with the correct form of the idioms in exercise 9.

1 My family has experienced a mixture of good things and bad things in life, but we're still together.

2 Instead of discussing me without my knowledge, why don't you say things to my face?

3 There's a great atmosphere in our volleyball team this year. All the players have a very friendly relationship.

4 John's housemates are always arguing because they don't share the same views on the European Union.

5 Jay and Poppy are completely different from each other. I was gobsmacked when they became a couple.

6 My grandparents have stayed with each other even when things were hard, and now they're enjoying their retirement.

7 Tim and I have known each other for years. We first met as playmates at nursery school.

8 Debbie and I have always been friends. We liked each other the moment we met.

9 I don't understand some of my school friends. We don't think the same way about things.

10 My best friend is familiar with everything about me, so I don't usually have to explain myself to her.

> ➡ **Vocabulary Builder** Love idioms: page 127

11 SPEAKING Work in pairs. Think of three people you know who fit the descriptions below. For each person, say how you met and how your friendship developed.

1 one of your closest friends in real life
2 a real-life friend you're no longer in touch with
3 a friend who you haven't met in real life

Reporting structures
I can report direct speech in a variety of ways.

1 **SPEAKING** What do you know about the play *Romeo and Juliet*? What kind of story is it? Does it have a happy ending?

2 Read the summary of a scene from *Romeo and Juliet*. What were the actual words used by the characters?

> Juliet called out to Romeo and ¹enquired what time she should send someone to get him. Romeo ²proposed that it should be at nine, and Juliet ³promised to do what he suggested. She ⁴confessed to not wanting to wait, complaining that it would be a very long time, and then ⁵admitted forgetting why she had called Romeo back. Romeo ⁶offered to stand there until she remembered the reason, and Juliet ⁷threatened never to remember it, so that he would have to stand there forever.

3 🎧 **1.20** Listen and check. How similar are your answers?

LEARN THIS! Reporting structures

We can use different structures to report requests, offers, promises, questions, etc. Some verbs use more than one structure, e.g. *recommend*, *suggest*.

1 verb + infinitive with *to*
   agree, refuse, *threaten* , *promise* , *offer*

2 verb + object + infinitive with *to*
   advise, beg, encourage, order, remind, urge

3 verb + gerund or verb + perfect gerund
   deny, mention, recommend, regret, suggest, *admit*
   We can also use a perfect gerund.
   He regretted having spoken harshly to her.

4 verb + preposition + gerund
   apologise for, insist on, *confess*
   NB we use an object pronoun or a possessive adjective for the subject of the gerund where it is different from the subject of the main verb.
   She insisted on Tom / him doing ...
   She insisted on Tom's / his doing ... (more formal)

5 verb + object + preposition + gerund
   accuse sb of, blame sb for, warn sb against

6 verb + *that* + *should* clause
   recommend, suggest, *propose*
   With these verbs we can also use a present subjunctive (infinitive without *to*) instead of a *should* clause.
   Romeo proposed she send a messenger at nine.

7 verb + question word / *if* or *whether*
   ask, wonder, *enquire*

4 Read the Learn this! box and complete it with the highlighted reporting verbs in exercise 2.

5 Read and report the direct speech. Use the verbs below. Where two reporting structures are possible, use both.

agree insist mention order recommend warn wonder

1 'You must marry Count Paris.' Juliet's father told her.
   Juliet's father *ordered her to marry Count Paris.*

2 'All right, I'll help you,' said Friar Lawrence to Juliet.
   Friar Lawrence *agreed to help Juliet* .

3 'The best thing to do is take a potion,' the friar told her.
   The friar *recommended that to take a potion* .

4 'Don't think like a child,' he said to Juliet.
   He *warned her to not think like a child* .

5 'Where have you been?' asked Juliet's father.
   Juliet's father *wondered where she had been* .

6 'I saw Paris while I was with Friar Lawrence,' said Juliet.
   Juliet *mentioned seeing Paris* .

7 'I must be alone in my room tonight,' Juliet said.
   Juliet *insisted on being alone* .

↪ **Grammar Builder 3.1** page 137

6 **USE OF ENGLISH** Complete the second sentence so that it means the same as the first. Write no more than six words and include the word in brackets. Use verbs from the Learn this! box. If a number of structures are possible, use all of them.

1 'I wish I had asked Lola for her phone number.' (not)
   I *regret not asking* for her phone number.

2 'I'm sorry I shouted at you,' Anouk told Mark. (to)
   Anouk *apologise to Mark for shouting* at him.

3 'Will you be dining alone?' the waiter asked her. (whether)
   The waiter *wondered if whether* alone. *she would be dining*

4 'It's your fault I lost my mobile,' Freya told me. (for)
   Freya *blamed me for the lost of* her mobile.

5 'Why don't you try the new Thai restaurant?' he told us. (that)
   He *recommended that we try* the new Thai restaurant.

6 'I won't lie to my friends for you,' Jack told Adam. (his)
   Jack *refused to lie to his friends* for Adam.

7 'Don't forget to take all of your belongings with you.' (leave)
   I must *remind you not to leave* any of your belongings here.

7 **SPEAKING** Work in pairs. Report the lines from famous films below. Then think of a line of your own. Report it and have the class guess the line and which film it comes from.

1 'I am your father!' (Darth Vader / Luke: *Star Wars*)

> Darth Vader admitted being Luke's father.

2 'I will find you, and I will kill you.' (Bryan / Marko: *Taken*)
3 'Just keep swimming.' (Dory / Marlin: *Finding Nemo*)
4 'Run, Forrest! Run!' (Jenny / Forrest: *Forrest Gump*)
5 'I see dead people.' (Cole Sear: *The Sixth Sense*)

Listening

Successful business partnerships

I can understand and react to a radio programme about successful business partnerships.

1 SPEAKING Work in pairs. What do you think are the advantages and disadvantages of starting a business on your own or with a friend?

> **Listening Strategy**
>
> To help you choose the correct answer, remember that the words in the options in the task will be paraphrased in the recording. This means that the speakers will use different words to express the same idea.

2 Read the Listening Strategy. Then look at the question below. Think of a way in which each of the options might be paraphrased.

Jerry was drawn towards Ben because Ben
a was the same age as him.
b came out with a funny remark.
c did not excel at P.E.
d shared his love of ice cream.

3 🎧 **1.21** Listen to the story of how the ice-cream company Ben & Jerry's was formed. Look at exercise 2 again and choose the correct answer. How was the correct option phrased in the recording?

4 🎧 **1.22** Listen to a radio interview about successful business partnerships. Choose the correct answer (a–d).

1 Margaret refers to Bill Gates and Paul Allen as 'partners-in-crime' because they
a failed their final year at school due to lack of work.
b deceived the I.T. teacher into giving them extra computer time.
c used their superior knowledge of I.T. to their advantage.
d stopped attending school to pursue their interest in I.T.
2 Margaret says that Steve Wozniak had to be persuaded by Steve Jobs
a to attend a Bob Dylan concert.
b to accept a third member into the partnership.
c to develop his second computer.
d to commercialise his new invention.
3 Margaret mentions Hewlett and Packard's holiday because it marks the moment the two founders
a sealed their friendship definitively.
b met for the first time.
c decided on a name for their new company.
d came up with the idea of opening a business.
4 According to Margaret, what happened on the first occasion of Brin and Page's acquaintance?
a They got on like a house on fire.
b They didn't exchange a single word.
c They refused to have anything to do with each other.
d They didn't see eye to eye.
5 Which statement is true for all four partnerships?
a The partners were born in the same year.
b The partners got acquainted during their studies.
c The partners bonded over a common interest.
d The partners graduated at the top of their class.

5 🎧 **1.22 VOCABULARY** Listen again. How are the underlined words and phrases paraphrased in the recording?

1 Having a common interest in computers …
2 The pair began to think about going into business together.
3 Allen convinced Gates to leave university before completing the course …
4 Jobs persuaded him to set up a company to sell it …
5 Ronald Wayne, who later withdrew from the deal …
6 The company became successful quickly …
7 … neither of the founders was alive to see this achievement.
8 Larry Page started the relationship badly with Sergey Brin …

6 Complete the sentences with the expressions in exercise 5.

1 Harry didn't finish the course. He *dropped out*.
2 They were delighted to attend their son's graduation as they had doubts that they would ever …
3 I was late on the first day of my work experience, so I …
4 Mia isn't sure whether to study law or not, but she's …
5 The project became too expensive, so in the end they …
6 The campaign was successful, so the new product …
7 I had no desire to go to the open day, but my friends …
8 As supporters of West Ham, Rob and Eddie never miss a match. They …

7 SPEAKING Work in pairs. Discuss the questions.

1 What do you think are the reasons for the success of the four business partnerships in the recording?
2 If you were setting up a business, which of the people you know would you choose as a partner? Why?
3 Number the qualities 1–10 in the order of their importance to a successful business relationship. (1 = most important.)

communication compatibility confidence co-operation
drive flexibility passion punctuality respect trust

➤➤ **Vocabulary Builder** Business collocations: page 127

Comparative and superlative structures

I can compare partners-in-crime from the past.

1 SPEAKING Work in pairs. Discuss the meaning of the word 'outlaw'. Why are outlaws often popular with the public?

2 Read part 1 of the text. What were the real names of Butch Cassidy and the Sundance Kid?

Robert Leroy Parker left home at thirteen. After working in a butcher's shop, where he earned the nickname Butch, he took a job as a farmhand. But earning a living was not as easy as he had imagined. Then he met Mike Cassidy, a horse thief. Mike seemed to be working only half as hard as Butch did on the farm, but earning a good deal more. Butch wanted as easy a life as Mike's, so he too turned to crime, and by the mid 1890s, he was leading a gang of outlaws called The Wild Bunch. It was at this point that Butch, who was now calling himself Butch Cassidy, met Harry Longabaugh, better known as the Sundance Kid, and invited him to join them. Together, they were as successful a band of robbers as ever seen in the American West. Soon, they were committing bigger and bigger robberies. And the more daring the crime, the more popular they became with the public.

3 Read the Learn this! box. Which comparative structures can you find in the text in exercise 2?

LEARN THIS! Advanced comparisons

a Comparatives can be followed by a clause. To avoid repetition, the clause may be reduced or it may include an auxiliary verb.

We arrived earlier than (we) expected.

They stole more from trains than they did from banks.

b We can use *half, twice, three times, ten times,* etc. to qualify a comparison with *as ... as ...* . With other comparative forms, we can use *three times, ten times,* etc. but NOT *half* or *twice.*

It took twice as long as we thought it would.

They're ten times richer than us.

NOT ~~They're twice richer than us.~~ ✗

c When we use *as ... as ...* with a singular countable noun, we need *a/an* before the noun.

It's as exciting a story as you'll ever read.

In the negative, we can either use *not as ... as ...* or *not such ... as ...* BUT note the different position of *a/an.*

She isn't as good a singer as she thinks.

She isn't such a good singer as she thinks.

d We can use double comparatives to show change.

They were becoming richer and richer / more and more reckless / less and less friendly.

The more she talked, the less I understood.

4 Find these comparatives forms in the text in exercise 2.

a a comparison with an adverb
b an irregular comparative form
c the comparative form of *much*

LOOK OUT!

1 We can use *as* or *like* + a clause to convey similarity. *Like* is more informal.

She hopes to study at Yale, as / like her mum did.

We can invert the subject and object of the clause after *as* (but not after *like*).

She hopes to study at Yale, as did her mum.

2 We can use *like* + noun / pronoun to convey similarity.

Like his friends, Tom is a huge basketball fan.

However, *as* + noun indicates identity, NOT similarity.

As your lawyer, I advise you to appeal. (I'm your lawyer.)

5 Read the Look out! box. Choose the correct word to complete each sentence. Choose both if both are correct.

1 His parents were farmers, **as / like** was his uncle.
2 **As / Like** a member of the Royal Family, Prince William receives public money each year.
3 Luke studied maths at university, **as / like** his sister had.
4 He has blond hair, **as / like** do all of his family.
5 Anna earns more **as / like** a waitress than she did **as / like** a receptionist.
6 Let's have a summer party, **as / like** we did last year.

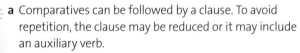 ➜ Grammar Builder 3.2 page 138

6 USE OF ENGLISH Complete part 2 of the text. Write one word in each gap.

Butch Cassidy and the Sundance Kid probably did not have
¹_____ a close friendship as depicted in the Hollywood film about them, but they certainly had plenty in common. Sundance had left home at a young age, as ²_____ Butch. And ³_____ Butch, he had spent time in prison. Sundance was considered to be as fast ⁴_____ gunfighter as anyone in the West, although the gang used less violence during their crimes than many other outlaws ⁵_____. But ⁶_____ more famous they became, the ⁷_____ desperate the police were to catch them. Pursued by detectives, they had ⁸_____ and ⁹_____ freedom. In 1901, Butch and Sundance fled to South America, where they were eventually killed in a shoot-out with police, ¹⁰_____ were many outlaws in those days.

7 SPEAKING Work in pairs. How do you imagine life as an outlaw in the Wild West was similar to or different from life as a modern criminial? Use comparative structures from the lesson.

As an outlaw, you were more ...
Like modern criminials, outlaws often ...
It wasn't such a ... life as people sometimes ...

Metaphors and similes

I can use metaphors and similes to make comparisons.

1 SPEAKING Work in pairs. Answer the questions. What are the advantages and disadvantages of sharing a talent with a sibling, for example, in art, music or sport?

2 Read the blog post and answer the questions.

1 What obstacles did the Singh Twins face in their youth?
2 How have they used these obstacles to their advantage?

The Singh Twins

Twins Amrit and Rabindra Singh are two artists I admire enormously. In my opinion, their work is as interesting as any single contemporary artist, if not more so. The sisters are identical, so they're like two peas in a pod to look at. As students, they had a bumpy ride through the education system: they were separated into different classes at school to enable the teachers to tell them apart, and also later at art college so that each would develop her own individual style. Life wasn't plain sailing for them because of their background either – as British Asians, they faced discrimination not only from classmates, but also from art college tutors, who insisted they ignore their own cultural heritage in favour of contemporary Western culture and way of life. Refusing to act like sheep, the sisters rebelled by wearing identical clothes to emphasise their union as twins and by taking inspiration for their art from a traditional Indian medium: the miniature. They borrowed the features of these tiny detailed paintings and mixed them with more up-to-date themes, such as consumerism and globalisation, to create a style they call 'past modern'. Today, these internationally acclaimed artists exhibit their works under a single name: the Singh Twins.

LEARN THIS! Metaphors and similes

- We use metaphors and similes to make comparisons.
- A metaphor describes a person or object as having similar characteristics to another person or object which it isn't usually associated with.
  A celebrity's life is an open book. (An open book has no secrets, a celebrity's life is the same.)
- A simile is a comparison that contains the words *as* or *like*. We can form similes in the following ways:
  1 noun + *like* + noun
  Tom's got a face like thunder. He must be angry.
  2 verb + *like* + noun
  My laptop worked like a dream before I dropped it.
  3 *as* + adjective + *as*
  Sorry, I'm as deaf as a post. Can you say that again?

3 Read the Learn this! box. Then answer the questions about the highlighted phrases in the blog post in exercise 2.

1 Are the phrases similes or metaphors?
2 What comparison is being made? How does it work?
3 How would you make the same comparison in your own language?

4 Read the sentences and decide if they contain similes or metaphors. Are any of them similar in your own language?

1 The lake was a mirror before we jumped in.
2 They get on like a house on fire and they never argue.
3 His hand was as cold as ice when I shook it.
4 For the old and infirm, a fourth-floor flat can be a prison.
5 The kitchen's a disaster area – will you clear up, please?
6 Lucy is as busy as a bee preparing for her party.
7 We're brothers, but we're like chalk and cheese.
8 At the end of the story, the hero dies of a broken heart.

5 VOCABULARY Match the nouns in A with their main characteristics in B. Then make similes with *as* or *like*.

a baby cries = cry like a baby

A		B		A		B	
1	baby	a	fight	6	feather	f	fit
2	bat	b	cry	7	glove	g	eat
3	bone	c	cool	8	horse	h	light
4	cats and dogs	d	blind	9	log	i	quiet
5	cucumber	e	dry	10	mouse	j	sleep

6 SPEAKING Work in pairs. Choose six similes from the lesson to describe people you know.

> My grandma is as blind as a bat and she's always losing her glasses.

Animal partnerships

I can understand and react to an article about symbiosis.

1 SPEAKING Look at the photos and answer the questions.

1 What is happening in each of the photos?
2 What does each species gain from the interaction?

Reading Strategy

When you are doing a gapped-paragraph task, read the text quickly, ignoring the gaps, to get a general idea of what it is about. Then read carefully the paragraphs before and after the gap to identify in them the topics and ideas the missing paragraph should refer to. Read through the options A–G to find the paragraphs about that topic. Try each paragraph in the gap until you find the one that fits best.

2 Read the Reading Strategy. Then read the first two paragraphs of the text before and after gap 1. Identify the topics and ideas which the missing paragraph needs to refer to. Then read paragraphs A–G and choose the correct one.

3 Read the text. Match paragraphs A–G with gaps 2–6. There is one extra paragraph. Remember to follow the procedure in the Reading Strategy.

4 Read the text again. Answer the questions.

1 Why does the writer say that the plot of *Finding Nemo* 'pales in comparison' with the real-life story of the clownfish?
2 At what stage in their lives are clownfish not in contact with sea anemones? Why not?
3 How many female clownfish are there in each group? What function do female clownfish perform?
4 The text states that it is 'easier said than done' for larvae to find a home on the reef. What dangers do they face?
5 Why are clownfish thought to be immune to the poison on the anemones' tentacles?
6 What differences did researchers notice between conditions when the clownfish and the sea anemone were together and when they were apart?
7 What conclusion did they draw from their observations?
8 How have these findings changed the way in which the symbiotic relationship between clownfish and sea anemone is viewed?

CRITICAL ANALYSIS

5 Look at the highlighted emphatic adjectives in the text. Read the sentences around them and try to work out their meaning. Then match them with the basic adjectives below.

entertaining difficult energetic great strict
surprising threatened tiny

[handwritten: frenetic profound rigid, miniscule, startling doomed]
entertaining – captivating

6 Why did the writer choose to use emphatic rather than standard adjectives in the text?

7 Complete the sentences with a pair of adjectives in exercise 6. In each case, say what effect each of the adjectives has.

1 The game began at a(n) __frenetic__ / __energetic__ pace and United took the lead after just three minutes.
2 The Earth is currently undergoing __great__ / __profound__ changes in its climate.
3 The cool air was damp with __miniscule__ / __tiny__ droplets of rain that left a shiny film on everything they touched.
4 I thought the book was boring, but the film was __entertaining__ / __captivating__. *[handwritten: doomed threatened]*
5 The expedition was __difficult__ / __daunting__ from the start due to a lack of planning.
6 Lost in the blizzard, the girl faced the __difficult__ / __daunting__ prospect of finding her way home alone.
7 His __rigid__ / __strict__ daily routine allows no time for dealing with the unexpected.
8 The police made the __surprising__ / __startling__ discovery that the victim had faked her own death.

8 SPEAKING Work with a partner. Look at the symbiotic relationships in exercise 1. Answer the questions.

1 What might cause the relationship to break down?
2 What might happen to each of the partners if the relationship breaks down?
3 What might happen to the surrounding environment if the relationship breaks down?

SYMBIOSIS: a mutual understanding

Anyone who has seen either of Disney's animated feature films *Finding Nemo* or *Finding Dory* will recognise a clownfish when they see one. In the first film, Nemo is caught by fishermen, prompting his father to set out on a daunting journey in order to bring Nemo home. Though captivating, the plot of the film pales in comparison with the real-life story of the clownfish, and the symbiotic relationship it has with its sea-anemone home.

1 *G*

Back at the reef, there is a rigid hierarchy among the half dozen or so clownfish that occupy each host anemone. At the top of the group is the largest fish, the dominant female, and next in line is the dominant male. When the female dies, a startling transformation takes place: the dominant male gets larger and changes sex, replacing its deceased partner as the dominant female.

2 *B*

However, finding a home on the reef is easier said than done. Not only do the larvae have to dodge predatory fish in search of their next meal, but they also face rejection from their own kind if they approach the wrong anemone. Clownfish are extremely protective of their group and will chase off other clownfish that don't fit into their hierarchy.

3 *E*

Although highly poisonous, these waving arms that move with the ocean currents do not seem to affect the clownfish. Apparently, the fish manage to avoid the toxin by rubbing against the anemone, covering themselves in its mucus. This coating seems to trick the anemone into thinking the fish is part of the anemone, allowing the clownfish to shelter inside.

4 *A*

But this is not the only service they provide. Scientists have recently found that the clownfish is much more valuable to the anemone than it was previously thought.

5 *F*

To understand this phenomenon, the team decided to film the behaviour of the clownfish within the anemone. What they witnessed left them stunned. At regular intervals, the clownfish would perform what appeared to be a kind of dance, flapping its fins while darting from one side to another. This caused the anemone to fill out and increase in size.

6 *C*

These findings highlight the profound importance of this symbiotic relationship for the sea anemone as well as for the clownfish. It has long been known that the clownfish would be lost without its anemone home, but now we are also aware that the anemone would be doomed without the clownfish.

A In exchange for this protection, the clownfish performs a series of functions beneficial to the anemone. The first of these is to scare off its greatest predator: the butterfly fish, which eats sea anemones. The clownfish does this by emitting a high-pitched sound that deters the butterfly fish from approaching.

B This movement up the hierarchical ladder affects every member of the group. A fish only gets bigger when a larger fish above it dies. When the dominant male replaces the female, the next-largest fish grows larger to occupy its place, and so on, until there is a vacancy at the bottom of the ladder for a tiny post-larva returning from the ocean surface.

C The researchers concluded that through its 'dance', the clownfish was helping the anemone to breathe. The fish's frenetic movements move the water around the stationary anemone, providing it with more oxygen, helping to speed up its metabolism, and enabling it to grow faster.

D Scientists have found sea anemones in all of the word's oceans. Related closely to coral and jellyfish, their bodies are hollow columns with a mouth and stinging tentacles at the top. They mostly live attached to rocks on the sea bed or on coral reefs, waiting for small fish and other prey to swim close enough to become trapped.

E Those larvae that fail to find a place in a host anemone will not survive. Clownfish need the anemone's protection because, although they are quite small, their neon colours make them highly conspicuous. Moreover, they cannot swim very fast, so they are easy prey for larger predators, such as grouper or barracuda. Among the tentacles of the anemone, they find refuge.

F The discovery was made by a team of marine biologists from Auburn University, Alabama, who were studying the amount of oxygen the clownfish and the anemone used, both individually and together. In the course of their research, they found that the two species used up far more oxygen when they were in contact with each other than either could use on its own.

G The fish's life begins when it hatches from the miniscule egg laid by its mother on the coral near the anemone she inhabits with her group. Remarkably, all clownfish larvae are male. As soon as a batch of larvae hatches, they all leave the reef and head for the ocean surface, where they feed on plankton for a few weeks – the only period they ever spend away from the anemones.

Collaborative task

I can maintain the interaction in a collaborative task and reach an agreement.

1 SPEAKING Describe the photo. How do you think the people are feeling? What are the advantages of doing this activity with a friend?

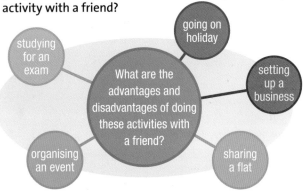

going on holiday

studying for an exam

What are the advantages and disadvantages of doing these activities with a friend?

setting up a business

organising an event

sharing a flat

2 🎧 **1.23** Read the task above. Then listen to two students doing the task. Answer the questions.

1 Which points in the task did they cover?
2 Which advantages and disadvantages do they give for each point?

> **Speaking Strategy (1)**
>
> In the discussion phase of a collaborative task, avoid repeating the words in the question. For example, when you are asked to discuss advantages and disadvantages, use synonyms for these words:
>
> It's a plus for me having a friend to study with.
>
> I find it difficult to stay focused when I study with a friend, so for me, it's a minus.

3 KEY PHRASES Read the Speaking Strategy. Then complete the phrases with the words below.

added   benefit   downside   drawbacks   main   outweigh
plus   pros

> Talking about advantages and disadvantages
> 1 the _____ (dis)advantage of ... is ...
> 2 one major _____ / drawback of ... is ...
> 3 the upside / _____ of ... is ...
> 4 weighing up the _____ and cons ... , I'd say ...
> 5 ... has some additional benefits / _____ , such as ...
> 6 ... has the _____ bonus of ...
> 7 the advantages _____ the disadvantages
> 8 for me, it's a _____ / minus

4 🎧 **1.23** Listen again. Which phrases from exercise 3 do the speakers use. How do they complete them?

5 SPEAKING Work in groups of four. Form two pairs, A and B.

Pair A make a list of:
a the benefits of setting up a business with a friend.
b the drawbacks of organising an event with a friend.
Pair B make a list of:
a the drawbacks of setting up a business with a friend.
b the benefits of organising an event with a friend.

6 SPEAKING Work in the same groups of four. Now form two new pairs, with one student from Pair A and one student from Pair B. Discuss the advantages and disadvantages of the two activities. Try to maintain the interaction by using the phrases in exercise 3.

> **Speaking Strategy (2)**
>
> When you are discussing the different options in this task, you and your partner may not share the same opinions. In this case, you should negotiate to try to reach an agreement. Negotiating involves:
> • disagreeing politely and justifying your opinion.
> • asking whether your partner agrees.
> • conceding a point.
> • concluding the discussion.

7 KEY PHRASES Read the Speaking Strategy. Complete the phrases with the words below.

along   come   disagree   fair   going   happier   help
point   suppose   way   wonder   wrap

> Disagreeing politely
> I can't ¹_____ thinking that ...
> That's one ²_____ of looking at it, I suppose, but ...
> Maybe, but I just ³_____ if ...
> Asking if your partner agrees
> Would you be ⁴_____ if ...?
> You wouldn't ⁵_____ with that, would you?
> Would you go ⁶_____ with that?
> Conceding a point
> Good ⁷_____ . I hadn't thought of that.
> ⁸_____ enough. I can accept that.
> Yes, I ⁹_____ you're right.
> Concluding the discussion
> So, have we ¹⁰_____ to a decision?
> Which one are we ¹¹_____ for, then?
> Let's ¹²_____ this up, shall we?

Which of the activities is likely to cause the greatest problems in a friendship?

8 🎧 **1.24** Read the question above. Then listen to the same two students answering it.

1 Which of the key phrases from exercise 7 do they use?
2 What decision to they come to?

9 SPEAKING Work in pairs. Turn to page 151 and do the speaking task. Use phrases from exercises 3 and 7.

Writing

A proposal

I can write a proposal.

1 SPEAKING Work in pairs. Think back to your first day at school. What were you anxious about? How might your school have made your first day easier?

The head teacher of your school is concerned about the length of time it takes new students to integrate. She has invited you to send in a proposal explaining why integration takes so long, suggesting what could be done to speed up the process and saying how your suggestions might affect the rest of the school community.

2 Read the task above and the proposal below. Answer the questions.

   1 In which paragraphs are the three elements of the task included?

   2 How are the recommendations in the proposal different from your ideas? Do you agree with them?

A warmer welcome

Introduction

In this proposal, I will present some of the difficulties new students face in integrating at our school, make some recommendations as to how the situation could be improved, and explain what effect the improvements may have on the rest of the school community.

Current situation

Feedback from students new to the school suggests that its sheer size is rather daunting at first. The majority come from surrounding villages, so few of them have friends at the school on their arrival. Most mention getting lost and some admit to not being familiar with the layout of the school until well into the first term.

Key needs to be addressed

New students should have access to a plan of our school before term starts. It would also help if they could meet some existing students. Moreover, the classrooms in the school need to be better signposted so that new students can find their way around more easily.

Recommendations

I would like to suggest the following:

- The school should organise a mentoring system by which an existing student shows a new student around the school and then checks on them every week.
- A plan of the school should be made available to new students either on our website or on the first day.
- Signs should be put up throughout the school, indicating the location of different areas. This would benefit all the school community, not only newcomers.

If these recommendations are carried out, the integration of new students is bound to be smoother.

3 Read the Writing Strategy. Then study the structure in the proposal. Work in pairs to think of an alternative title and alternative sub-headings.

4 KEY PHRASES Complete eight of the phrases with the words below. Then complete the remaining phrases with words from the proposal in exercise 2.

aim focus implemented ought proposal recommend results survey

Stating the purpose
The main ¹_____ of this proposal is to …
This ²_____ is intended to …
In this proposal, I will ³_____ …
Background information
Comments made during ⁴_____ groups show that …
⁵_____ from … suggests that …
Following a ⁶_____ of … it was revealed that …
Making recommendations and suggestions
There ⁷_____ to be …
I ⁸_____ that …
… ⁹need / _____ + passive infinitive
Final recommendation
Unless these ideas are ¹⁰_____, it is unlikely …
The ¹¹_____ of … suggest that … would be the best option
If these ¹²_____ are carried out, …

The head teacher is concerned about the number of cases of bullying in your school. She has invited you to send in a proposal explaining why bullying occurs in the school, suggesting what could be done to stop it and saying how your suggestions might affect the rest of the school community.

5 Read the task and follow the instructions below.

   1 Underline the three elements to be included in the proposal.
   2 Brainstorm three answers for each of the elements.
   3 Write a paragraph plan for the proposal.
   4 Choose a title and sub-headings for each paragraph.

6 Now write your proposal (220–260 words). Use your notes from exercise 5.

CHECK YOUR WORK

Have you …
- written 220–260 words?
- followed the structure in the Writing Strategy?
- included phrases for writing proposals?

Reading

1 Read the strategy and question 1 in exercise 2. Identify the two pieces of information you need to find. Read the text in exercise 2 and identify the section which contains a paraphrase of both parts of the question.

2 Read the article and match sections A–E with questions 2–9.

Which section …
1 mentions two similar productions that preceded *Game of Thrones* and were highly successful? *B*
2 comments on a feature of the genre which influences the appreciation of the audience? *C /A*
3 implies that the reason for *Game of Thrones*' popularity is not apparent at first glance? *A*
4 reveals that there may be an ulterior motive for the TV adaptation of *Game of Thrones*? *D*
5 indicates several strategies used to adapt the material from one medium to another? *B*
6 uses aspects of the real world to make a point about *Game of Thrones*? *F*
7 suggests that *Game of Thrones* may not have been destined for success from the start? *A*
8 describes a well-loved character who refuses to let others get the better of him or her? *D*
9 compares *Game of Thrones* to another genre which is more problematic to adapt for TV. *C*

Why is *Game of Thrones* so popular?

A critic explores how a niche book series became a TV phenomenon.

A American TV network HBO took a risk in adapting George RR Martin's *A Song of Fire and Ice* novels for the screen. Despite being bestsellers, the books belong to the epic fantasy genre, which attracts a fraction of the audience needed to make a profit on television. Set in an imaginary world, the story involves multiple plots and a dense web of characters made up of kings and queens, brave warriors and magical creatures, such as dragons. Yet, producers saw through the elaborate fairy story to spot a theme with a potential for huge success: old-fashioned escapism. In the world of *Game of Thrones*, you can solve all of your problems if you have a horse and a sword.

B On-screen fantasy sagas are not new, of course. Cinema has seen plenty of them, such as William Wyler's 1959 epic movie *Ben Hur*, and the 1938 classic *The Adventures of Robin Hood*. *Game of Thrones* has the drama and gravitas of the first and the wit and wordplay of the second. To boost the appeal of Martin's tale of warring families, executive producers David Benioff and DB Weiss added extra ingredients to the mix: romance and bloody battle scenes, and increased the pace of the action to have viewers sitting on the edge of their seats.

C Unlike *Game of Thrones*' style of escapism, the typical costume drama is most often based on, and constrained by, historical fact, which often stands in the way of viewers' enjoyment, as they are obliged to recall stuff that sent them to sleep in school. It's a tedious reliance upon history that slowed down battle-focused TV shows that preceded *Game of Thrones*, firstly *Rome* and then *Spartacus*. As a fantasy, *Game of Thrones* does not suffer from this restriction: it is unchained from history.

D It helps, of course, that *Game of Thrones* features many fine actors. Chief among them is Peter Dinklage, whose Tyrion Lannister has a strong inclination for revenge. He absorbs any ridicule of his diminutive height not by getting mad but by getting even – a fantasy for anyone who's suffered bullies. Less well-known actors, such as Maisie Williams as the brave tomboy Arya Stark, and Lena Headey as mistress of deceit Cersei Lannister, also quickly established themselves as fan favourites. And the presence of esteemed actors like *The Jewel in the Crown*'s Charles Dance and *The Avengers*' Diana Rigg shows how *Game of Thrones*' producers are as keen to make show-business history as they are to adapt Martin's novels to the small screen.

E At its core, there is a primitive appeal to the story. Author George RR Martin's web of characters and their relationships may be confusing, but there's a moral simplicity to *Game of Thrones* that attracted audiences to it. If your primary concern is staying alive, all your other problems and worries seem minor indeed. At a time when people fear upsetting the boss, or are struggling to make the monthly mortgage payment, the escapism of a programme in which bosses can be cut down to size holds an instinctive attraction. That particular fantasy of revenge and triumph is very real – and most of us can relate to it. Even if you'll never get to ride a dragon.

Listening

3 Read the strategy above and the two tasks in exercise 4. Identify the question asked in the rubrics of each of the tasks. Then read A–H and think about how the options answer these questions.

4 🎧 **1.25** You will hear five short extracts in which people are talking about writing courses they have attended.

TASK ONE: For questions 1–5, choose from the list (A–H) each speaker's main reason for attending the course.

Speaker 1	1 _____		Speaker 4	4 _____
Speaker 2	2 _____		Speaker 5	5 _____
Speaker 3	3 _____			

A build on existing skills   E prove someone wrong
B fulfil an ambition   F replace someone
C get a book deal   G spend time with similar people
D make contacts   H take on a challenge

TASK TWO: For questions 6–10, choose from the list (A–H) how each speaker feels about the course they attended.

Speaker 1   **6** _____   Speaker 4   **9** _____
Speaker 2   **7** _____   Speaker 5   **10** _____
Speaker 3   **8** _____

A delighted with the instructor
B eager to put new techniques into practice
C encouraged by feedback from peers
D glad to have had doubts resolved
E grateful for practical information
F hopeful about future success
G reassured by the level of others
H surprised by the progress made

Use of English

5 Read the strategy and look at gaps 1–8 in the text. What do you need to complete each gap: an idiom, a collocation, a set phrase or a phrasal verb? Complete the text. Choose the correct answers (a, b, c or d).

Brothers make Irish sporting history

Two brothers ¹_____ Irish sporting history at the 2016 Rio Olympics by winning their country's first Olympic medal in rowing. Gary and Paul O'Donovan from Skibbereen in County Cork finished less than a second behind Olympic ²_____ France in the final of the lightweight double sculls. Gary and Paul became involved with rowing in 2001 when they were eight and seven ³_____, and until 2013 they were coached by their father. Their first ⁴_____ competition was in 2008, when they were ⁵_____ for the Irish junior team to compete at the Home International Regatta ⁶_____ in Cardiff, Wales, where they won a gold medal. Since their ⁷_____ in Brazil, the brothers have gained a considerable following due to the ⁸_____ entertaining interviews they have been giving both to the press and on TV.

1 a did b earned c got d made
2 a champions b medalists c winners d victors
3 a accordingly b correspondingly c proportionately d respectively
4 a influential b major c outstanding d principal
5 a appointed b elected c named d selected
6 a celebrated b conducted c held d run
7 a display b performance c portrayal d realisation
8 a deeply b highly c strikingly d terribly

Speaking

6 Read the strategy. Add another example to each of the techniques.

7 Work in pairs. Do the task below. Use the ideas in the strategy to improve your interaction.

How effective are these ways of meeting new people?
• joining the gym   • getting a part-time job
• taking up a hobby   • using social media
• volunteering
Decide which two of these ways of meeting new people is likely to be the least successful.

Writing

8 Read the strategy and the task below and write an example of each of the persuasive techniques.

The head teacher of your school has announced that the school will buy two apps that would be useful for your studies. Write a proposal to the head teacher with your recommendations. Your proposal should describe each of the apps, saying why they would benefit the students. It should also explain which of the apps is most useful, in case there isn't enough money for both.

9 Write the proposal (220–260 words) for the task above.

4
Changes

Unit map

4A Vocabulary
Changing world
I can talk about global issues.

1 SPEAKING Work in pairs and discuss this quotation. Do you agree with it? Why? / Why not?

> Progress is impossible without change, and those who cannot change their minds cannot change anything.

2 SPEAKING Work in pairs. Look at the charts below. Match the labels below with the correct charts.

global population   PC and smartphone users   people living in poverty

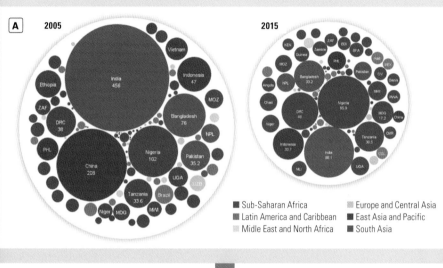

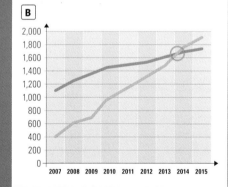

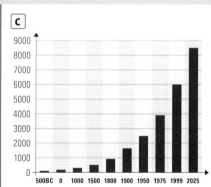

3 VOCABULARY Work in pairs. Match the verbs below with the meanings (A–C). Which verb can mean both increase and decrease?

Rise and fall (verbs) crash dwindle escalate flatline fluctuate level off mount mushroom outpace outstrip overtake plateau plummet plunge (sky)rocket surpass tumble

A: increasing	B: decreasing	C: staying the same
escalate	crash	flatline

4 SPEAKING Work in pairs. Use verbs from exercise 3 to explain what the graphs in exercise 2 show.

> The first chart shows that in most countries ... has plunged.

4A

5 VOCABULARY Complete the text with the global issues below. What does 'declinism' mean and what causes it?

Global issues armed conflicts   climate change   epidemics   famine   global capitalism   life expectancy   population growth   poverty   refugees   terrorism

When you ask people if the world is getting better or worse, the majority (around 70%, according to surveys) say worse. Psychologists even have a term for this belief that things are not as good as they used to be – declinism – and they believe it is due to people overestimating past happiness. Perhaps the media is also partly to blame. As the number of 24-hour news outlets continues to soar, we are constantly exposed to anxiety-inducing reports and analysis. We see thousands of ¹ _refugees_ being forced to leave their homes. The number of wars and ² ~~terrorism~~ _armed conflicts_ appears destined to spiral for ever, while the threat of ³ _terrorism_ makes some of us afraid to go about our daily lives. There are other worries too. Can food production possibly keep pace with ⁴ _population growth_ or will there be widespread ⁵ _famine_ , made worse by the droughts caused by ⁶ _climate change_

But despite appearances, we actually live in a golden age for humans. Average ⁷ _life expectancy_ now well over 70 years, whereas for 99% of human history it remained constant at around 25. Even at the start of the 20th century, it was still only 31 years, and millions of lives were cut short by ⁸ _epidemics_ like flu and cholera. In the past few decades, life expectancy has surged, and although poor countries still lag behind rich countries, the gap is narrowing. Contrary to appearances, the modern era is not particularly violent. In prehistoric times, about 500 people out of every 100,000 were killed each year by other humans. This figure nose-dived when people began to live in nations rather than tribes. Today the global average is around 7 per 100,000, and even lower in developed countries. And although ⁹ _global capital_is often the target of protests – especially against huge multinational companies – global inequality is actually falling as the poorest countries in the world get richer, allowing more and more people to escape ¹⁰ _poverty_ .

6 Add the six highlighted verbs to the correct group (A–C) in exercise 3.

FLUENCY!
Some words are near, but not exact, synonyms. They share the same basic meaning but are used in different contexts or have slightly different implications. To sound natural, you need to choose exactly the right word for the context. For example, the verbs *amend* and *adjust* both mean 'change', but *amend* is used mainly for written text, whereas *adjust* can be used for physical objects.
He had to adjust the monitor before he could read the document.
The company has amended the user agreement for this software.

7 VOCABULARY Read the Fluency! box. Then look at the verbs and nouns below and choose the correct answer to questions 1–5. Use a dictionary to help you if necessary.

Change (verbs and nouns)   adapt / adaptation   adjust / adjustment   alter / alteration   amend / amendment   convert / conversion   evolve / evolution   transform / transformation   modify / modification   mutate / mutation   revise / revision   vary / variation

Which noun and verb ...
1 imply gradual change over a long period of time? _adjust/evolve_
2 imply a complete change rather than a partial change? _transform_
3 do we use for changes we make when we find ourselves in new circumstances? _adapt / adjust_
4 do we use for small changes – for example, to an item of clothing? _vary_
5 do we use if somebody changes to a different religion? _convert_

8 🎧 **1.26** Choose the best verb to complete the questions. Then listen and answer them.

Which speaker ...
A found it hard to **adapt** / modify to living in a new country?
B often helps companies to revise / **transform** their publicity material?
C has **converted** / modified his or her approach because of the internet?
D finds that his or her work evolves / **varies** depending on the time of year?
E had to adjust / **convert** his or her expectations soon after starting work?

9 SPEAKING Work in pairs. Discuss the questions.

1 Do you agree that we live in a 'golden age' or do you think the world is getting worse? Give reasons.
2 What have been the most significant changes in the history of the world?
3 What will be the most significant changes in the world during your lifetime, do you imagine?

Compound future tenses

I can use compound future tenses for predictions and suppositions.

1 **SPEAKING** What is a 'utopia'? Do you think humans have ever built or will ever build one? Why? / Why not?

2 Read the text. Which future seems more likely to you: utopian or dystopian? Why?

> In *Utopia*, Thomas More envisaged a perfect society. Science fiction often predicts the opposite: a dystopia. What is your own view? A century from now, will the world have improved or not? Will we be living in a utopia or a dystopia?

UTOPIA: Humans will be living longer, healthier lives. Most diseases will have been eradicated years before. Since then, scientists will have been working on ways to halt the ageing process.

DYSTOPIA: Humans will be suffering from diseases linked to obesity and inactivity. Infectious diseases will be returning as bacteria will have developed resistance to antibiotics.

3 Read the Learn this! box below. Complete the examples with the correct form of the verbs in brackets. How many more examples of these tenses can you find in exercise 2?

LEARN THIS! Compound future tenses

When we talk about the future, we can use the:

1 future continuous for an action in progress.
   This time tomorrow, you **will be playing** (play) football on the beach.

2 future perfect simple for a completed action.
   By the end of this month, they **will have finished** (finish) the project.

3 future perfect continuous to say how long an action has been in progress by that time.
   By December, Emma **will have been worked** (work) at NASA for five years.

   Note that we often use the future perfect simple in the passive but not the other two tenses:
   The email will already have been sent. ✓
   NOT ~~The email will be being sent tomorrow.~~ ✗

4 Complete the sentences using the correct form of a compound future tense from the Learn this! box, active or passive. Then say whether each sentence belongs to a utopian or dystopian view of the future.

1 People **will be living** (live) in 'smart cities', surrounded by helpful technology. Humans **won't be doing** (not do) manual jobs any more.

2 Cities **will have become** (become) desperately overcrowded. More and more people **will be competing** (compete) for fewer and fewer jobs.

3 Climate change **will have caused** (cause) the weather to be dangerously unstable.

4 Combustion engines **will have been banned** (ban) and governments **will be tackling** (tackle) climate change successfully.

5 Artificial intelligence (AI) **will have surpass** (surpass) human intelligence long ago, and for years, computers **will have been helping** (help) humans to improve the world.

6 Humans **will have lost** (lose) their position as the most intelligent creatures on Earth for ever and **won't be making** (not make) any important decisions about the world.

LOOK OUT!

We can also use compound future tenses to speculate about the present.
I expect Jo will have finished her homework by now.
We must phone Dad. He'll be worrying about us.
Don't ask Tom what the plan is. He won't have been listening!

5 Read the Look out! box. Then decide if the underlined verbs refer to the present (P) or the future (F).

1 You'll have finished your packed lunch by the time we get on the coach! P

2 I'm sure my aunt will be staying at the very best hotel when she goes to Paris. F

P 3 They've cancelled my bus. I'll be waiting here for ages!

P 4 Seth looks so tired. He'll have been revising since about six o'clock this morning.

F 5 I can't wait for my summer holiday. I'll have been working hard for months by then!

P 6 This is such an exciting match. Do you think your friends will be watching it too?

→ Grammar Builder 4.1 page 139

LOOK OUT!

We often use adverbs and adverbial phrases to modify the meaning of compound future tenses. They usually come immediately after *will* but before *won't*.
She'll no doubt have read your email.
He probably won't be working in London next year.

6 Read the Look out! box. Then complete the sentences with the correct form of the verb. Include the adverb.

1 If you arrive at 9 p.m., I (do / most likely) all my homework.

2 It's snowing now, but it (not snow / probably) by the morning.

3 He (not eat / hopefully) all the pizza before we arrive!

4 Don't worry if you missed the lecture, he (repeat / definitely) it next week.

5 Make sure Tom changes his T-shirt when he gets home. He (wear / probably) the same one for two days!

6 I've sent Lucy a message, but (not read / no doubt) it.

7 **SPEAKING** Work in pairs. What will the world will be like 100 years from now? Try to include adverbial expressions from exercise 6.

1 What kinds of cities do you think people will be living in?

2 Will people be working? If so, what jobs will they be doing?

3 What other major changes will most likely have happened?

4C

Online campaigns

I can infer information which is implied rather than overtly stated.

1 SPEAKING What is an online petition? Have you ever signed one? Why? / Why not?

2 SPEAKING Read the text. What's the difference between a grassroots campaign and 'astroturfing'. Why do you think it is called 'astroturfing'?

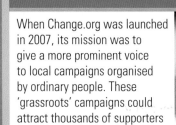

When Change.org was launched in 2007, its mission was to give a more prominent voice to local campaigns organised by ordinary people. These 'grassroots' campaigns could attract thousands of supporters a day using online petitions and, for the first time, exert genuine influence on government and big business. There have been some notable successes and, as the idea has caught on in more and more countries, the number of users has skyrocketed. But there have also been criticisms. Some people say the choice of domain name implies that Change.org is a charity, whereas in reality it is a commercial organisation. Also, it has been claimed that companies use the site for 'astroturfing'– that is, using multiple fake identities in order to make a commercial campaign resemble a grassroots campaign. But perhaps the most damaging criticism, strenuously denied by Change.org, is that what began as a way of challenging the power of large multinational corporations has itself become one, and has in the process lost sight of its original mission.

Listening Strategy

Sometimes information can be implied rather than clearly stated. For example, a subsequent contrast or concession can make the speaker's opinion clear:

We spent the morning shopping for souvenirs, but then we had a relaxing afternoon at the beach.
(Implication: the morning was not relaxing.)

3 ◯ 1.27 Read the Listening Strategy. Then listen and choose the correct implication. Justify your choices. Does everyone in the class agree?

1 The speaker's brother **was / wasn't** keen to help with the petition.
2 The speaker **was / wasn't** happy his sister came to stay.
3 The speaker found the first term's topic **interesting / uninteresting**.
4 The speaker **is / isn't** a fan of modern classical music.
5 The speaker thinks climate change **is / isn't** an important issue.
6 Numbers have **surged / dwindled** at the speaker's athletics club since last year.
7 The speaker **wants / doesn't want** to go on holiday in May.

4 ◯ 2.02 Listen to five people talking about Change.org. Were their petitions successful or unsuccessful? Is the information clearly stated or only implied?

5 ◯ 2.02 Listen again. For questions 1 and 2, choose the correct answer (A–H) for each speaker (1–5). There are three extra sentences.

1 Why does each speaker start the petition?
   A to prevent a new building development ___
   B to help preserve a public facility ___
   C to prevent somebody from coming to the UK ___
   D to stop antisocial behaviour ___
   E to help a family remain in the country ___
   F to protect small businesses in the area ___
   G to generate publicity for a business ___
   H to force an amendment to a new law ___

2 What surprises each speaker about the experience?
   A the technical difficulty of setting up the petition ___
   B the number of people who signed ___
   C the ruthless tactics of a commercial company ___
   D an absence of support from friends and family ___
   E a lack of gratitude ___
   F the accusations of bullying ___
   G the feeling of anti-climax afterwards ___
   H the media interest in the petition ___

6 SPEAKING Work in pairs. Think of a petition you would like to start on Change.org. It can relate to a local, national or global issue. Use the examples below to help you.

SAVE OUR SWIMMING POOL!

Invest in education.   **NO MORE HUNTING.**

BAN INSECTICIDES.   *Equal rights for all!*

MAKE OUR STREETS SAFER!

7 KEY PHRASES Complete the phrases with verbs below. Then decide on the wording of your petition and make a list of reasons why it is important. Use the key phrases to help you.

bring cut initiate make provide put raise reverse

Politics and change
1 _____ the red tape (surrounding …)
2 _____ a stop to …
3 _____ the trend (towards …)
4 _____ in legislation (to …)
5 _____ it easier / harder / illegal for people to …
6 _____ more funding (for …)
7 _____ / reduce taxes (so that …)
8 _____ a project to …

8 SPEAKING Share your ideas with the class and explain why your petition is important. Take a class vote with each student voting for their three favourite petitions. Which petition gets the most support?

4D Grammar

Quantity

I can use articles and quantifiers correctly.

1 SPEAKING Work in pairs. Discuss these questions: Do you always behave in a logical way? Can you think of a time when you or somebody else behaved illogically?

2 Read the text. What is the main difference between a 'nudge' and a WPI?

For ¹many years, psychologists have known that ²a lot of our behaviour is influenced by factors we are not consciously aware of. Sometimes, we get into bad habits which we cannot seem to break, however ³much effort we make. Simply telling ourselves to change has ⁴little or no effect. But there are ⁵a few psychological tricks which can help us on the road to self-improvement.

In 1982, a professor at the University of Virginia tried an experiment. He showed ⁶half his class (Group A) statistics which demonstrated that new students always struggle at first but then improve. Group B received ⁷none of this information. Over the next year, Group A's grades improved faster than Group B's and ⁸fewer of them dropped out of university. Why? Because they did not blame themselves for ⁹any of their early failures; they saw them as normal. This experiment was an early example of what psychologists now call 'wise psychological interventions' or WPIs, which enable self-improvement by removing mental blocks.

'Nudges' are similar to WPIs but their effect is more immediate. Governments have shown ¹⁰a great deal of interest in 'nudges' because they offer a way of altering people's behaviour without the need for new laws. In one study, researchers wondered whether 'nudges' could improve the health of people who were not eating ¹¹enough fruit and vegetables. They drew a line across the middle of supermarket shopping trolleys and wrote 'fruit and vegetables' on one side. Because it looked as if ¹²one half of the space in the trolley was for fruit and vegetables, shoppers bought more.

3 Look at the highlighted quantifiers in the text. Tick the alternatives below which make sense in the context and are grammatically correct.

1 a) some ✓	b) a lot of ✓	c) much ✗
2 a) any of	b) much of	c) a good deal of
3 a) lots of	b) more	c) some
4 a) hardly an	b) hardly any	c) a little or no
5 a) several	b) some	c) some of the
6 a) a half	b) half of	c) one half of
7 a) not any of	b) any of	c) neither of
8 a) any	b) enough	c) nearly every
9 a) all of	b) none of	c) more of
10 a) some of	b) all of	c) lots of
11 a) many	b) either	c) no
12 a) a good deal	b) a lot	c) much

LEARN THIS! Quantifiers

The choice of quantifier will depend not only on meaning but also on:
- register (formal or informal).
- countability or uncountability of the noun.
- whether the sentence is affirmative or negative.
- whether it is a question.

4 Read the Learn this! box. Then look at the list below and say which quantifier(s):

1 is the most informal?
2 can only be used with countable nouns? (×3)
3 can only be used with uncountable nouns? (×2)
4 is used more often in negative sentences and questions than in affirmative sentences.

a good deal of   all   any   both   enough   every   fewer   half   less   loads of   most   none of   some

➜ Grammar Builder 4.2 page 140

5 Explain how the choice of article or quantifier alters the meaning or register of the sentences below. (Both are correct English.)

1 We found **a / one** restaurant near the hotel.
2 I spent **an / the whole** afternoon tidying my room.
3 The teacher asked **each / every** student to name a film.
4 **Not all / None of** my friends went to the party.
5 **A few / Few** people visit the islands in winter.
6 Strangely, she couldn't remember **both / either** of her own email addresses.
7 **Loads of / Many** people who tried to buy tickets for the event were unsuccessful.
8 I had never had the chance to study Drama at **any / either** of my previous schools.
9 To be honest I hadn't realised that **both / neither** of my parents had visited the USA.

6 SPEAKING Complete the short text about a psychological experiment using the words below. Then in pairs, discuss questions 1–3.

any   both   little   most   neither   some

You are given £100 and told that you can keep ¹_____ of it as long as you offer ²_____ of it – however ³_____ – to a stranger. If the stranger rejects your offer, ⁴_____ of you gets ⁵_____ money. ⁶_____ of you know the rules.

1 What is the most logical way for the people to behave?
2 How do you think people in the experiment actually behaved in practice? Why?
3 How would you behave in each of the two roles in the experiment?

Word Skills

Binomial pairs

I can use a two-part set phrase correctly.

1 **SPEAKING** Work in pairs. Try to work out the meaning of the underlined phrases in the sentences below. Think of a single word to replace each phrase. What part of speech is it?

1 She's recovered from pneumonia now, but it was touch and go for a while.

2 When my dad starts to rant and rave about politics, I always stop listening.

3 We haven't really got anything for dinner – just a few odds and ends in the fridge.

2 Read the Learn this! box. Does this type of phrase exist in your own language? If so, think of examples.

> **LEARN THIS! Binomial pairs**
>
> 1 Binomial pairs are fixed expressions made from two grammatically similar words (nouns, adjectives, etc.) joined by a conjunction (*and, or*, etc.).
> aches and pains   neat and tidy   make or break
>
> 2 The order of words is fixed and cannot be reversed.
>
> 3 Binomial pairs function as nouns, adjectives, verbs, etc.
> You won, fair and square. (adverb)
> I'm sick and tired of your rudeness! (adjective)

3 Read the text. Work in pairs. Discuss the question in the final sentence. Do you agree?

CHANGING PLACES

Money can't buy happiness, or so the saying goes, and there are certainly pros and cons to being rich. But by and large, people from wealthy backgrounds have easier lives than people who are born and bred in poverty. For example, Haruki (not his real name) enjoyed the benefit of private tutors and a university education, all part and parcel of growing up in an affluent family. Now, at the age of sixty, he is head of a successful property company. In contrast, Katashi (also a pseudonym) experienced far more ups and downs during his early years. His father died when he was two, and although his mother supported Katashi and his brothers through thick and thin, they had very little money. Katashi was obliged to do shift work here and there in order to pay for night school, eventually finding a job as a driver. Neither Haruki nor Katashi knew the shocking truth: that they had been swapped at birth in a hospital mix-up. Sooner or later, however, it was bound to emerge. It was Haruki's brothers who first requested a DNA test, but Katashi who sued the hospital for damages. The ins and outs of the case are complex, but basically, once the DNA evidence was available, the result was cut and dried and Katashi was awarded ¥38 million in compensation (which is more or less €335,000). He had asked for a great deal more. The question is: how much compensation should you receive for being given the wrong life?

4 Find ten more binomial phrases in the text in exercise 3. Decide whether each one is equivalent to a verb, a noun, an adjective or an adverb.

pros and cons – noun

5 Match the binomial pairs in exercise 4 with the equivalent phrases below.

1 minor details ins and outs
2 completely settled
3 in general
4 approximately
5 born and raised
6 advantages and disadvantages
7 good luck and bad luck
8 before long
9 an essential aspect
10 all circumstances
11 in various places

6 **VOCABULARY** Complete the sentences with the binomial pairs below.

Binomial pairs dead and buried   dos and don'ts
high and dry   live and learn   pick and choose
rough and ready   safe and sound   short and sweet
through and through   wear and tear

1 I'd have preferred to go to a university nearer my home, but I wasn't in a position to _____.

2 In our first chemistry lesson, the teacher explained all the _____ of the laboratory.

3 I've written down some ideas for our brochure. They're a bit _____ but they're a start.

4 I didn't realise you had to pay for Wi-Fi at the hotel. Oh well, you _____.

5 When their taxi failed to appear, they were left _____ in the centre of Cairo.

6 The school's plan to build a new swimming pool was _____ as soon as the council withdrew their support.

7 I know you all need to get back to work, so I'll keep this speech _____.

8 They charged us €800 to rent the apartment for a week, plus €100 for _____.

9 My dad is a Londoner _____ and would hate to live anywhere else.

10 Our cat went missing for eight days, but then turned up _____.

7 Work in pairs. Check your answers to exercise 6. Try to think of a single word or phrase to replace each binomial pair.

8 **SPEAKING** Work in pairs. Tell your partner about:

1 a place you go when you want peace and quiet.
2 something you achieved by trial and error.
3 a hard and fast rule in your home.
4 an occasion when you hummed and hawed about the best thing to do.
5 a famous person who is on the up and up.
6 an activity which is often hit and miss.

How language changes us

I can understand a text about languages and the brain.

1 SPEAKING Work in pairs. Agree on a definition of 'bilingual'. In what different circumstances do people usually become bilingual?

2 Read the text. Then decide which two pieces of information in the text you find most interesting and/or surprising. Give reasons for your choices.

> **Reading Strategy**
>
> Remember that multiple-choice questions about a text:
> - always follow the order of the text.
> - sometimes specify what part of the text they refer to by mentioning a paragraph.
> - may relate to the overall meaning of the text rather than to a specific part. (If so, this will be the final question.)

3 Read the Reading Strategy. Then read questions 1, 3 and 4 in exercise 4 (but not the options a–d). In which paragraphs would you expect to find the answers? How did you work it out?

4 Read the text. For questions 1–6, choose the correct option (a–d).

1 Speaking more than one language has an effect on
   a the part of the brain where language is processed.
   b the part of the brain which makes decisions.
   c several parts of the brain equally.
   d the way all the different parts of the brain are organised.

2 The studies described in paragraph 2 suggest that, compared to monolingual people, bilingual people
   a recover from a stroke more quickly.
   b are less likely to suffer from dementia.
   c have fewer lasting effects from a stroke.
   d develop less severe forms of dementia.

3 The theory that people cannot understand a concept if their language has no word for it
   a has become more widely accepted since 1940.
   b was superseded by the idea that language changes the way you see the world.
   c was disproved during the first decade of this century.
   d was discovered to be true for people whose native language is Greek.

4 Studies suggest that speakers of different languages
   a have different levels of skill at reasoning.
   b all have an equally good sense of direction.
   c do not all have the ability to categorise objects into groups.
   d may think about time in different ways.

5 According to the research described in paragraph 6, bilingual people
   a describe their own personality differently depending on which language they're speaking.
   b have a more outgoing personality than monolingual people.
   c tell stories in a more emotional way than monolingual people.
   d are better at understanding other people's feelings in one of their languages than in the other.

6 What is the main point of the text as a whole?
   a What languages you speak has an effect on how your brain functions.
   b How many languages you speak is far more significant than what those languages are.
   c The similarities between speakers of different languages are more significant than the differences.
   d Learning another language is possibly the best way to improve the functioning of your brain.

5 VOCABULARY Find the verbs below in the text. Then match them with the definitions (1–6).

Paragraph 2: caution, conjecture
Paragraph 4: probe
Paragraph 6: elicit, highlight, rumour

1 to explore whether something is true (e.g. by asking questions about it)
2 to speculate
3 to say that something is true without knowing for sure
4 to draw attention to something
5 to warn
6 to cause or encourage somebody to say something

⮕ **Vocabulary Builder** Speech verbs: page 128

CRITICAL ANALYSIS

6 Find examples of direct speech in the text. Answer the questions:

1 Why do you think the writer includes quotations in the article?
2 What tense are the speech verbs which follow the quotations? Is this the same as you would expect to find in a fictional text? If not, why is it different?

7 SPEAKING Work in pairs. Discuss the quote below from the text. What you do think it means? Do you agree? Why? / Why not?

> 'To have another language is to possess a second soul.'

Can learning a language rewire your brain?

1 As our species evolved, parts of our brain expanded, resulting in more computing power for language. It's what makes us hard-wired for communication. What is perhaps more surprising is how language can shape our brains throughout our lives. Most of the evidence for this comes from studies of people who are bilingual. Brain scan studies show that switching between two languages triggers different patterns of brain activity compared with speaking in one language, particularly in the prefrontal cortex. That part of the brain, at the very front of our skulls, is involved in organising and acting on information, including using memory, reasoning and planning. Other studies show that people who are bilingual are faster at getting to grips with a new language.

2 It may also make the brain more resilient. Ellen Bialystok at York University in Toronto, Canada, has found that lifelong bilinguals tend to be diagnosed with dementia on average 4.5 years later than monolinguals, and have more cerebral white matter, including in their prefrontal cortex. White matter is made of nerve fibres that connect different brain regions, shuttling information back and forth between them. So boosting language skills appears to build more connected brains – although Bialystok cautions that this still needs to be confirmed. More evidence for the benefits of speaking a second language came last year from a study of 608 people who had had a stroke. Thomas Bak of the University of Edinburgh found that of the bilinguals among them, 40% recovered fully, compared with only 20% of monolinguals. Bak conjectures that the mental gymnastics involved in speaking several languages could build extra connections that improve function and help cope with damage. 'The idea is that if you have a lot of mental exercise, your brain is trained and can compensate better,' says Bak.

Can language influence how you see the world?

3 Time flows from back to front for English speakers: we 'cast our minds back' to the 1990s, and 'hope for good times ahead'. It's an example of a cultural concept encoded in language, but can language in turn influence how we think? Maria Sera is a native Spanish speaker who grew up believing all squirrels were female. The Spanish word for squirrel, *ardilla*, is feminine. As a linguist at the University of Minnesota, she has found some substance for her childhood belief. Studies of French and Spanish speakers, whose languages attribute genders to objects, suggest they associate those objects with masculine or feminine properties.

4 The idea that the language you speak could influence how you think dates back to 1940, when linguist Benjamin Lee Whorf proposed that people whose languages lack words for a concept would not understand it. It was relegated to fringe science until the early 2000s, when a few people began probing a related but more nuanced idea: that language can influence perception. Greek, for instance, has two words for blue – *galázio* for light blue and *ble* for a darker shade. A study found that Greek speakers could discriminate shades of blue faster and better than native English speakers.

5 Language even seems to affect our sense of space and time. For example, one Aboriginal tribe in the north of Australia doesn't have words for relative space, like left and right, but does have terms for north, south, east and west. Studies have shown that they tend to be unusually skilled at keeping track of where they are in unfamiliar places. There is also some evidence that the direction in which your first language is written can influence your sense of time, with speakers of Mandarin more likely to think of time running from top to bottom (with earlier events at the top) than English speakers. More generally, language helps us understand the world by allowing us to categorise things. Children are better at grouping objects if they have already learned the names of the categories they belong to. Conversely, after a stroke, people who have lost language skills can have trouble grouping objects. 'It's not that language just affects the high-level reasoning part of the brain,' says Gary Lupyan of the University of Wisconsin-Madison. 'It's changing our basic perceptual representations.'

Does your language shape your personality?

6 'To have another language is to possess a second soul,' Charlemagne is rumoured to have said. He may have been on to something. In the 1960s, sociolinguist Susan Ervin-Tripp of the University of California at Berkeley asked English–Japanese bilinguals to describe what was going on in ambiguous pictures. One person, for example, described the picture differently depending on which language they were using. A picture of a woman leaning against a couch elicited a story in Japanese about a woman contemplating suicide after the loss of her fiancé. The same person, asked to respond at a separate session in English, said the woman was completing a sewing project for a class. 'In general, there was more emotion in the Japanese stories,' Ervin-Tripp wrote in a description of the experiment. 'The switch in language draws with it the cultural baggage associated with that language.' Nairán Ramírez-Esparza at the University of Connecticut asked bilingual Mexicans to rate their personalities using both English and Spanish questionnaires. English responses highlighted openness and extroversion, while Spanish responses were more humble and reserved. 'Language is such a powerful thing. It obviously makes you see yourself differently,' Ramírez-Esparza says. Paula Rubio-Fernández of the University of Oslo, meanwhile, has found that bilingual children perform better on tests that require them to understand a situation from someone else's perspective.

7 Evidence is mounting that the words we speak and think shape our brains, perceptions and personalities. Who knows what else? Perhaps also our tastes, habits or values. The door is wide open to future investigation.

4G Speaking
Discussion
I can discuss a topic and express opinions.

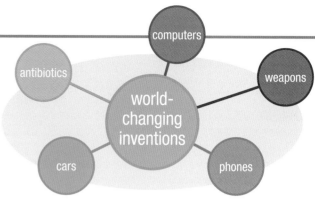

1 **SPEAKING** Work in pairs. Look at the diagram on the right. Which of the inventions has changed human society the most? Discuss your reasons and try to agree on one invention.

> **Speaking Strategy**
> When you are expressing opinions, you can use rhetorical questions to emphasise your points. Remember:
> - rhetorical questions do not require answers, but you can sometimes add an answer in order to emphasise your view. If you do not give an answer, it must be clear what answer you have in mind:
>   *What have you done to help today? (Nothing!)*
>   *Would you let a child watch that video? (Of course not!)*
>   *How much time do people waste on the internet? (Far too much)*
> - do not over-use rhetorical questions.

2 **SPEAKING** Work in pairs. Read the Speaking Strategy. Then complete the rhetorical questions to emphasise points 1–5 below. Include answers if appropriate.

1 Antibiotics have saved a lot of lives.
   How many lives have antibiotics saved since they were invented? Millions!
2 Cars are polluting our cities.
3 We rely too heavily on computers in our daily lives.
4 People spend too much time staring at their phones.
5 Governments spend too much money on weapons.

3 🎧 **2.03** Work in pairs. Listen to two students talking about the inventions in exercise 1. Answer two questions each.

Student A's questions
1 Do they choose the same invention as you in the end?
2 Do you agree with their reasons? Why? / Why not?
Student B's questions
1 Which invention from exercise 1 is not mentioned at all?
2 How many rhetorical questions do you hear? Are the answers stated or just implied?

4 **SPEAKING** Work in pairs. Tell your partner the answers to your questions from exercise 3.

5 🎧 **2.03** **KEY PHRASES** Complete the phrases with the words below. Then listen again. Which of the phrases do you hear?

case down end even fair so take view

Acknowledging without agreeing
That's a ¹_____ point, but I still think …
True, but what it really comes ²_____ to is …
Maybe ³_____, but what it really boils down to is …
Perhaps, although in my ⁴_____ …
I see what you mean, but at the ⁵_____ of the day, …
That may be the ⁶_____, but for me, it's more about …
I ⁷_____ your point, but at the same time, …
That could well be true, but ⁸_____ so, I think …

6 **SPEAKING** Work in pairs. Ask and answer the questions below. Use phrases from exercise 5 in your conversation.

1 Can you imagine something that hasn't been invented, but if it were, it would change the world for the better?
2 If the technology existed to alter the human body and make people faster and stronger, would that be a good or bad thing? Why?
3 Do you think robots are going to take over most people's jobs in the future? Why? / Why not?

7 🎧 **2.04** Listen to the students answering the questions in exercise 6. Do you agree or disagree with their answers?

8 **VOCABULARY** Look at the list of adjectives for describing changes. Decide whether they imply a big or small change.

Adjectives to describe change cosmetic dramatic drastic fundamental marginal marked minimal momentous profound radical subtle sweeping

9 🎧 **2.04** Listen again. Which adjectives from exercise 8 do they use to talk about changes? Complete the sentences.

1 Although to be honest it would have a _____ effect on the world in general.
2 That would have a _____ effect on some developing countries.
3 Perhaps it's OK to make _____ changes, but I wouldn't be happy with anything fundamental.
4 There are going to be _____ changes in all areas.
5 I think there's going to be a really _____ overhaul of society.

10 **SPEAKING** Work in pairs. Ask and answer two questions each from the list below. Try to include adjectives from exercise 8 in your answers.

1 Do you think the world has changed a lot so far during your lifetime?
2 Some people talk about wanting to 'put the clock back'. Would you like to do this? (Why? / Why not?)
3 Do you think technology is moving too quickly? (Why? / Why not?)
4 Do you think technology has changed the ways humans think and behave? If so, in what ways?
5 What single thing that you've bought or received has changed your life the most?

11 **SPEAKING** Work in pairs. Discuss the question below.

> If you could 'uninvent' one piece of technology, what would you choose and why?

Writing

Letter to an editor

I can write a letter about a local improvement scheme.

1 SPEAKING Work in pairs. If you could change the place you live by adding a new facility, what would you choose? Decide what would be best for:

1 teenagers and young adults
2 families with young children
3 elderly and retired people

2 Read the task and the letter below. What does the writer suggest as a way of getting a range of good ideas for the new development?

> You have read an article in a local magazine about plans to create a nature reserve in a run-down area of town by the river. You feel these suggestions do not sufficiently cater for younger people and decide to write a letter to the editor explaining your opinion.

To the editor,

Having read your article outlining suggestions for a new riverside development, I feel I must write to express my disappointment at the plans in their current form. Pleasant as a nature reserve may be, it would have limited appeal for the younger members of our community and, for this reason, I would like to suggest that the current proposal be reconsidered.

How often have people accused teenagers in our town of antisocial behaviour? What is undeniable is that there is a serious lack of leisure facilities for young people, with the result that they are often reduced to congregating in the shopping centre. Only when young people have access to a wider range of possible activities will this problem be resolved. A skate-park next to the river would be a low-cost, low-maintenance means of achieving this.

An alternative idea would be to allow cafés and restaurants to open along that stretch of the river. This would bring a lively and appealing atmosphere to an area which is currently rather gloomy and foreboding. Provided there were a number of reasonably priced cafés, there is no reason why this should not prove popular with local residents of all ages.

In short, this is a once-in-a-generation opportunity to make a radical improvement to this area of town. I firmly believe that, were the council to embark on a full consultation with local residents, a wide variety of exciting and viable schemes would be suggested.

3 Find more formal equivalents for the clauses and phrases below in the letter.

1 I want to tell you how disappointed I am …
2 … young people wouldn't be too keen on it.
3 … that's why I'm asking you to change your mind.
4 … there are not enough facilities for young people.
5 … so they just hang around in the shopping centre.
6 … this should go down well with both young and old.

> **Writing Strategy**
>
> In a formal letter, in addition to avoiding inappropriately colloquial language, you should:
>
> - avoid using rhetorical questions.
> - use inversion to add emphasis: *Only rarely have they allowed the public to visit.*
> - include passive forms to make the style more impersonal.
> - emphasise your opinions using formal expressions like *What is clear / undeniable is that … , I have no doubt that … ,* and *I firmly believe that … .*

4 Read the Writing Strategy. Then find in the letter:

1 a rhetorical question and rewrite it using a passive form.
2 an example of inversion.
3 two opinions given emphasis by using two of the expressions in point 4 of the Writing Strategy.
4 an opinion in the letter that you could rewrite using one of the formal expressions in the Strategy.

> ➡ **Vocabulary Builder** Formal and informal equivalents: page 128

> You have read an article in a local magazine about plans to redevelop a large, disused power station as a block of luxury flats. You feel there are far more imaginative uses for the building which would be of more benefit to the community. Write a letter to the editor explaining your opinion.

5 SPEAKING Work in pairs. Read the task. Then think of six imaginative uses for a large, empty building. Choose the best two or three to include in your letter.

6 Plan your letter using the model in exercise 2 to help you. Include an introduction and a conclusion. Use the main paragraphs to propose and justify your ideas.

7 Now write your letter (220–260 words) using your ideas from exercise 5 and your plan from exercise 6. Remember to use appropriately formal vocabulary and syntax.

> **CHECK YOUR WORK**
> Have you …
> - written 220–260 words?
> - used appropriately formal language, including syntax?
> - checked the spelling and grammar?

5

Battles

5A Vocabulary
War and conflict
I can talk about military conflicts.

1 SPEAKING Work in pairs. Describe the photos of the war in Afghanistan. What do you know about the war? Try to answer the questions.

1 Which countries were involved?
2 Why and how did it start?
3 What was the eventual outcome?

2 VOCABULARY Complete the text with the nouns below. Check your ideas from exercise 1.

War and conflict allies asymmetric warfare atrocities border civilian government coalition guerrilla raids insurgency invasion leader occupation security special forces terrorist-training camps terrorists troops

Following the 9/11 attacks in New York, when ¹_____ flew planes into the World Trade Center and the Pentagon, killing nearly 3,000 people, the USA issued an ultimatum to the Taliban government in Afghanistan to hand over Osama bin Laden, the ²_____ of Al Qaeda, which, having a few years earlier declared war on the USA, now claimed responsibility for the ³_____. When the Afghan government refused the request, the USA invaded Afghanistan in order to remove the government from power and destroy the ⁴_____, where it was claimed the 9/11 hijackers had spent time. The USA was supported from the outset by its closest ⁵_____, including the UK, and from 2003 by a ⁶_____ of NATO forces. In all, ⁷_____ from 43 different countries were involved in the ⁸_____ and subsequent ⁹_____ of Afghanistan. The Americans were determined to capture or kill Osama bin Laden, but he fled to the mountains on the Afghan–Pakistan ¹⁰_____. The Taliban, who had seized power in 1996, were replaced by a ¹¹_____. Though outgunned and outnumbered, the Taliban launched an ¹²_____ against the new government and the forces of occupation, mounting ¹³_____ and staging ambushes in the countryside and carrying out suicide attacks in towns and cities. This type of ¹⁴_____ was difficult to counter and the Taliban took control of much of the south and east of the country. In May 2011, élite American ¹⁵_____ killed Osama bin Laden in Pakistan, and in 2012 the USA took the decision to withdraw their forces from Afghanistan. The Americans and their allies ended combat operations in 2014 and the Afghan government in the capital, Kabul, assumed full responsibility for the country's ¹⁶_____.

FLUENCY!

Choosing the right verb-noun collocation will make you sound more precise. For example, you can say *start an attack* or *cause casualties*, but using the collocations *launch an attack* and *inflict casualties* will make you sound more like a native speaker.

3 DICTIONARY WORK Read the Fluency! box. Then read the dictionary entries below. Look again at the text in exercise 2 and find six collocations from the entries.

- VERB + ULTIMATUM **deliver, give sb, issue, present (sb with), send** *The government denied that it had presented the union with an ultimatum.* | **get, receive** | **comply with** | **ignore** | **withdraw**

- VERB + WAR **be in, fight in** *My grandfather fought in two world wars.* | **fight, make, wage** *The two countries fought a short but bloody war.* | **win** | **lose** | **declare** | **go to** *The country went to war in 1914.*

- VERB + POWER **come to, rise to** *When did this government come to power?* | **assume, seize, take** *The Crown Prince assumed power in his father's place.* | **fall from, lose** *They fell from power in 1992.* | **give up, relinquish, renounce** | **delegate, devolve** *The new law delegates many of these powers to school governors.*

- VERB + AMBUSH **lay, prepare, set up** *The soldiers set up an ambush in the road.* | **lie in, wait in** *The soldiers lay in ambush for the enemy troops.* | **carry out, stage** *They staged an ambush on an army patrol.* | **be caught in, run into, walk into** *We ran into an ambush in the valley.*

- VERB + ATTACK **carry out, launch, lead, make, mount, spearhead** *The soldiers mounted an all-out attack on the village.* | **come under, suffer** *They came under sustained attack from the air.*

- VERB + FORCE **assemble, create, form, mobilise** *A large expeditionary force is now being assembled.* | **send** *The decision to send forces over the border.* | **deploy, use** *A small peacekeeping force will be deployed in the area.* | **withdraw**

4 Complete the sentences with the nouns below and the correct form of the verbs from the dictionary entries in exercise 3. Sometimes more than one verb is possible.

an ambush   attack   forces   power   the ultimatum   war

1 The port _____ under _____ from missiles fired from ships out to sea.
2 The dictator went into hiding after _____ from _____ in 2012.
3 Last night two soldiers were injured when they _____ in _____ as they entered the town.
4 The president decided to _____ armed _____ into the disputed territory.
5 NATO demanded that the government withdraw its troops within 24 hours. But the government refused to _____ _____.
6 The terrorists said they were _____ _____ on Western civilisation.

5 🎧 **2.05** **SPEAKING** Work in pairs. Can you answer the questions about the Vietnam war below? Then listen to an account of the war, and check or find out the answers.

1 Until the Second World War, Vietnam was a colony of which country?
2 Which political system did North Vietnam adopt?
3 In which decade did the Vietnam war end?
4 Who won the Vietnam war, the North or the South?

6 🎧 **2.05** Listen again. Complete the sentences with a word or short phrase.

1 The tactic which Ho Chi Minh used against the Japanese and French was to wage _____.
2 The French abandoned Vietnam in the mid 1950s after they lost _____.
3 The Americans supported South Vietnam because they were afraid that it and other countries in the region might turn to _____.
4 Air raids on the North started after the North attacked _____.
5 _____ helped the North to defend themselves against air strikes.
6 In the USA, demonstrations against the war were organised by _____.
7 50% of the Vietnamese casualties were _____.

7 VOCABULARY Complete the collocations from the listening with the verbs below.

break   claim   inflict   lose   make   occupy   put up   stage   station   suffer   supply

Collocations: conflict and war

1 _____ a country / area	7 _____ resistance
2 _____ arms (to)	8 _____ losses
3 _____ troops (in)	9 _____ a protest
4 _____ a breakthrough	10 _____ victory
5 _____ the stalemate	11 _____ one's life
6 _____ casualties	

8 Work in pairs. Take turns to use the collocations from exercise 7 in sentences.

> My great-grandfather lost his life in the Second World War.

9 SPEAKING Work in pairs. Discuss the quotations and sayings below. Do you agree with them? Give reasons for your opinions.

1 'The purpose of all war is peace.'
2 'An eye for an eye and the whole world goes blind.'

Passive structures
I can use passive structures.

1 **SPEAKING** Have you ever seen a Star Wars film? Did you enjoy it? Why? / Why not? What are the films about? How many Star Wars characters can you name? Do you have a favourite?

2 Read the text. In what order were the three Star Wars trilogies released?

MAY THE FORCE BE WITH YOU

Star Wars is a series of science-fiction films set in the distant past, 'in a galaxy far, far away'. The first film, *Star Wars*, was released in 1977 and was the first of a trilogy of films released over the next six years. The films follow the classic plotline of an evil power being taken on by a 'small guy' who eventually triumphs. They were phenomenally successful, to the point where phrases from them like 'the Evil Empire' and 'May the Force be with you' have become part of everyday language. The first film was awarded seven Oscars, including one for the visual effects, which were ground-breaking and incredibly convincing for the time. The film has had praise heaped on it from all quarters, and can be regarded as instrumental in launching the science-fiction boom of the late 1970s and early 1980s. Three more films (a prequel to the first trilogy) followed in the late 1990s and early noughties, and since 2015 they have started to release a sequel trilogy. It is widely rumoured that there are plans for the Star Wars franchise to be kept alive for many years to come!

3 Find examples of passive structures 1–7 below in the text. Sometimes more than one answer is possible.

1 a passive gerund, e.g. *I dislike being photographed.*
2 a verb with two objects which is used in a passive construction, e.g. *I was promised the job.*
3 a passive construction with *regard, say, consider,* etc., e.g. *Spielberg is seen as …*
4 a passive construction with introductory *it* and *regard, believe, consider,* etc., e.g. *It was thought that …*
5 a passive phrasal verb, e.g. *I was woken up by …*
6 a phrase with a past participle used in place of a passive construction, e.g. *a film directed by Almodóvar*
7 a passive or perfect passive infinitive, e.g. *(to) be seen, (to) have been seen*

➡➡ **Grammar Builder 5.1** page 141

4 In your notebook, rewrite each sentence twice, making each object the subject of the passive verb.

1 The sales assistant sold me a defective TV.
   I was sold …
   A defective TV was …
2 The lifeguard has thrown a lifeline to the swimmer.
3 We'll offer the job to the most experienced applicant.
4 The farmer was feeding the chickens with corn.
5 After the poor performance, the crowd showed the players little respect.
6 They are sending me my exam results in the post.

LEARN THIS! Auxiliary passive

1 With verbs with two objects we can also use a passive construction with *have*.
   They gave me a book. > *I had a book given (to) me.*
2 The following can also become the subject of the auxiliary passive:
   a The prepositional object of a verb. *They explained the situation to us.* > *We had the situation explained to us.*
   b A possessive (*your, Jo's*). *They confiscated Tom's iPad.* > *Tom had his iPad confiscated.*

---

5 Read the Learn this! box. Find an example of 2a in the text in exercise 2. How would it be expressed as a standard passive structure?

6 In your notebook, rewrite the sentences using the auxiliary passive. Start with the words in brackets.

1 A close friend gave me this CD for my birthday. (I)
   I had this …
2 Someone had stolen Sally's car from right outside her house. (Sally)
3 They always read stories to us at primary school. (We)
4 They won't return Tom's iPad to him until the end of the lesson. (Tom)
5 They'll refuse Ed permission to miss the P.E. lesson. (Ed)
6 They played a practical joke on Liam. (Liam)

7 Where possible, rewrite the sentences in exercise 6 with a standard passive construction.

1 *I was given … / This CD was …*

8 **SPEAKING** Work in pairs. Take turns to read a sentence from below to your partner with his / her book closed. Your partner reforms it using a passive structure. If you can, invent more active sentences for your partner to make passive.

1 Someone should tell her the truth.
2 They say that Harry didn't do any revision.
3 He always wants people to praise him.
4 I hate it when people stare at me.
5 They should take the car for repair immediately.
6 The critics gave the film poor reviews.

> Someone should tell her the truth.

> She should be …

Arguments
I can understand people talking about arguments.

It's only a scratch.

1 SPEAKING Work in pairs. What do you think the following people most often argue about amongst themselves? Give examples.

1 siblings
2 teenage friends
3 parents and their teenage children
4 married couples

> **Listening Strategy**
> Listening tasks often include language that reports or summarises things people say in the recording. It is important therefore to have a good knowledge of reporting verbs, adjectives and adverbs that describe feelings, and verbs that report opinions.

2 🎧 2.06 Read the Listening Strategy and check the meaning of the reporting verbs below. Then listen to eight people talking and complete the sentences with a reporting verb. Use the past simple.

Reporting verbs admit advise announce argue boast claim complain concede confirm deny dismiss doubt enquire fear inform insist mention object (to) observe propose protest question recommend regret remark remind resent reveal threaten warn

1 The woman _____ to punish the children if they didn't stop misbehaving.
2 The boy _____ his innocence and _____ breaking the window.
3 The woman _____ to the plan to build a supermarket near her house.
4 He _____ that he was at fault for starting the argument.
5 The teacher _____ the students that they had a test coming up.
6 The man _____ to the waiter that his food was cold and smelled odd.
7 The woman _____ that she and her boyfriend were going to get married.
8 The man _____ them not to swim in the river.

➤➤ **Vocabulary Builder** Reporting verbs: page 128

3 🎧 2.07 Listen to three conversations and choose the correct answers. There are two questions for each conversation.

Conversation 1: You hear two people talking about how to avoid arguments.
1 The woman insists that
  A it's always possible to avoid getting into a rage.
  B articles like this always contain good advice.
  C the man has misunderstood the advice in the article.
2 The man concedes that
  A the article may contain some truth.
  B he needs some advice and help himself.
  C arguments are always avoidable.

Conversation 2: You hear two people talking about an argument that got out of control.
1 What does the woman say/think about an argument she had with her partner?
  A She admits that it was her fault.
  B She resents having to apologise to her partner.
  C She fears that they'll split up.
2 The man reveals that he and his partner
  A take a long time to make up.
  B also have serious rows.
  C don't feel any anger towards each other.

Conversation 3: You hear two people talking about making up after arguments.
1 The woman claims that
  A her partner spends too much time with his friends.
  B she and her partner don't need to make up after an argument.
  C her partner never apologises to her.
2 What does the man think of the woman's attitude to arguments?
  A He argues that it may have long-term negative consequences.
  B He doubts that their relationship will survive.
  C He advises her to give in to her partner.

4 SPEAKING Work in pairs. Which of the opinions expressed in the recordings do you agree or disagree with? Why?

5 SPEAKING Work in pairs or small groups. Discuss the questions below and then report your ideas to the class.
1 Is it a good thing to be passionate about your beliefs?
2 Do you enjoy 'playing devil's advocate' (pretending to be against an idea that others support)?
3 Do you get along with argumentative people?
4 Are you easily persuaded in an argument or debate?

Uses of *it*

I can use a range of structures with it.

THE TEN TORS CHALLENGE is an annual weekend hike for teenagers, organised by the British Army. It takes place on Dartmoor, a vast area of moorland in south-west England. Teams are made up of six people. The aim is to visit ten points on the moor within 34 hours, walking a total of 56, 72 or 88 km (depending on the age group). Participants have to carry everything with them: tent, food, clothes and water. It isn't a race but a test of endurance, and of navigation and survival skills, though teams often compete to see who can finish first.

1 SPEAKING Read about the Ten Tors Challenge. Would you like to take part in it? Why? / Why not? Do you know any similar challenges or races? What do they involve?

2 🎧2.08 Listen to Elin talking about the Ten Tors Challenge. Complete the sentences.

1 People regard it _____ the distance in such a short time.
2 It isn't easy _____ the length of Dartmoor.
3 It was really hard work _____ for the challenge.
4 It's anybody's guess _____ will be like.
5 It's important _____ strong.
6 You have to help if one of the team is finding it hard _____.
7 It was kind of her friend _____.
8 She loved it _____ the finish line.

3 Read the Learn this! box. Match the sentences in exercise 2 with the uses of preparatory *it*.

> **LEARN THIS!** Uses of *it*
>
> **1** We can use *it* to introduce a gerund, infinitive or clause that is the subject of the sentence.
> *It was fun going to the cinema with you.*
> *It isn't important whose fault is it.*
>
> **2** We can use *it* to introduce an adjective, adding *of / for* + noun to say who or what the adjective refers to.
> *It was kind of you to invite me.*
> *It wasn't easy for me to pass the test.*
>
> **3** *it* can also stand for a clause or infinitive that is the object of a sentence.
> *I love it when you smile.* ✓ NOT ~~I love when~~ ... ✗
> *I hate it that he's so rude.*
> *I'd appreciate it if you'd send me more information.*
>
> **4** We use *it as* + noun / adjective + clause or infinitive with *see, take, regard, accept* and *view.*
> *I see it as insulting / an insult that he didn't invite me.*

➡ Grammar Builder 5.2 page 143

4 Use the phrases below and prompts 1–7 to write sentences with preparatory *it*. Use the correct tense of the verb *be.*

a pain fascinating fun hard work no use not worth well worth

1 dance / at the party. We had a great time!
   It was fun dancing at the party. We had a great time!
2 hear / all about his adventures in Africa. I can't wait.
3 dig / the new vegetable patch. It took us two whole days.
4 buy / a travel card. We'll hardly use it.
5 have to / go all the way to London to get a new passport.
6 ask / Tom to sponsor you. He never has any spare money.
7 visit / Venice. There's so much to see.

5 In your notebook, rewrite the sentences using *it* + adjective / noun + *of* or *for* and an infinitive.

1 Joe didn't say sorry, which was very rude.
   It was rude of Joe not to say sorry.
2 I'm not usually so tired in the morning.
3 Kate remembered my birthday. How thoughtful!
4 Joe's thinking of quitting his job, which would be a mistake.
5 You fixed my iPhone. That was so clever!
6 We really ought to leave the party now. Look at the time!
7 She did a very silly thing, leaving the cup of tea on the edge of the table.

6 USE OF ENGLISH In your notebook, rewrite the sentences using the word in brackets and a structure with *it.*

1 Going to the gym after work is very relaxing for her. (finds)
   She finds it very relaxing going to the gym after work.
2 You don't need to clear up. I'll do it. (leave)
3 She discovered that she just wasn't able to make ends meet. (found)
4 Using a mobile whilst driving is against the law. (illegal)
5 In his opinion, her failure to apologise is unacceptable. (regards)
6 You have a responsibility to your parents to let them know where you are. (owe)
7 What I hate is when you refuse to talk to me. (can't stand)

7 SPEAKING Work in pairs. Complete the sentences with your own ideas.

1 I find it hard …
2 It isn't worth …
3 I hate it when …
4 I see it as unlikely …
5 It's always fun …
6 I'd appreciate it if …
7 It's strange …

Word Skills
Dependent prepositions
I can use a range of dependent prepositions.

1 **SPEAKING** Work in pairs. Discuss the question: Is violent protest ever justified? Give reasons for your opinions.

2 **2.09** Listen to two teenagers, Nathan and Becky, answering the question in exercise 1. In what circumstances do they believe that it is justified? Do you agree?

3 **2.09** Complete the phrases from the listening with the correct prepositions. Then listen again and check.

1 opposed _____ violence
2 disapprove _____ people breaking the law
3 responsible _____ our own actions
4 discourage the victim _____ a gross injustice _____ taking the law into their own hands
5 result _____ more violence
6 a danger _____ democracy
7 have/lose sympathy _____ a cause
8 preferable _____ any form _____ violent protest
9 restrict themselves _____ non-violent protest
10 a disregard _____ human rights
11 the threat _____ imprisonment without trial
12 excuse them _____ resorting _____ violence
13 no other means _____ protest available _____ them
14 justified _____ defending themselves _____ the people who were intent _____ annihilating them
15 no threat _____ life and liberty
16 protests _____ GM crops
17 limit themselves _____ civil disobedience

4 Cover the dictionary entry below. Answer the questions about the verb *agree*, and think of examples.

1 How many different prepositions can be used after *agree*?
2 Can *agree* take an object without a preposition, i.e. *agree something*?

---

agree /əˈɡriː/ **verb**
• SHARE OPINION [I,T] to have the same opinion as sb; to say that you have the same opinion: *When he said that, I had to agree.* <> + **speech** '*That's true,*' *she agreed.* <> ~ (**with sb**) (**about/on sth**) *He agreed with them about the need for change.* <> ~ **with sth** *I agree with her analysis of the situation.* <> ~ (**that**)… *We agree (that) the proposal was a good one.* <> '*It's terrible.*' '*I couldn't agree more!*' (= I completely agree.)
> SAY YES [I,T] to say yes; to say that you will do what sb wants or that you will allow sth to happen: *I asked for a pay rise and she agreed.* <> ~ **to sth** *Do you think that he'll agree to their proposal?* <> ~(**that**)… *She agreed (that) I could go early.* <> ~**to do sth** *She agreed to let me go early.*
> DECIDE [I,T] to decide with sb else to do sth or to have sth: ~**on sth** *Can we agree on a date?* <> ~**sth** *They met at the agreed time.* <> *Can we agree a price?* <> *They left at 10, as agreed.* <> ~**to do sth** *We agreed to meet on Thursday.* <> ~**what, where, etc.** … *We couldn't agree what to do.*
> ACCEPT [T] ~**sth** to officially accept a plan, request, etc. **SYN approve**: *Next year's budget has been agreed.*

---

5 **DICTIONARY WORK** Look at the dictionary entry and check your answers to exercise 4.

6 Look at the prepositions in bold in the sentences below. Then complete the sentences with the correct forms of the words below. Use each word twice.

appeal differ improve warn

1 I _____ **with** Kate on the best way to organise direct action.
2 This essay is certainly an _____ **on** your last one.
3 Mum _____ me **about** the impending bad weather.
4 Left-wing politics have never really _____ **to** me.
5 There's been an _____ **in** human rights.
6 Dave _____ me **against** getting involved with the anti-war demonstrators.
7 The president has _____ **for** calm following the riots.
8 Your views on violent protest _____ **from** Joe's.

7 Complete the sentences with the correct prepositions. All of the adjectives are in exercises 3–6.

1 The terrorists were responsible _____ several bombings.
2 We're agreed _____ our opposition to violent protest.
3 People in some countries face the threat _____ terrorism every day.
4 The army is intent _____ crushing all opposition.
5 I have no sympathy _____ people who take the law into their own hands.
6 My dad discouraged me _____ attending the march.
7 Is living under capitalism preferable _____ living in a socialist state?
8 Across the country there were protests _____ the austerity measures.

8 **SPEAKING** Work in pairs. In what, if any, circumstances would you be prepared to use violence? Give reasons for your views. Use the ideas below to help you.

To protect:
• yourself
• your family or friends
• a stranger
• your property
• your country
• to prevent a crime

5F

'Why?' 'Because it was there!'
I can understand a text about mountaineering.

1 SPEAKING Describe the photos and read the title of the lesson. Why do you think people attempt dangerous challenges like this? What qualities do you need to achieve them?

Reading Strategy

In gapped text tasks, you sometimes have to choose carefully between two paragraphs and decide which is the most logical paragraph to fill the particular gap. Look for words and phrases which indicate the logical development of the text, e.g. adverbs of time and reason, words that express contrast, pronouns that point forwards or backwards to nouns, paraphrasing of vocabulary, repetition of names or ideas and the use of verb tenses.

2 Read the Reading Strategy. Read the text on page 59 before and after the first missing paragraph. Decide which paragraph, F or G, matches it. Explain your reasons.

3 Read the text again and match gaps 2–6 with the remaining paragraphs. There is one extra paragraph.

CRITICAL ANALYSIS

4 The text is the introduction by a famous mountaineer, Joe Simpson, to a book by another mountaineer, Heinrich Harrer. Find examples in the first five paragraphs of the completed text of the following devices that Simpson uses to draw the reader in and make them want to read Harrer's book.

1 emphasising his personal reaction to the book
2 talking about the effect it has had on his life
3 giving us a taste of highly dramatic or gruesome events without giving too much away about the story
4 using colourful dramatic language, with metaphors and similes
5 drawing a parallel with a book he himself has written
6 a rhetorical question

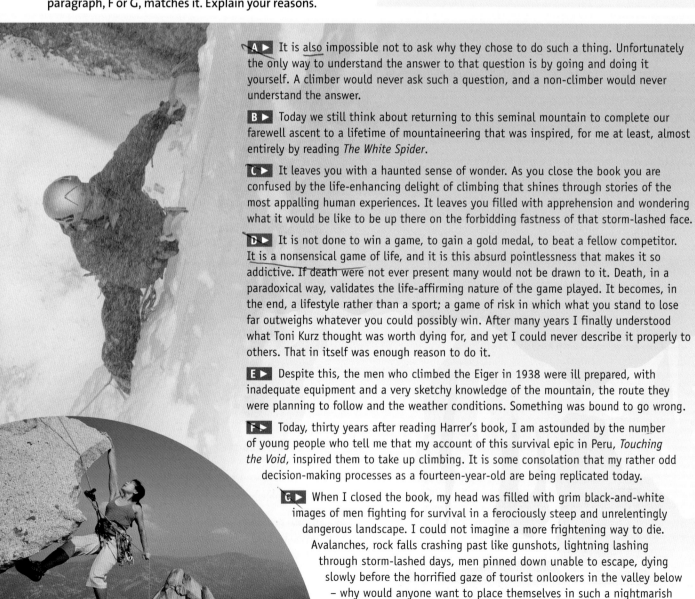

A ▶ It is also impossible not to ask why they chose to do such a thing. Unfortunately the only way to understand the answer to that question is by going and doing it yourself. A climber would never ask such a question, and a non-climber would never understand the answer.

B ▶ Today we still think about returning to this seminal mountain to complete our farewell ascent to a lifetime of mountaineering that was inspired, for me at least, almost entirely by reading *The White Spider*.

C ▶ It leaves you with a haunted sense of wonder. As you close the book you are confused by the life-enhancing delight of climbing that shines through stories of the most appalling human experiences. It leaves you filled with apprehension and wondering what it would be like to be up there on the forbidding fastness of that storm-lashed face.

D ▶ It is not done to win a game, to gain a gold medal, to beat a fellow competitor. It is a nonsensical game of life, and it is this absurd pointlessness that makes it so addictive. If death were not ever present many would not be drawn to it. Death, in a paradoxical way, validates the life-affirming nature of the game played. It becomes, in the end, a lifestyle rather than a sport; a game of risk in which what you stand to lose far outweighs whatever you could possibly win. After many years I finally understood what Toni Kurz thought was worth dying for, and yet I could never describe it properly to others. That in itself was enough reason to do it.

E ▶ Despite this, the men who climbed the Eiger in 1938 were ill prepared, with inadequate equipment and a very sketchy knowledge of the mountain, the route they were planning to follow and the weather conditions. Something was bound to go wrong.

F ▶ Today, thirty years after reading Harrer's book, I am astounded by the number of young people who tell me that my account of this survival epic in Peru, *Touching the Void*, inspired them to take up climbing. It is some consolation that my rather odd decision-making processes as a fourteen-year-old are being replicated today.

G ▶ When I closed the book, my head was filled with grim black-and-white images of men fighting for survival in a ferociously steep and unrelentingly dangerous landscape. I could not imagine a more frightening way to die. Avalanches, rock falls crashing past like gunshots, lightning lashing through storm-lashed days, men pinned down unable to escape, dying slowly before the horrified gaze of tourist onlookers in the valley below – why would anyone want to place themselves in such a nightmarish situation? I had no idea, so I read the book again.

5 Read from the sixth paragraph of the completed text to the end. Answer the questions.

1 How do we know that *The White Spider* was written a long time ago? *because the photographs*
2 In what ways does Simpson believe that climbing is much more than a sport? *the pointlessness makes*
3 What does *The White Spider* allow readers to do?
4 What evidence of previous climbing accidents is described in *The White Spider*?
5 What happened when Simpson and his climbing companion attempted the same route up the Eiger?

6 **VOCABULARY** In the second and eleventh paragraphs of the completed text, find intensifying adverbs that qualify the following adjectives.

1 _____ steep   3 _____ gripping
2 _____ dangerous

➡ **Vocabulary Builder** Intensifying adverbs: page 128

7 **SPEAKING** Work in pairs. Having read Joe Simpson's introduction to *The White Spider*, would you now like to read the whole book? Why? / Why not?

The North Face of the Eiger has always held a lingering fascination for me from the moment I finished reading Heinrich Harrer's *The White Spider* at the age of fourteen. This gripping account of the first ascent in 1938 and the subsequent and often disastrous attempts that followed should really have put me off mountaineering for life. Only a week earlier I had been taken rock climbing on a small limestone crag on the edge of the North York Moors. I was unaware that the arcane world of extreme mountaineering even existed, let alone that I would consider devoting the rest of my life to it.

1 G
I was no better informed at the end of the second reading, but I knew one thing: I wanted to find out. Despite the terrible hardship and awful deaths, I was forcibly struck by the fact that these men had chosen to be there. They couldn't all be idiots. There must be something very special about mountaineering for these people to think that such risks are worth it. I became a mountaineer inspired by the most gripping and frightening mountaineering book I have ever read. *— annoyance*

Eleven years later, much to my chagrin, I found myself hanging helplessly from a rope, battered by avalanches and storm winds, badly injured, and about to plunge into a nightmare every bit as bad as those described in *The White Spider*.

2 F
In many ways *The White Spider* is an unlikely success. The language can seem archaic and incongruous today. The grainy black-and-white photographs seem old-fashioned compared to the sumptuous photography in modern mountaineering literature. Today, standards of climbing have far outstripped anything that would be found on the 1938 route. It should really be a relic of mountaineering history accessible to only the most avid of climbing aficionados. And yet it is these very criticisms that make it such a fascinating and seminal book. *— important*

It is not solely about mountaineering. It is about humanity, courage, strength in adversity, and the power of the mind. It is impossible to read this book without being awed by the single-minded determination of a small band of poorly equipped climbers struggling to survive in a world that few of us can imagine.

3 A
When I read of Toni Kurz enduring such a terrible, drawn-out death, hanging alone on a rope, his companions dead around him, his rescuers tantalizingly out of reach, I was horrified and fascinated in equal measure. This, I was later to discover, is the essence of mountaineering: that strange mixture of fear and excitement, the addiction of apprehension and anticipation without which mountaineering would simply be another sport. It is far, far more than sport.

4 D
The White Spider is at once the most exciting and compulsively gripping of books and at the same time repellent and disturbing. Heroic in scale, legendary in the stories of long-lost lives that it recounts, it allows readers to experience vicariously the terror and the exultation of mountaineering from the warm comfort of their armchairs.

5 C
Harrer writes about the aura of fatality of the Eiger's North Face and of the 'hunted' feeling that climbers experience on the climb. The grim history lies scattered all around. Broken pitons, the shattered rocks strewn with the debris of past ascents, torn rucksacks, tattered ropes drifting in the wind, indistinguishable scraps of colour-drained clothing, the unshakable sense of other people's tragedies found in lonely spots all over the face. I had always been haunted by the North Face of the Eiger.

In September 2000, when Ray Delaney and I made our first attempt on the 1938 route, it was less of a climb and more of a pilgrimage in the footsteps of our heroes. It was exciting and frightening and loaded with the psychological baggage of all that we knew about it. We too felt that hunted sensation as we mutely witnessed the deaths of two young men, then crept, cowed and haunted, back to the safety of the valley. We tried again during the following two summers, beaten back each time by foul weather and cold, uncomfortable bivouacs. *— camp without tent*

6 B
One successful ascensionist described his time on the face: 'I seemed to have been in a dreamland; not a dreamland of rich enjoyment, but a much more beautiful land where burning desires were translated into deeds.' That to me was inspirational. The words of an intelligent, sensitive man who had 'in complete harmony ... a perfectly fashioned body, a bright, courageous mind and a receptive spirit.' A man who thought that sometimes in life it was worth gambling far more than you could ever possibly win.

Joe Simpson, Sheffield, September 2004

5G   Speaking
Photo comparison
I can describe, compare and speculate about photos.

1   **SPEAKING**   Work in pairs. Read the Speaking Strategy. What difficulties would you face trying to speak for one minute without stopping?

> **Speaking Strategy**
>
> You should accustom yourself to:
> - speaking for a minute on a subject without interruption.
> - using fillers (*Well,* …) and paraphrasing (*It's kind of* …) to help you keep pauses to a minimum.
> - listening to other students speak for a minute and then commenting or asking questions based on what you have heard.

2   **SPEAKING**   Work in pairs. Do the task below.

1   **Students A and B:** Choose one of the topics below (not the same one) and spend two minutes preparing to speak on it for one minute.

> my dream job   my bedroom   my favourite school subject
> last summer holidays   a present I received
> a hobby of mine   shopping   the internet

2   **Student A:** Using a watch, time Student B while he/she speaks for one minute. Listen carefully and ask a question based on what you have heard.

    Student B: Speak for one minute on the topic you chose. Use the phrases below to help you. Then answer Student A's question.

> **Fillers**
> Well, …   Let's see, …   Let me think, …
> What else? …   You know, …   Actually, …
> if you see what I mean …   You see, …   I suppose
> **Paraphrasing**
> What I mean is, …   It's a kind of …   You use it to …
> it looks a bit like a …   it's similar to a …   How do you say?
> I'm not sure what it is in English …   those things that you …

3   Swap roles and repeat the task.

3   **SPEAKING**   Work in pairs. Read the task below. Then look at the photos and agree on two qualities and two challenges.

> Compare the photos. What challenges might these people face in their jobs and what qualities might they need to carry them out successfully?

4   🎧 **2.10**   Listen to a student doing the task in exercise 3. What challenges and qualities did she think of? Were any the same as yours?

5   🎧 **2.10**   **KEY PHRASES**   Look at the key phrases below. Listen again. Which ones did the speaker use?

> **Speculating**
> I wonder, in fact, if …
> No doubt …
> In all probability, …
> I daresay …
> The chances are …
> I imagine that …
> My best guess would be that …
> It's highly unlikely that …
> My initial impression is that …
> His expression suggests that …
> It's not entirely clear if / how / what, etc.

6   **SPEAKING**   Take turns to do the task in exercise 3. Speak for one minute about the photos below. Your partner should time you.

7   **SPEAKING**   Work in pairs. Read the question below.
Student A: answer it in relation to the photos in exercise 4.
Student B: answer it in relation to the photos in exercise 6.

> Which job is the most rewarding job do you think?

8   **SPEAKING**   Work in pairs. Turn to page 151 and do the picture comparison task.

Writing
For and against essay
I can write a for and against essay.

1 SPEAKING Work in pairs. Try to answer these questions.

1 Which four of these countries don't have nuclear weapons?

Britain China France Germany India Israel Italy Japan North Korea Pakistan Ukraine the USA

2 When and where have nuclear weapons been used in a war?

2 Read the essay task below. Answer the questions.

1 What does 'unilaterally' mean? *sth that involves one group*
2 Can you think of one advantage and one disadvantage? *or one country*

Some people think that the world would be a safer place without nuclear weapons. What are the advantages and disadvantages of countries that have nuclear weapons disarming unilaterally?

3 Read the essay. Does the writer mention any of your ideas from exercise 2?

MANY PEOPLE believe that nations with nuclear arsenals should get rid of their weapons without waiting for other countries to do so. There are drawbacks to this approach, but also strong arguments that it would make the world a safer place.

To begin with, it is often argued by peace campaigners that countries would benefit from disarming. One argument in favour of this approach is that nuclear weapons pose a danger to everybody. If one country renounces the weapons, the risk to everybody is reduced and the world is made safer. By the same token, other nations will feel less threatened and will have no reason to keep their own weapons. Last but not least, it is simply unthinkable that any politician would 'press the nuclear button'. That would provoke retaliation resulting in the destruction of both countries. In other words, they are redundant.

By contrast, it can be argued that unilateral disarmament is against any one country's national interest. The reasoning is as

follows. In the first place, it would jeopardise that nation's security and leave them defenceless in the event of a nuclear attack. Secondly, nobody knows the nature of future threats and holding nuclear weapons is like an insurance policy. The only way forward, it is claimed, is a multilateral approach to disarmament, whereby all countries dispose of their weapons simultaneously.

Overall, I am convinced that the advantages of nuclear powers disarming unilaterally outweigh the disadvantages. Despite the risk to their own security, it will encourage others to follow their example and will lead to a safer world.

Writing Strategy
Make sure your essay has a clear, logical structure.

Paragraph 1: Introduction. Rephrase the question and/or give an example of the situation it describes to show that you have understood it.
Paragraph 2: Give two or three pros (arguments for). Include evidence and/or examples where appropriate.
Paragraph 3: Give two or three cons (arguments against). Include evidence and/or examples where appropriate.
Paragraph 4: Conclusion: sum up the most important or convincing arguments and give your opinion.

4 Read the Writing Strategy. How many pros and cons does the writer mention? Which of them are supported by examples or evidence?

5 KEY PHRASES Complete the key phrases with the words below. Which does the writer use in the essay?

argued case compelling contrast favour hold least place reasoning said simply token words

Introducing one side of the argument
It is often/sometimes [1] _argued_ that …
Some people maintain / [2] _hold_ / believe that …
There is a strong [3] _reasoning_ for ↑ _claim_

Listing arguments _case_
One argument in [4] _favour_ of / against …
Another [5] _compelling_ argument / reason for … is …
The [6] _case reasoning_ is follows. To begin / start with, …
In the first / second [7] _place_, …
Last but not [8] _least_, …

Introducing a similar point
Similarly, … Likewise, … In the same way, …
By the same [9] _token_, … Equally, …

Introducing an opposing point
By [10] _contrast_, … Alternatively, … All the same, …
On the other hand, … Having [11] _said_ that, …

Putting the same idea in a different way
In other [12] _words_, … To put it (more) …
[13] _simply_, … In a nutshell, …

6 Read the essay task below and think about the question. Then make a paragraph plan like the one in the Writing Strategy.

Some people believe that nuclear weapons have helped to prevent a third world war. Write an essay which presents the advantages and disadvantages of nuclear weapons.

7 Write your essay (220–260 words) using your plan from exercise 6.

CHECK YOUR WORK
Have you …
• followed the plan in the Writing Strategy?
• included key phrases for introducing arguments?
• checked your spelling and grammar?

Exam Skills Trainer

Reading

1 Read the strategy above and the question below. Follow the instructions in the strategy to answer the question.

Which athlete has a similar attitude to B towards the effect of pain on the outcome of a race?

2 You are going to read four extracts from articles in which ultra-endurance athletes describe their techniques for getting through the pain barrier. For questions 1–4, choose from the athletes A–D. The athletes may be chosen more than once.

Which athlete …

1 has the same attitude as B about the probability of encountering problems in a big race?
2 has a different attitude from the others towards self-motivation?
3 has a similar view to C on how to plan a competition?
4 experienced a similar difficulty to athlete A when competing in a big race?

Mind over matter

Four ultra-endurance athletes describe what they do to get through the pain barrier.

A Tina Whitby *Ultra-endurance runner*

When you're competing, you need to be able to turn negative experiences into positive ones really fast. It's imperative not to let the pain enter your head, or you'll find reasons to pull out. The most mentally demanding moment I've ever experienced was while I was doing the long stage of the Gobi March, a 250 mile race through the Gobi desert in China. At the time, I was running with another endurance runner from Australia, Rachel Phelps, and we'd been running for twelve hours. It was really hot, I was injured and night was coming. The only thing that kept me going was the certainty that I needed to stick with Rachel, so I was dragging myself along to keep up with her. At that stage of a race, my brain usually needs something concrete to focus on – attempts at encouraging myself just distract me in the end.

B Chris Tomlinson *Endurance racing cyclist*

When you're cycling the 3,000 miles of the Race Across America, something's bound to go wrong. The important thing is not to think about the problems too much and keep moving, every moment you're stopped is time wasted. Something I do is to break the race up into stages: I know I'm going to get up every day, ride my bike and then get off at night and sleep for two hours. During the race there are moments when you're in extreme discomfort, and that's where mental toughness comes in. You need to be able to mentally overcome your brain, which is telling you to stop, and keep pushing yourself forward, even though things aren't going well. Things got really bad during my last Race Across America, so I just told myself that it would get better – I find giving myself a pep talk helps to motivate me.

C Jonathan Wilde *Long course triathlete*

When you're doing a 1.2 mile swim, a 56 mile bike race and a 13.1 mile run, you're likely to get into difficulties at some point. Before each race, I visualise it and divide it up into as many key points as I can: at the halfway point I want to feel like this, for example. The greatest challenge for me personally has been winning my third Wildflower Triathlon with a broken foot. It started hurting three miles into the race, but there was no way I was giving up the chance for a third win, so I battled to the end of the race. It definitely helped that I kept on yelling 'Great stuff! You're killing it!', so that I was hearing it as well as saying it. That kind of thing always works when it comes to getting me going. The fundamental thing for me is the ability to deal with pain and process it.

D Philippa Dale *Elite CrossFit athlete*

CrossFit isn't an endurance sport as such, but as a CrossFit athlete, you have to push your body and mind to the limit to qualify for and take part in the annual CrossFit Games. You're competing against the top 50 athletes in the world, and it's tough! To get through the workouts you have to forget about all the negativity in your life and focus on the task in hand. The toughest workout I've ever done is the rowing challenge in the last CrossFit Games. We had to do a half marathon on stationary rowing machines, which took me about an hour and a half. I couldn't see straight by the end of the workout! Every now and then, I'd check my progress on the scoreboard and tell myself, 'Come on! You've done this much, you can do this much more'. Reasoning with myself tends to have the effect of pushing me forward.

Listening

3 🎧 **2.11** Read the strategy. You will hear a radio interview about a soldier called Desmond Doss. For questions 1–6, choose the best answer (A, B, C or D). As you listen, decide which option matches what is said and why the other options are wrong.

1 Desmond Doss became an army recruit because
   A he had considerable experience repairing ships.
   B his age obliged him to do so.
   C he was eager to serve his country.
   D his father expected him to follow in his footsteps.

2 Desmond eventually went to the front because
   A he had surpassed all his peers in physical trials.
   B he had frustrated all attempts to discharge him.
   C he had shown promise in military training.
   D he had agreed to comply with orders.
3 On his first placement, Desmond was a prime target for the enemy owing to
   A the negative attitude of his comrades.
   B his refusal to carry a weapon.
   C his haste to rescue the wounded.
   D the intrinsic nature of his job.
4 Desmond's miscalculation of the men he rescued in Okinawa reveals that he was
   A modest about his achievement.
   B proud of his bravery.
   C desperate for military recognition.
   D ashamed of his performance.
5 As a casualty, Desmond
   A expected a medic to attend to him immediately.
   B went on treating others while he was waiting.
   C demanded the stretcher of another patient.
   D continued to put the well-being of others first.
6 After the war, Desmond's fragile health
   A restricted his future life considerably.
   B required him to make frequent hospital visits.
   C limited his freedom only a little.
   D obliged him to leave the army.

Use of English

Strategy
Key-word transformations test your knowledge of advanced grammar and vocabulary. Each question tests two different language points and one mark is allocated to each one. Before you answer each question, try to identify the two language points being tested to help you transform the sentence.

4 Read the strategy and questions 1–6. Which language points are being tested in each question? Complete the second sentence so that it has a similar meaning to the first sentence, using the word given. Do not change the word given. You must use between three and seven words.

1 I don't remember her name, so I can't have met her before.
   BELL
   If I'd met her before, her name _____.
2 My brother and I don't usually agree on what to watch on TV.
   EYE
   My brother and I tend _____ what to watch on TV.
3 'Don't get involved in other people's problems,' my mum said to me.
   AGAINST
   My mum _____ in other people's problems.

4 Nobody has ever treated me with such disrespect before.
   I
   Never before _____ with such disrespect.
5 We hadn't expected the film to be so good.
   TURNED
   The film _____ than we'd expected.
6 I couldn't find a cheap holiday deal anywhere.
   PICK
   Nowhere _____ cheap holiday deal.

Speaking

Strategy
When you compare two photos, you have to speculate about the topics and themes related to the photos and not just describe the photos. Use a variety of modal verbs and phrases for speculating to demonstrate your range of language.

5 Read the strategy and look at the photos below. Write a sentence speculating on the people in the photos using each of the key words below.

   must   might   seem   look like / as if   appear   can't

6 Compare two of the photos which show major life changes and say how the people might be feeling and in what ways their lives might change.

Writing

Strategy
When you write a letter to the editor of a newspaper, you should finish with a conclusion with an impact. You can make an impact in the conclusion by using a summary, an opinion, a closing statement or a rhetorical question.

7 Read the strategy above and the task below and write a conclusion using each of the techniques for making an impact.

You have read a magazine article which argues that protest demonstrations are a waste of time. Write a letter to the editor in which you explain whether you agree or disagree with this view. You should describe a protest march that illustrates your opinion.

8 Write the letter to the editor (220–260 words) for the task above.

6

Dreams

6A · Vocabulary

Life's too short

I can talk about dreams and ambitions.

1 SPEAKING Work in pairs. Read the quote. What do you think the actor meant? Do you agree with the quote?

'Dream as if you'll live forever. Live as if you'll die today.' – James Dean

2 Read the synopsis of a film called *The Bucket List*. What is a bucket list? Which of the characters succeeds in 'completing' the list? How does he manage this?

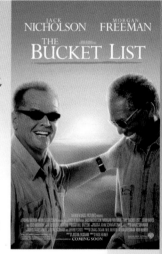

Diagnosed with a life-threatening illness, penniless car mechanic Carter Chambers is living on borrowed time. Having led a very ordinary life, he writes a bucket list of everything he would like to see and do, but decides not to ¹fulfil his dreams when he discovers that he has less than a year to live. However, life has more in store for Carter, as he is in the right place at the right time when billionaire Edward Cole is admitted to hospital. At first, Edward has no time for Carter, but in time the two strike up a friendship. Finding Carter's list, Edward adds some objectives he would like to ²accomplish too, and finances a trip for the two of them, a race against time, to ³meet all of their aspirations. The pair have the time of their lives ⁴realising their ambitions: they go skydiving, drive a racing car, ride motorbikes along the Great Wall of China and fly over the North Pole, until Carter confesses that he wants to go home because he is missing his wife. He arrives in the nick of time to be reunited with his family before being rushed to hospital, where Edward visits him. As Carter is taken off for an unsuccessful operation, Edward promises to ⁵complete their mission and finish the bucket list without him. First, he makes up for lost time by reconciling with his daughter and granddaughter. Then, at Carter's funeral, he expresses his joy at having been able to help his new friend ⁶attain his goals. Edward succeeds in ⁷achieving all but one of the aims on the bucket list before he passes away at the age of 81. The film ends with Edward's assistant helping him ⁸reach his target of completing the list. The assistant climbs to the top of a mountain in the Himalayas and places a coffee tin with Edward's ashes next to a similar one containing Carter's, so that the two could 'witness something majestic'.

> **FLUENCY!**
>
> When you use synonyms to avoid repetition, remember that a synonym can be a whole phrase (for example, a verb + a noun) rather than a single word:
>
> *to realise your dream = to achieve your objective*
>
> More than one verb + noun collocation may be possible, but not all combinations sound natural.

3 VOCABULARY Read the Fluency! box. Then complete the collocations below with the verbs highlighted in the text and Fluency! box.

> **Achievements: verb + noun collocations**
> achieve, ¹ *realise* , ² *fulfil* a dream
> ³ *achieve* , ⁴ *accomplish* , attain, fulfil, meet, reach an objective
> achieve, fulfil, ⁵ *meet* , realise an aspiration
> achieve, fulfil, ⁶ *realise* an ambition
> accomplish, ⁷ *complete* a mission
> achieve, ⁸ *attain* , reach a goal
> ⁹ *achieve* , fulfil an aim
> achieve, meet, ¹⁰ *reach* a target

4 VOCABULARY Complete the questions with a suitable verb + noun collocation from exercise 3. Then match the people with their achievements.

Jane Austen   Ludwig van Beethoven   Vincent van Gogh
Jennifer Lawrence   Valentina Tereshkova   Harriet Tubman
Jamie Vardy   Stevie Wonder

Who ...

1 fulfilled their ambition of becoming a premier league footballer despite being told they were too short?
2 _____ *Jennifer Lawrence* _____ of becoming an actor against the wishes of their parents?
3 was able to _____ *Ludwig van Beethoven* _____ of composing music despite losing their hearing?
4 _____ of being a music legend although they are visually impaired?
5 _____ *Harriet Tubman* _____ of saving hundreds of slaves despite being one themselves?
6 _____ *Jane Austen meet her* aspiration of publishing a novel at a time when writing was not considered appropriate for their gender?
7 _____ *Vincent van Gogh* _____ of gaining recognition as a talented artist, but only after their death?
8 _____ of piloting a spacecraft to become the first woman in space?

5 VOCABULARY Find eight idioms that include the word 'time' in the text in exercise 2. Match them with the definitions below.

1 Their trip is something that has to be done quickly. *a race against time*
2 Carter is in the best position to take advantage of an opportunity. *in the right place at the right time.*
3 Edward compensates for many wasted years by reconciling with his daughter. *makes up*
4 At first, Edward dislikes Carter. *has no time*
5 Carter arrives home just before something bad happens. *in the nick of time.*
6 Carter and Edward enjoy themselves very much. *had the time of their life*
7 Carter was expected to have died before now.
8 Eventually, Carter and Edward start to get along. *in time*

6 SPEAKING Work in pairs. Which of the items on Carter and Edward's bucket list would you most like to do? Would you like to see this film? Why? / Why not?

7 🎧 **2.12** Listen to the introduction to a radio documentary about a real-life person who wrote a bucket list. Answer the questions.

1 How many goals were on John Goddard's bucket list?
2 How many of his ambitions did he realise?

8 SPEAKING Work in pairs. Look at the photos illustrating some of John Goddard's dreams. What do you think the photos represent?

9 🎧 **2.13** Listen and check your answers to exercise 8. Which of the dreams did he realise?

10 🎧 **2.13** Replace the underlined verbs in the sentences below from the recording with the synonyms. Then listen again and check your answers.

circumnavigated¹   conducted³   endured⁶   mastered²
piloted⁸   retraced⁴   scaled⁵   traversed⁷

1 He went round the globe no less than four times ...
2 He learned three foreign languages ...
3 He led fourteen major expeditions to remote areas ...
4 ... he followed the steps of Marco Polo and Alexander the Great ...
5 ... he climbed twelve of the world's highest mountains ...
6 ... he suffered a major blizzard to reach the summit of the Matterhorn in the Swiss Alps.
7 ... he crossed eleven countries in north-eastern Africa ...
8 ... he flew one of the world's fastest aircraft.

11 SPEAKING Work in pairs. Answer the questions.

1 Which of the verbs in exercise 10 could you use to describe the photos in exercise 8?
2 What is John Goddard's most impressive achievement in your opinion? Why?

12 Write your own bucket list of at least ten items. Use the synopsis of *The Bucket List* and the story of John Goddard to help you, or use your own ideas.

13 SPEAKING Work in pairs. Compare your list with a partner. Discuss the likelihood that you will ever fulfil each of the goals on your list.

Grammar
Relative clauses and reduced relative clauses
I can use relative clauses and reduced relative clauses.

1 **SPEAKING** Work in pairs. Which famous person do you think is a good role model for his or her fans? Why?

2 Read the story behind the book club. How did it begin?

Leah Moloney never expected to fulfil her dreams, one of which was to create an online bookshop; the other was to meet the singer of Florence and the Machine, a band that Leah is very keen on. But then, in July 2012, a photo of Florence Welch, captioned 'Booksbooksbooksbooks', appeared on Leah's Twitter feed. It showed the singer standing in front of a well-known independent bookshop. Leah responded and proposed that she and Florence start a book club based on suggestions that the star sent in. To her surprise, Florence agreed and Between Two Books was born. Since then, members have read dozens of books by various authors, the most recent of which has been *The Descent of Man* by Grayson Perry. Since Florence has a busy career in music, the person writing the posts on the website is often Leah. She has run the group for several years now, and believes that reading is much trendier today, thanks to the co-operation of her new friend, to whom she will always be indebted.

3 Read the text again and find five relative clauses. Which are defining and which are non-defining?

4 Read the **Learn this!** box. Which relative clauses from the text in exercise 2 can be rewritten with the prepositions in a different position? What effect does this have on the sentence?

LEARN THIS! Prepositions in relative clauses

1 When we start a relative clause with a preposition, we use *which* or *whom* as the relative pronoun. It sounds quite formal.

She phoned the man from whom she had bought the car.

2 Less formally, we put the preposition at the end of the clause. We often omit the relative pronoun or use *that*.

She phoned the man (that) she'd bought the car from.

3 We never put the preposition at the start of the clause when it is part of a phrasal verb or when the relative pronoun is the subject of a passive verb.

She went out to buy some milk, which she had run out of.

I put the photo, which hadn't been looked at, in my bag.

4 In non-defining relative clauses, we can use *of which* and *of whom* after a number, a quantifier (*some, many, a few*, etc.) or a superlative.

She collects jewellery, some of which is valuable.

I've got three brothers, the eldest of whom is a doctor.

➡ **Grammar Builder 6.1** page 143

5 In your notebook, write the two sentences as one with a relative clause. Which can be written in two ways, one more formal than the other?

1 Leah juggles her work on the book club with her studies. She looks forward to her work immensely.

2 Florence often makes time to chat to Leah. Florence has a good relationship with her.

3 The book club receives numerous posts daily. Some of the posts are from the authors of the chosen books.

4 Florence has conducted interviews with famous authors. Their books have been sold all over the world.

5 Once, Florence invited Leah up on stage in front of the fans. She was introduced to them as a 'special guest'.

6 Florence has recorded more than fifty songs. The most popular of them is *Never Let Me Go*.

6 Read the **Learn this!** box and study the two highlighted examples in the text in exercise 2. Are the reduced relative clauses defining or non-defining? How would write them as full relative clauses?

LEARN THIS! Reduced relative clauses

1 A relative clause formed with a participle and no relative pronoun is called a reduced relative clause. A present participle (*-ing*) replaces an active tense and a past participle (*-ed*) replaces a passive tense.

2 A reduced relative clause can be defining or non-defining. If non-defining, it is written between commas.

A car belonging to the police was stolen. (= which belonged to the police)

The castle, built in 1300, is still standing. (= which was built in 1300)

➡ **Grammar Builder 6.1** page 144

7 Complete each sentence with a relative clause, defining or non-defining, using one of the verbs below. Then rewrite each sentence using a reduced relative clause.

bury   finance   hold   recommend   want   wear

1 My whole family went to the fundraising event _____ in our school.

2 The city of Pompeii, _____ under volcanic ash nearly 2,000 years ago, is a popular tourist attraction.

3 The person _____ the project is a well-known figure.

4 I've read all of the books _____ by my teacher.

5 The singer, _____ a thick coat, got into the car hurriedly.

6 People _____ tickets for the concert will have to get them well in advance.

8 **SPEAKING** Work in pairs. Prepare a description of a famous person who has made a positive contribution in some way. Include three relative clauses in your description.

9 **SPEAKING** Describe your person to another pair. Then decide which person has made the greatest contribution.

Against all odds

I can understand and react to a radio programme about female explorers in history.

1 **SPEAKING** Discuss the points below. To what extent might they prevent a person from achieving their goals?

gender   health   money   race   society   time

2 🎧 **2.14** Listen to the introduction to a radio documentary and answer the questions.

1 What kind of people are featured in the documentary?
2 Which obstacle did these people have to overcome to achieve their goals?

3 🎧 **2.14** **VOCABULARY** Listen again. Complete the table with six adjectives from the recording.

Synonyms	Antonyms
¹_____ distinguished	insignificant unknown
fearless ²_____	cowardly fainthearted
³_____ hair-raising	dismal dreary
liberal unbiased	⁴_____ intolerant
escorted chaperoned	alone ⁵_____
becoming fitting	⁶_____ unsuitable

Listening Strategy

In a true and false listening task, the statements may contain words that are synonyms or antonyms of words in the recording. While you are listening, look out for synonyms and antonyms for the key information.

4 Read the Listening Strategy and the statements below. Which synonyms or antonyms from exercise 3 might you hear instead of the highlighted words?

1 The leader of the expedition that Jeanne Baret joined was a distinguished explorer.
2 Having completed the expedition's botany research in Mauritius, Baret sailed home to France unaccompanied.

5 🎧 **2.15** Listen to the first part of the documentary. Are the sentences in exercise 4 true (T) or false (F)? Which words in the recording helped you decide?

6 🎧 **2.16** Listen to the rest of the documentary. Are the sentences true (T) or false (F)?

1 Advised to go on a voyage for health reasons, Isabella Bird travelled to America.
2 On completing her world travels, Bird returned home and had a somewhat dreary retirement.
3 Excluded from American flying schools for her gender, Bessie Coleman gained her pilot's licence in Europe.
4 Practising for a demonstration of her flying skills, Coleman was killed in an accident.
5 Clashing with the narrow-minded attitude of her parents, Freya Stark started out by seeking adventure in books.
6 Having spent much of her life away from Europe, Stark decided to go back there to live out her final days.

7 🎧 **2.16** Listen again. What words in the recording indicate the correct answers? Compare your answers and explain why the sentences are true or false.

8 Read the Learn this! box. Match sentences 1–6 in exercise 6 to rules a–c. Say whether each participle clause gives information about reason or timing.

LEARN THIS! Participle clauses

Participle clauses contain a present, past or perfect participle rather than a subject and verb. Clauses with a past participle have a passive meaning.

a Present and past participle clauses can contain a **reason** or **condition**, or give information about **timing**.
b Perfect participle clauses emphasise that one action is complete before another begins.
c Present participle clauses can be introduced by *after*, *before*, *by*, *on*, *since*, *when*, *while* or *without*. Past participle clauses can be introduced by *once* or *until*.

9 🎧 **2.16** Rewrite the information from the recording using participle clauses. Then listen again and check.

1 Because she suffered from multiple ailments, Bird was urged by her doctors to undertake a sea voyage.
2 She vowed to take off again because she had had her curiosity piqued by her first experience of travelling.
3 Coleman learned French and travelled to France as she was banned from flying in the USA because of her colour.
4 She performed aerial tricks all over the USA because she had vowed to finance an African-American flying school.
5 Stark became fascinated with Arab culture when she received *One Thousand and One Nights* for her birthday.
6 She explored and mapped uncharted areas of the Islamic world while she was living in Baghdad.

10 **SPEAKING** Work in pairs. Answer the questions.

1 Apart from gender, which obstacles did the women in the recording have to overcome to achieve their goals?
2 Which of the women do you admire the most? Why?

➡ **Vocabulary Builder** Gender and language: page 129

Modal verbs: speculation
I can speculate about different possibilities.

A

B

1 SPEAKING Work in pairs. Look at photo A of a dream home and answer the questions.

1 What kind of person do you think it belongs to?
2 Where do you think it is?
3 What do you think it might be like living there?
4 Would you like to live in a house like this? Why/Why not?

2 Read the comments made by two students speculating about the dream home in exercise 1. Choose the best modal verb for each comment.

1 It _____ be one of those stately homes in the UK.
  a should   **b** can't   **(c)** must
2 It _____ be the house of some aristocratic family or other.
  (a) can   **b** 'll   **c** can't
3 It _____ belong to an ordinary person like you or me.
  (a) can't   **b** might   **c** must
4 I suppose the owner _____ be inside waiting for visitors.
  (a) might   **b** can   **c** can't
5 It's midday, so they _____ be arriving soon ...
  a can't   **b** can   **(c)** should
6 I guess the house _____ be empty.
  a can   **(b)** may   **c** should
7 Those houses _____ be really expensive to maintain.
  (a) can   **b** should   **c** can't
8 I guess the family _____ be living somewhere else, then.
  a can   **(b)** could   **c** can't

3 🎧 2.17 In pairs compare your answers in exercise 2. Try to explain why the other modal verbs do not fit. Then listen and check your answers.

4 Look at your answers to exercise 2. Which modals can we use to talk about ...

1 what we assume to be true? (_____)
2 what we can deduce is definitely true? (_____)
3 what we can deduce is definitely not true? (_____)
4 what we can deduce is possible? (_____ / _____ / _____)
5 what we expect? (_____)
6 what sometimes happens? (_____)

➡ Grammar Builder 6.2 page 145

5 Look at photo B of part of the same home one morning in 2015. Read the comments made by people speculating about the incident and complete them with *can't, may* or *must.*

1 There _____ have been a fire.
2 It _____ have been caused by a match.
3 The owners _____ have been expecting this to happen.

6 Read the Learn this! box. Match sentences 1–3 in exercise 5 to rules a–c below.

> **LEARN THIS!** Past modal verbs of speculation
> To speculate about past situations, we use:
> **a** modal + perfect infinitive (*have* + past participle)
> **b** modal + perfect continuous infinitive (*have been* + -ing)
> **c** modal + passive infinitive (*have been* + past participle)
> We only use *can* to speculate about the past in questions or with *hardly, only* or *never*.

7 In your notebook, write sentences speculating or making deductions about the fire. Use language from the Learn this! box and the prompts below.

1 The fire (hardly / start) by the owner.
2 The owners (sleep) when the fire started.
3 The roof (catch fire).
4 They (save) all of the furniture.
5 Fire fighters (try) to put out the flames for hours.

8 🎧 2.18 Listen to a news item about the fire. Does it contain any information that either confirms or contradicts your speculations in exercises 5 and 7?

9 USE OF ENGLISH Complete the second sentence so that it has a similar meaning to the first sentence, using modal verbs in exercise 4. Write between three and six words.

1 I'm sure the roof fell in.
  The roof *must have fallen in*
2 Perhaps someone was working in the basement.
  Someone *might have been* in the basement.
3 I expect they're re-opening the house soon.
  They *might reopen* the house soon.
4 I'm sure they didn't have time to save the larger pieces of furniture.
  They *can't have had* *time to save* the larger pieces of furniture.
5 Some people say it was possible to prevent the fire.
  Some people say the fire *could have been prevented*

10 SPEAKING Work in pairs. Read the headline. Use modal verbs to speculate about the house. Think about the previous owner and events that may have happened there.

Portsmouth's 'haunted' manor house fails to sell

Phrasal verbs (2)

I can recognise and use literal and idiomatic phrasal verbs correctly.

1 SPEAKING Work in pairs. Answer the questions.

1 What's the last thing you <u>switch off</u> at night?
2 Do you usually <u>leave out</u> your clothes for the next day?
3 Did you ever <u>fall out</u> of bed when you were younger?
4 Who's the first person to <u>get up</u> in your family?
5 What time does your alarm <u>go off</u> on a school day?
6 What's the first thing you <u>put on</u> in the morning?

LEARN THIS! Phrasal verbs: literal and idiomatic meanings

Some phrasal verbs have multiple meanings. One of the meanings may be more literal, i.e. the words mean exactly what they say.

Hold on to the railing when you're on the stairs.

The other meaning or meanings are idiomatic, i.e. the words mean something different from the original meaning of the individual words. Sometimes, the literal meaning can help you understand the idiomatic meaning.

Hold on! I'll only be a minute.

DION MCGREGOR has ¹gone down / settled down in history as the world's greatest sleep-talker. Anxious to ²get on / get over as a songwriter in New York in the 1960s, McGregor's career was slow in ³taking in / taking off. Short of cash, he moved in with a colleague, who recorded McGregor's dreams and played the tapes to friends. Eventually the dream stories came to the attention of a record company, which ⁴put out / went down a selection of them in 1964 on a disc called *The Dream World of Dion McGregor*. The same year, a publishing house heard about his dreams, but insisted that he see a psychiatrist to prove he wasn't ⁵making them up / taking them off. Once convinced that they weren't being ⁶put out / taken in, they released a volume of dreams, but it soon went out of print. The LP, however, became a cult record, which has recently been rediscovered. McGregor died in 1994, never living to see the renewed interest, but by then he had already ⁷made up / got over his sleep-talking. Once he had met and ⁸settled down / got on with his life partner, his strange habit subsided.

2 Read the Learn this! box. Replace the underlined words with the correct form of the phrasal verbs in exercise 1. Are their meanings generally more or less idiomatic than their meanings in exercise 1?

1 Don't drink that milk – it's <u>become bad</u>. *gone off*
2 My essay didn't get full marks because I <u>didn't include</u> something important. *left out*
3 The talk was so boring that I <u>stopped paying attention</u>. *switched off*
4 The wind <u>increased in strength</u> last night, waking everybody up. *got up in strength*
5 I'm not talking to my sister – we've <u>had an argument</u>. *fallen out*
6 She isn't really ill; she's just <u>faking (it)</u>. *putting it on*

3 Complete the sentences with the correct form of the literal phrasal verbs below.

get on   get over   go down   make up   put out
settle down   take in   take off

1 I slid on the slope and <u>went down</u> with a bump.
2 The bus was already at the stop, so I had to run to <u>get on</u>.
3 We <u>took off</u> our shoes and left them at the front door.
4 Don't forget to <u>put</u> the rubbish <u>out</u> in the morning.
5 They needed somewhere to sleep, so we <u>settled</u> ~~put~~ them <u>down</u> ~~up~~.
6 Our school community is <u>made up</u> of many different nationalities.
7 Nobody knows how he managed to <u>get over</u> the fence.
8 I <u>settled down</u> on the sofa, waiting for the film to start.

4 Read the article and choose the correct idiomatic phrasal verbs. What was the man's strange talent?

5 Match the phrasal verbs in exercise 4 with the definitions.

a publish or broadcast something *put out*
b start having a quieter way of life *settled down*
c invent a story *making them up*
d be successful in a career *taking off*
e deal with or gain control of something *get over*
f become successful or popular *get on*
g be recorded and remembered *gone down*
h make somebody believe something that is not true *take in*

6 Rewrite the questions below using phrasal verbs from exercise 4 to replace the underlined words. Use a dictionary to help, as their meanings may be different from the meanings in the text.

1 How <u>well are you doing</u> at school this year? *Are you getting on*
2 What's the longest it's taken you to <u>recover from</u> an illness? *get over*
3 How do you feel when you tell a joke that <u>isn't received</u> very well? *go down*
4 If you don't study one day, do you <u>compensate</u> the next? *make up for*
5 How do you feel when you notice you're <u>causing extra work for somebody</u>? What do you usually do about it? *putting someone out*
6 How long does it usually take your class to <u>become calm</u> at the start of lessons? Why? *settle down*
7 When you see an acquaintance, do you stop and chat or <u>leave in a hurry</u> before they see you? *take off*
8 Are there any subjects in which you find it hard to <u>understand everything</u>? Which ones? *take in*

7 SPEAKING Work in pairs. Discuss the questions in exercise 6.

I have a dream

I can understand and react to the opinions of four historians about a speech.

I HAVE A DREAM

THE MARCH ON WASHINGTON FOR JOBS AND FREEDOM
AUGUST 28 1963

1 SPEAKING Work in pairs. Read the quote in the photo above. Who said it? What did he do? What happened to him?

2 🎧 2.19 Listen to a historian talking about an important event at the memorial in exercise. 1. What's the name of the memorial? What happened there and when did it happen?

3 🎧 2.19 Listen again and answer the questions.
1 How did the setting enhance King's speech?
2 Why was the memorial relevant to King's speech?
3 In what way does King compare the Emancipation Proclamation to a 'bad cheque'?

4 Read the text. Do any of the four historians clearly express the opinion that Martin Luther King's speech is the greatest speech in history?

> ### Reading Strategy
> In this task you have to read four texts to identify similar or different opinions and attitudes. Take each question in turn and follow the procedure below:
> 1 Underline the key words in the question.
> 2 Note whether you need to find a similar or a different opinion.
> 3 Find and underline the opinion in the text specified in the question. If no text is specified, read all the texts.
> 4 Find and underline the same opinion in the other three texts.
> 5 Compare the opinions and choose the correct answer.

5 Read the Reading Strategy and the question below. Follow the instructions in the Strategy and answer the question.

Which historian has a similar view to Brian Ward about how the speech should be considered?

6 Match the historians A–D with questions 1–4. The historians may be chosen more than once.

Which historian ...
1 has a different opinion from Webb about the quality of King's voice as he gave the speech? ____C____
2 shares Lewis's view about the attention paid to the 'dream' part of the speech? ____D____
3 agrees with Houston about the part of the speech dedicated to the debt owed to African-Americans? ____C____
4 disagrees with Lewis's opinion of King's use of phrases and ideas that people had used before? ____A____

7 Read the text again. Answer the questions in your own words.
1 Which of King's particular skills does Houston think the speech exemplifies?
2 According to Houston, what did King mean by 'cashing a cheque'?
3 According to Webb, what significance do all the experts attribute to the March on Washington?
4 What was the importance of the new technology that Webb mentions?
5 What does Lewis consider the main strength of King's speech?
6 According to Lewis, what contrasting impressions did King convey during his speech?
7 What was the cause of the underlying dissatisfaction that Ward mentions?
8 What veiled threat does Ward detect in the speech?

CRITICAL ANALYSIS

8 Look at the highlighted adjectives and nouns and the underlined verbs in the text. How would you describe this language? What effect does it have on the text? How could it improve your own writing?

9 Match the highlighted words in the text with their synonyms below. Use the context to help work out the meaning.

~~consternation~~ ~~demeanour~~ ~~dire~~ ~~dismayed~~ ~~spectre~~
anxiety   attitude   critical   disappointed   ghost   ideas
insignificant   quiet   notions
negligible   subdued

10 Try to work out the meaning of the underlined verbs in the text. Then match them with the highlighted words below.
Crys tallises   blends
1 The picture combines modern and traditional styles.
2 Military activity is a sign of an imminent attack. foreshadows
3 The two groups of protesters come together at the town hall. converged
4 What can be done to make the economy strong again? rev
5 Do not criticise others before listening to their reasons.
6 The words of a great speech can echo in your mind for days after.
7 The sea mist will prevent the boats from being seen. obscur
8 As she listened, a plan took shape in her mind.

11 SPEAKING Work in pairs. Answer the questions.
1 To what extent do you think Martin Luther King's dream of racial equality has been achieved?
2 In your view, what makes a good speech?

Is Martin Luther King's 'I HAVE A DREAM' THE GREATEST SPEECH IN HISTORY?

A BENJAMIN HOUSTON

Calling King's address 'the greatest in history' is a tall order for any historian and for any speech to live up to. It certainly should be classed as among a handful of momentous speeches in US
5 history, perhaps second only to the Gettysburg Address.

The speech crystallises some of King's greatest gifts, not least of which an ability to address diverse audiences with one voice – to
10 both revive the souls of the march participants and to stir the consciences of the greater public beyond, to speak eloquently to the African-American experience and yet also to the wider American spirit. *— clear*

15 He meant to give 'new meaning', as he said in the speech, to old words and clichés that nonetheless were rooted in broader notions of the American Dream.

His soaring oratory at the March on
20 Washington spoke of cashing a cheque, of laying claim to the economic aspirations that remained largely out of reach of African-Americans.

It foreshadowed King's deepening critique of American society that would dominate his
25 thoughts and the social and political conflicts of the 1960s.

B CLIVE WEBB

On 28 August 1963, a quarter of a million demonstrators, black and white, converged on the capital of the United States to participate in
30 the March on Washington for Jobs and Freedom.

Almost singing the words in his great baritone voice, Dr Martin Luther King, Jr. described his dream of a United States that a century later finally fulfilled the promise of President Abraham
35 Lincoln's Emancipation Proclamation.

King's inclusive vision of a country united across its racial and religious divide emphasised the idealism and determination of a civil rights movement that had over a decade of struggle
40 developed an unstoppable political and moral momentum.

While many commentators observe that the March on Washington had a negligible impact on the eventual passage of the Civil Rights Act
45 of 1964, none deny the importance of the event in awakening the national consciousness to the question of civil rights.

King's speech resonated not only throughout the United States but also across the world. A
50 Telstar communication satellite performed what one British newspaper described as 'its most dramatically historic duty so far' and enabled audiences in the UK to witness the march, although only the end was live.

C DR GEORGE LEWIS

55 For many of the strategists who were close to King and activists who were present, this was not even the greatest speech at the March on Washington, let alone of King's career.

In terms of oratorical style it was curiously subdued, lacking the tone and rhythm that characterised the southern Baptist church where King was a preacher.
60 In terms of content, the most significant section of the speech was not its 'Dream' section but an earlier passage which detailed the real reason that lay behind the gathering at the March on Washington: that black Americans had been given a 'bad cheque' at the time of their supposed emancipation 100 years previously, which they were now coming to Washington to demand to be cashed.
65 The idea of a 'Dream' caused consternation: King's colleagues judged it repetitive to the point of cliché; radical student activists were dismayed to hear a black leader dreaming of a far-off future.

For those who had not heard King's oratory previously, however, the reaction was altogether different, and this is where the genius of the speech truly lies.
70 Deep in the White House, President John F. Kennedy openly declared that King was 'damn good'. Northern white liberals, who provided much of the Democrats' electoral base, were deeply impressed by his level-headed demeanour and statesmanlike tone.

D BRIAN WARD

'I Have a Dream' is rightly considered one of the most important speeches of modern
75 history, yet its significances and meanings are often misunderstood.

While it is impossible not to sympathise with the sentiments expressed in the stirring finale, as King imagines a world of interracial harmony where people 'will not be judged by the color of their skin but by the content of their character,' too much emphasis on the 'Dream' can obscure other important aspects of King's
80 magnificent oration.

The speech is filled with barely concealed frustration at the slow pace of federal action to support black civil and voting rights.

Brilliantly blending politics with his inspiring social vision, King starts by reminding white Americans of the continuing abuse of black rights (African-
85 Americans generally did not need reminding). He goes on to condemn the gap between America's democratic ideals and the realities of its racial practices. Finally, he hints at the dire consequences of failing to address these issues immediately (the speech is haunted by the spectre of more militant black protest if
90 non-violent demands for basic citizenship rights are not met).

6G Speaking
Debate

I can use a range of discourse markers to give my opinion in a debate.

1 SPEAKING What did you want to be when you were younger? Have your ambitions changed? Why? / Why not?

2 SPEAKING Read the quotes below. Explain in your own words what they mean. Do you agree or disagree with the statements?

1 'If you want to live a happy life, tie it to a goal, not to people or things.' (physicist Albert Einstein)
2 'Extreme hopes are born from extreme misery.' (philosopher Bertrand Russell)
3 'Being realistic is the most commonly travelled road to mediocrity.' (actor Will Smith)
4 'The only thing limiting your aspiration is your imagination.' (author Stephen Richards)

> **Speaking Strategy**
>
> In a debate, you have some time to plan your answer. Decide if you are for or against the statement and think of four or five arguments to support your view. Start with one of your weaker arguments and move onto the stronger ones as the conversation progresses.

3 Read the Speaking Strategy and look at the first quote in exercise 2. Imagine you are for the statement. In pairs, make a list of four or five points to support your argument.

4 (2.20) Listen to a student giving her view on the first quote. Which of her points did you think of? Which other points does she make? Do you agree with what she says? Why? / Why not?

5 (2.20) Listen again and complete the extracts from the interview with the discourse markers below.

all the same   as a result   as for   certainly   I mean
on the whole   to start with   what's more

1 _____, I'd like to say that I completely agree with Einstein's statement.
2 ... the latter are not always permanent. _____, our friends are likely to change as we get older, ...
3 ... partners may not be around for ever. _____ things, they can wear out or break.
4 _____, I believe that a goal is more likely to make us happy than people or things.
5 ... a person without friends might get very lonely. _____, there's a need to have some people ...
6 ... extra baggage makes it more difficult for us to pursue our goals. _____, we can lose our way ...
7 ... bring you down rather than lift your spirits, I think. _____, I believe that goals are important.
8 ... make it more achievable. _____, there's nothing more satisfying than fulfilling a dream ...

6 KEY PHRASES Add the discourse markers from exercise 5 to the correct group below.

Adding further information
Besides, ...   ¹_____, ...   As well as that, ...
Announcing the subject in advance
²_____ ...,   As far as ... is concerned, ...
Regarding ...,
Clarifying
³_____,   that is to say, ...   in other words, ...
Concession
It's true, ...   ⁴_____, ...   Of course, ...
Counter-argument
⁵_____, ...   Even so, ...   Still, ...
Explaining the reason for something
⁶_____, ...   Because of this, ...   Consequently, ...
Generalising
⁷_____, ...   By and large, ...   Broadly speaking, ...
Structuring
⁸_____, ...   For one thing, ...   For another thing, ...

7 Choose the correct discourse markers to complete the speech against the first statement in exercise 2.

> First of all, I'd like to say that I'm against the statement. ¹Of course / As well as that, it's important to have a goal in life, but not to the detriment of the people around us. ²By and large / As far as, it's our families and friends who give our lives meaning. ³For one thing / Even so, family provides us with a base from which to go out and experiment with life. ⁴Still / Consequently, we can return to the nest if things go wrong. ⁵In other words / It's true, family is a kind of safety net on which our happiness depends. ⁶Regarding / Broadly speaking friends, they also provide us with a kind of support network. ⁷Besides / That is to say, spending time with friends can be extremely rewarding. ⁸Because of this / For another thing, I believe that tying our lives to people, in the form of family and friends, is better than tying it to a goal.

8 Choose a quote from exercise 2. Decide if you are for or against the statement and prepare four or five points to support your argument.

9 SPEAKING Work in pairs. Present your argument to your partner. Use your notes from exercise 8 and the discourse markers from exercise 6.

An informal email

I can show empathy in an informal email.

1 SPEAKING Work in pairs. What are you looking forward to in the next few months? What are you dreading?

2 Read the task. In pairs, answer the two questions in the task.

> You have received an email from an English friend.
>
> *As for my final exams, I'm really not looking forward to them! I'm scared stiff I won't get the marks I need to get into university. What about you – how are you feeling about your exams? Are you doing anything special to cope with the stress – if so, what?*
>
> Write your email in reply.

3 Read the email. Explain in your own words how Rose is feeling about her exams and why.

 To: ellie@email.com

Hi Ellie,

Sorry for not getting back to you before – I've only just seen your email. I've been trying to keep away from the internet so that I can focus on my exams.

If it's any consolation, you aren't the only one who's got exam nerves. I know what you mean about worrying you might not get into uni – I need really high marks for veterinary science too, so we're in the same boat! I don't know what I'll do if I don't make the grade, but I'll cross that bridge when I come to it. For now, there's no point in worrying about things that may never happen. All we can do is buckle down and give it our best shot on the day.

I see where you're coming from with your question about stress – nearly everyone I know is a nervous wreck at the moment. I don't know about you, but I'm trying to focus on one thing at a time. I've also made a revision timetable, which is helping to keep me on track. If it helps, I've found it's easier to concentrate in my room if I'm wearing headphones, whether I'm listening to music or not!

On that note, I'd better get back to biology – I've got another two pages to study before I can call it a day.

Keep at it, Ellie, and I'm sure everything will turn out all right in the end.

Lots of love,

Rose

---

4 Read the Writing Strategy. Then find expressions in the email to replace the words below.

1 replying
2 in the same difficult situation
3 reach the necessary standard
4 worry about a problem when it happens, not before
5 start to do something seriously
6 try as hard as we can
7 a person suffering from stress
8 doing the right thing to achieve a particular result
9 stop doing something
10 continue working at something

5 KEY PHRASES Complete the useful phrases from the email.

> Showing empathy
> I don't ¹_____ about you, but I ...
> If it's any ²_____, you aren't the only one who ...
> I see where you're ³_____ from with ...
> I'm sure ⁴_____ will turn out all right in the end.
> If it ⁵_____, ...
> I know what you ⁶_____ about ...

6 You are going to write an email. Read the task below. Make notes about how you could answer the two questions.

> You have received an email from an English friend.
>
> *As for leaving home next year to go to uni, I'm dreading it! I'm petrified I won't get on with my housemates. What about you? How are you feeling about leaving home? Are you doing anything special to prepare for moving out – if so, what?*
>
> Write your email in reply.

7 Now write your email (220–260 words). Use your notes from exercise 6.

 CHECK YOUR WORK

Have you ...
- written 220–260 words?
- used four paragraphs?
- used the appropriate informal style?
- included phrases for giving advice and showing empathy?
- checked the spelling and grammar?

➡ Vocabulary Builder Colloquial language and slang: page 129

7
Journeys

Unit map

● **Vocabulary**
Road travel
Parts of a bicycle
Types of holiday
On holiday
Travel problems

● **Word Skills**
Verb patterns

● **Grammar**
Modal verbs
Talking about ability

● **Listening** Crossing borders

● **Reading** Time traveller

● **Speaking** Collaborative task

● **Writing** Letter of complaint

● **Culture 7** Lewis and Clark

● **Literature 7**
On the Road, Jack Kerouac

● **Vocabulary Builder** page 129

● **Grammar Builder and**
Reference page 145

7A Vocabulary

Road travel
I can talk about roads and road users.

1 SPEAKING Work in pairs. Ask and answer the questions. Do you agree or disagree with these regulations? Would you change any of them? Why? / Why not?

In your country …
1 at what age can you legally a) drive a car and b) ride a motorbike?
2 what do the driving tests consist of?
3 are there any regulations about riding a bicycle on the road?

2 Read the text. Complete the compound nouns using the words below. Do you know any similar stories about people who failed their test?

aid   atlas   car   drivers   maintenance   safety   seat   stop   test   traffic   users

For many teenagers and young adults in the UK, taking (and sometimes retaking) your
¹driving _____ is a rite of passage. The test was introduced in the 1930s in
response to public concerns about ²road _____ because around 7,000 people
a year were dying in ³road _____ accidents. That is roughly twice the present
level, even though there are twelve times as many ⁴road _____ today! The test
has changed over the years. For example, since 1996, learners have had to sit a theory
test which includes questions on ⁵first _____ and ⁶vehicle _____.
Currently, more than half the ⁷learner _____ who take the test each year
fail. However, some fail more spectacularly than others. For example, one candidate,
who was taking the test in an ⁸automatic _____, selected 'drive' too early and
crashed into the driving test centre. The whole test lasted less than two seconds. On
another occasion, when the candidate made an ⁹emergency _____, a heavy
¹⁰road _____ flew forwards from the ¹¹back _____ of the car and hit
the examiner on the back of the head. The candidate had to rush the unconscious
examiner to the nearest hospital!

3 VOCABULARY Divide the words below into two groups: parts of the road network (A) and verbs related to driving (B).

Road travel accelerate   brake   central reservation   change gear   crossroads
cul-de-sac   dual carriageway   flyover   give way   hard shoulder   indicate   kerb
lay-by   level crossing   overtake   pull over   reverse   side street   slip road
speed bumps   stall   steer   T-junction

4 🎧 **2.21** Listen to six people talking about their driving test. For each speaker complete:
- the first sentence with a word from exercise 3 group A;
- the second sentence using a verb from exercise 3 group B in the correct tense.

Speaker 1
1 The key events took place at a _____.
2 She failed because she _____ by mistake.

Speaker 2
1 The key events took place in a _____.
2 He _____ while trying to park.

Speaker 3
1 The key events took place at a _____.
2 She made a mistake when she tried to _____.

Speaker 4
1 The key events took place in a _____.
2 He had to _____ a long way because of a lorry.

Speaker 5
1 The key events took place on a _____.
2 She forgot to _____.

Speaker 6
1 The key events took place at a _____.
2 He _____ a car that was slowing down.

5 Work in pairs. Compare your answers to exercise 4. Which speaker was, in your opinion, the unluckiest and/or the worst driver?

> **FLUENCY!**
> - English speakers often choose to use a phrase instead of a simple verb. The meaning is the same.
>   *Look at this photo. / Take a look at this photo.*
> - Other common phrases include:
>   **have** *a walk / a talk / a chat / a try / a think*
>   **make** *a start (on) / a comment (about) / a call*
>   **pay** *a compliment / a visit (to)*
> - Sometimes we use different prepositions for the simple verb and the phrase:
>   *He commented on my appearance. / He made a comment about my appearance.*

6 **VOCABULARY** Work in pairs. Read the Fluency! box. Then complete phrases 1–6 with the verbs below.

call   come   give   have   make   shoot

| to ¹_____ a halt to something (= to halt something) |
| to ²_____ another attempt (= to attempt again) |
| to ³_____ a glance at sb/sth (= to glance at sb/sth) |
| to ⁴_____ to a halt (= to halt) |
| to ⁵_____ a shriek (= to shriek) |
| to ⁶_____ a left turn (= to turn left) |

7 🎧 **2.21** Listen again. Check your answers to exercise 6.

8 Rewrite the sentences using a phrase from the Fluency! box instead of the underlined verbs. Use a different preposition if necessary.

1 Did the teacher <u>comment</u> on your exam result?
2 It's time to <u>start</u> our homework.
3 We decided to <u>visit</u> the fish and chip shop on our way home.
4 He refused to <u>look</u> at the map.
5 We <u>talked</u> to the flight attendant about moving seats.
6 We <u>attempted to open</u> the door of the carriage.

9 **VOCABULARY** Work in pairs. Label the photo above using the words below. Which of the words could you also use to describe a) a car and b) a motorbike?

Parts of a bicycle brake levers   chain   gears   handlebars   pedals   pump   reflector   saddle   spokes   stand   tyres   valve

10 **SPEAKING** Work in pairs. Discuss the pros and cons of:

1 riding a bicycle vs driving a car.
2 riding a motorbike vs riding a bicycle.
3 driving a car vs riding a motorbike.

Think about the issues below and add your own ideas.

comfort   cost   pollution   repairs   speed
safety of the driver / rider   safety of pedestrians
traffic congestion

> One advantage of riding a bicycle is that, unlike cars, they don't cause any pollution.

➡ **Vocabulary Builder** Phrasal verbs: travel: page 129

Modal verbs

I can use modal verbs correctly for advice and prohibition.

1 SPEAKING Work in pairs. Imagine you are going travelling with friends for a few months. Discuss why it would be a good or bad idea to:

- book all your accommodation.
- take a sleeping bag.
- arrange to travel at night.
- buy travel insurance.

2 Choose the correct modal verbs to complete the messages from an online forum. Does their advice match your ideas from exercise 1?

TRAVEL FORUM

I travelled around Europe for seven months, staying in youth hostels. Before I left, I thought, '¹**I'd better** / I need take my sleeping bag.' But every hostel I visited had a sign saying: 'Guests ²**had better** / must not use sleeping bags.' So in fact, I ³mustn't / **needn't** have taken mine with me – I didn't use it once!

Before leaving, you definitely ⁴**ought** / should to plan the first few weeks of your trip and make some reservations online. But you ⁵must / **needn't** book all your travel and accommodation in advance. In fact, sometimes ⁶**you're better off** / you should being flexible.

You really ⁷**must** / ought arrange travel insurance for the whole trip, in case you ⁸**need** / ought to claim for hospital bills. I bought insurance for six months but extended my trip to eight months. In the last week, I fell ill and ⁹**had to** / must spend three nights in hospital. My insurance had run out!

You ¹⁰have to / **should** try to travel at night as much as possible because it saves money. When I travelled around Italy, I booked three overnight train journeys. For those three nights, I ¹¹**didn't need to** / mustn't pay for accommodation. Looking back, I ¹²needn't / **should** have booked more.

➤ Grammar Builder 7.1 page 145

3 Choose the better option, a or b. Why is the other option less suitable or incorrect?

Travel Plan

1 When travelling abroad, you _____ always share your itinerary with friends and family.
   a had better   (b) should ✓

2 _____ I book a single ticket or a return, do you think?
   a Ought   (b) Should ✓

3 Do you want this spare bus ticket? I _____ it.
   (a) didn't need to use   b needn't have used ✓

4 The festival isn't this weekend. It _____ next weekend.
   a must happen   (b) must be happening

5 You _____ show your passport at the border.
   (a) often have to ✓   b must often

6 If you book online, it _____ expensive to stay in hotels.
   a mustn't be   (b) needn't be

7 You _____ your passport at the hotel. I'll go and get it.
   a 'd better not have left   (b) shouldn't have left

LOOK OUT!

We can combine *need to* or *have to* for obligation with modal verbs like *might (have)* or *should (have)*.
Tom's still in town. He might be having to wait for Sam.
If you hadn't offered me a lift, I might have needed to walk home.
In my opinion, everyone should have to pass a test before riding a bike on the road.

4 Read the Look out! box. Then complete the sentences with the phrases below.

can't have had to   may be having to   might not have to   must have needed to   should have to

1 We've already got our tickets, so we **might not have to** queue up.

2 In my opinion, everyone **should have to** learn a foreign language.

3 You **must have needed to** book that hotel months ago. It's always full!

4 She's still in customs. She **may be having to** open her bags.

5 He **can't have had to** pay full price for his ticket – he's only fourteen.

5 Explain how the choice of verb slightly changes the meaning of the sentences below.

1 Someone has accessed my email. They **should have had to** / **can't have had to** enter a password.

2 In the future, tourists **may not need to** / **won't have to** obtain a visa.

3 You **'d better** / **needn't** check the tyres before using your bike.

4 We **didn't need to plan** / **needn't have planned** any outings for our visitors. They're only going to stay with us for one day.

5 You **'d better not** / **don't have to** walk back to the hotel on your own.

6 In your notebook, rewrite the sentences using modal verbs from exercise 2 and the Look out! box.

1 It isn't necessary to take cash with you when you travel.
2 It probably won't be necessary to carry ID all the time.
3 It would have been a good idea to buy a local SIM card for your phone.
4 It isn't a good idea to keep in daily contact with your family.
5 Perhaps it was necessary for him to leave his passport at the hotel reception.

7 SPEAKING Work in pairs. Complete the sentences with your own ideas. Then discuss them with the class.

1 Before you leave, you really should have …
2 However, you needn't have …
3 When you're travelling, you really must …
4 However, you definitely shouldn't …
5 You needn't …
6 You may have to …

Crossing borders

I can understand first-person accounts by migrants.

1 SPEAKING Work in pairs. Do you think people should be able to live and work in whichever country they choose? Why? / Why not?

2 Read the text. Look at the gaps and decide what part of speech each missing word might be. Can you guess what word it is?

The idea that governments should control who enters their country is a ¹_____ recent one. For most of history, authorities have worried more about people ²_____ than arriving. Laws in medieval England prevented ³_____ from leaving their farms in search of better work or more money. It was not until the French Revolution of 1789 that the idea of having passports for leaving or entering a country was introduced. Other countries introduced ⁴_____ regulations. However, during the Industrial Revolution of the 19th century, many countries, including Britain, needed workers, and in 1872, the British foreign secretary wrote, 'All foreigners have the ⁵_____ right of entrance into and residence in this country.' The United States ⁶_____ a similar approach. It was not even clear that ⁷_____ had the legal right to control people's international ⁸_____. But as Europe headed towards war in the early 20th century, everything changed. Foreigners were considered to be ⁹_____ spies. Passport controls were applied and never lifted again.

3 🎧 **2.22** Listen and complete the text in exercise 2. During which periods of history were there no controls on international travel?

> **Listening Strategy**
>
> To help you understand unknown words, ask yourself:
>
> 1 Is the general meaning of the word clear? For example:
> *'That's typical!' he retorted.* ('Retorted' is a speech verb.)
> *He wore a red cravat.* ('Cravat' is an item of clothing.)
>
> 2 Is the word part of a pair or list of more familiar words?
> *His clothes were old, dirty and dishevelled.* ('Dishevelled' must be related in meaning to 'old and dirty'.)
>
> 3 Is the word followed by a result or explanation?
> *I felt so befuddled that I wasn't even sure why I was there.* ('Befuddled' must broadly mean 'confused'.)

4 Read the Listening Strategy. Then try to work out what the missing words are in the sentences below. What clues helped you work them out? What kind of story do the sentences come from?

1 I put all my belongings into a _____ and set off on foot.
2 There were so many people in the _____ that I feared it would sink.
3 My grandparents stood on the _____ and watched us move away from the shore.
4 The coastguards sailed closer and called to us through a _____.
5 After so long at sea, we were cold and _____.

5 🎧 **2.23** Check the meaning of the words below and use five of them to complete the sentences in exercise 4. Then listen and check.

jetty delinquents loudhailer persecute mortar
haversack doctorate contaminated dinghy
disconsolate

6 🎧 **2.24** Listen to five people telling their own stories of migration. Which speaker moved:

1 to a different continent? _____
2 to a different island in the same country? _____
3 to a neighbouring country? _____
4 to a different country in the same continent (but not a neighbouring country)? _____
5 from the city to the country? _____

7 🎧 **2.24** Listen again. Choose the correct answer (A–H) for each speaker. There are three extra sentences.

1 Why did each speaker leave home?
   A His/Her parents hoped to improve their employment prospects by moving country. _____
   B An increase in crime threatened his/her safety. _____
   C He/She hoped to send money back home. _____
   D He/She wanted to escape from an armed conflict. _____
   E A serious shortage of food forced him/her to move. _____
   F There was no supply of fresh drinking water. _____
   G The village was occupied by soldiers. _____
   H He/She was being targeted because of their race. _____

2 What current concern or challenge does each speaker mention?
   A Not feeling that he/she belongs anywhere. _____
   B Worrying that another natural disaster will occur. _____
   C Trying to keep himself/herself occupied. _____
   D Overcoming a language barrier. _____
   E Earning enough money to support all the family. _____
   F Obtaining medical treatment for a sick child. _____
   G Not forgetting the culture of their homeland. _____
   H Feeling unhappy about the interruption to his/her children's education. _____

8 SPEAKING Work in pairs. What challenges might be faced by somebody coming to live in your country? What advice would you offer? Discuss your ideas with the class.

7D Grammar

Talking about ability

I can talk about past, present and future ability.

1 SPEAKING Work in pairs. Discuss the questions.

1 Why are some people so keen to be the first to reach inaccessible places like the North Pole?
2 Do you think there are many inaccessible places left in the world? Can people still be 'explorers'?

2 Read the text. What challenges will Jim McNeill face when he attempts his journey?

The northern 'Pole of Inaccessibility' is the name given to the very centre of the Arctic Ocean – the furthest point from land. It ¹cannot be reached by boat because the sea is frozen. Trekking for hundreds of kilometres over sea ice is extremely dangerous, and so far nobody ²has been able to complete the journey. However, if all goes according to plan, British explorer Jim McNeill ³could be the first. McNeill has tried twice before without success. On the first occasion, he became ill and ⁴couldn't continue. At the next attempt, the ice began to melt before he ⁵managed to reach his destination. For three days, he ⁶was unable to sleep because he ⁷could hear the ice cracking beneath him at night! This time, McNeill plans to set off in winter. During an Arctic winter, it is dark for 24 hours a day and temperatures ⁸can plummet to -50°C. But McNeill has to begin his journey then because if he goes in the summer, the ice will start to melt and he ⁹won't be able to complete his return journey.

3 Work in pairs. Which of the verbs below would be just as natural as the underlined verbs 1–9 in the text in exercise 2? Use the Grammar Builder to help you if necessary.

1 is not able to
2 a could   b has managed to
3 can
4 was not able to
5 a could   b was able to
6 couldn't
7 a managed to   b was able to
8 a are able to   b could
9 a can't   b couldn't

➡ **Grammar Builder 7.2** page 147

4 USE OF ENGLISH Choose the correct words to complete the text. Explain why the other options do not work.

During the 19th century, there were several expeditions to explore the Arctic but nobody ¹ __b__ the North Pole. In the first decade of the 20th century, two rival explorers both claimed success: Frederick Cook and Robert Peary. Cook ² __b__ proof of his achievement, which was widely disbelieved. Peary ³ __b__ convince more people of his claim, but so far nobody ⁴ __b__ verify it. In fact, most modern explorers argue that he ⁵ __a__ reached the pole: even professional skiers with modern equipment ⁶ __a__ complete the journey so quickly. It seems that we ⁷ __a&b__ prove it one way or the other. The first people who we ⁸ __b&a__ be sure set foot on the North Pole were the members of an expedition in 1948, who ⁹ __b__ complete the journey in a few hours because they flew there by plane!

1 a could have reached   b was able to reach
2 a can't have provided   b was unable to provide
3 a could   b managed to
4 a could   b has been able to
5 a couldn't have   b can have
6 a can't   b would be able to
7 a can never   b 'll never be able to
8 a can   b are able to
9 a could   b managed to

> **LOOK OUT!**
>
> We use *be able to* to express ability in structures which require an infinitive or *-ing* form:
> *Imagine being able to fly!*
> *He'd love to be able to dance.*
>
> We use *be able to* after modal verbs like *should* or *must*:
> *If I stand on a chair, I should be able to reach the shelf.*
> *All participants must be able to swim.*

5 Read the Look out! box. Then in your notebook rewrite the sentences below using the verb in brackets and *be able to*.

1 It's essential that all employees can drive. (must)
2 It's impossible that he was able to hear us. (can't)
3 I really dislike the fact that I can't skate. (hate)
4 It's likely that the doctor can see you today. (should)
5 It appears that she can understand Chinese. (seems)
6 She'd be happy if her children could play the piano. (wants)

6 SPEAKING Work in pairs. What would be the best and worst things about a polar expedition? Include some of these phrases when you express your ideas:

You might (not) be able to …
You could probably … / You probably couldn't …
You might (not) manage to …

Verb patterns

I can use various different verb patterns correctly.

1 SPEAKING Work in pairs. Look at the title of the text in exercise 2 and speculate about a) why the man decided to do this and b) what problems and dangers he faced.

2 Read the text and compare your ideas with the facts.

3 Choose the correct verb forms in the text. Choose both if both are correct. Then match them with verb patterns a–e in the Learn this! box below.

THE MAN WHO POSTED HIMSELF TO AUSTRALIA

In 1964, Australian athlete Reg Spiers longed [1]to return / returning home from London to Adelaide, but he couldn't afford [2]to buy / buying a ticket – and he couldn't face [3]to work / working for months in order to save up. So he decided to return home by airmail. He asked a friend, John McSorley, to help him [4]to arrange / arrange it. Spiers had his friend build a wooden box designed to let Spiers open it from the inside, as the plan depended on him being able to get out when necessary. Spiers expected [5]to have / having a difficult journey but in fact it was worse than he'd imagined. His friend had no trouble [6]to check / checking the box in at Heathrow Airport. But because of thick fog in London, Spiers then spent 28 hours [7]to wait / waiting for somebody to load the box onto his flight. Later in the journey, the box was left [8]to sit / sitting for hours in blazing sunshine on the runway in Bombay. When he heard the airport workers talking, he considered [9]to turn / turning himself in – but resisted. In some ways he was lucky, though. By 1964, airlines had started [10]to heat / heating the cargo areas on flights, which saved him from freezing to death. After 63 hours, Spiers arrived at Perth Airport. He managed [11]to get / getting out of the box without being seen and, once he'd had his passport checked, was free [12]to leave / leaving!

LEARN THIS! Verb patterns

a verb + infinitive 1, 2 5
b verb + gerund   3
c verb + infinitive or gerund
d verb + object + base form or infinitive 4, 6, 7
e be + adjective + infinitive
f verb + object + gerund
   I heard them chatting happily.
g verb + preposition + object + gerund
   They insisted on everybody staying for dinner.
h verb + object + preposition + gerund
   The noise of the storm stopped me from sleeping.
i verb + object + infinitive
   We encourage all students to take part.
j verb + preposition + object + infinitive
   I've arranged for them to stay an extra night.
k verb + object + base form
   They made him open his suitcase.
l verb + object + past participle
   He's getting all his hair shaved off for charity.

4 Study patterns f–l in the Learn this! box and find one example of each in the text in exercise 2.

5 Complete the sentences. Use *at, for, in, of* or *on* in the first gap, and then the infinitive or gerund of the verbs in brackets.

1 The protesters have succeeded _in forcing_ (force) the government _to change_ (change) its plans. ✓
2 The guards shouted _at_ him _to stop_ (stop) _running_ (run). ✓
3 I was longing _for_ my parents _to decide_ (decide) _to move_ (move) house. ✓
4 Have you ever heard _of_ a teenager _spending_ (spend) so much time _doing_ (do) homework? ✓
5 Our business depends _on_ the public _wanting_ (want) _to buy_ (buy) our products. ✓

LOOK OUT!

In verb patterns, we sometimes need to use a passive form or a perfect form of the infinitive or gerund.
She detests being photographed. (passive gerund)
He wants to be loved. (passive infinitive)
He confessed to having lied. (perfect gerund)
She appears to have left. (perfect infinitive)

6 Read the Look out! box. Then complete the sentences in your notebook with the correct form of the verbs in brackets. Use the passive infinitive, passive gerund, perfect infinitive or perfect gerund.

1 The flood caused several houses (damage).
2 He strenuously denied (steal) the man's car.
3 I clearly remember (teach) the alphabet when I was five.
4 The criminal is believed (escape) in a white car.
5 In shops, I always insist on (give) a receipt.
6 His cycle helmet saved him from (injure) more seriously.

7 Complete the text with the infinitive, gerund, base form or past participle of the verbs in brackets. You need to include passive and perfect forms.

In 1965, a Welshman called Brian desperately wanted [1](return) home to the UK but was penniless. Inspired by the story of Reg Spiers, he vowed [2] (try) the same journey in the opposite direction. But he didn't really stop [3](consider) the dangers. He had a similar box [4](build), but it was more cramped because he insisted on [5](take) a suitcase with him. He spent 22 hours [6](hang) upside-down before he'd even left Australia! En route, he narrowly escaped [7](freeze) to death in an unheated cargo hold. Many hours later, Robson believed himself [8](arrive) in England but in fact he was in Los Angeles. He tried [9](check) the time on his watch but couldn't because he dropped his torch. An official saw the light [10](shine) through the box and shouted at his colleagues [11](help) him [12](open) it. When they saw Robson [13](lie) in the box, he appeared [14](die). But in fact, he recovered, and after spending some time [15](treat) in hospital, he ended up [16](give) a free ticket back to London.

8 SPEAKING Work in pairs. Think of other, less dangerous ways to make a long journey for free.

7F Reading

Time traveller

I can understand a text about a person who claimed to be a time traveller.

1 SPEAKING How many books, films and TV programmes can you think of which include the idea of time travel? Why do you think the idea is popular in fiction? For what reasons do characters usually go time-travelling?

> **Reading Strategy** TOPIC SENTENCES !
> When a text is organised into paragraphs, the first one or two sentences of each paragraph often indicate what information it will contain. Use these paragraph openers to get a general understanding of what the text is about and to help you find your way around longer texts.

2 Read the Reading Strategy. Then read the first two sentences of paragraphs 1–7 and match one of the summaries below to each paragraph.

   a Titor continues to make predictions for the coming years. 5
   b People start to believe Titor is telling the truth. 4 4
   c On internet forums Titor describes aspects of the world in 2036. 2
   d John Titor claims to be a time traveller. 1
   e People try to uncover who was really behind the messages. 7
   f Titor gains support and makes an offer to his supporters. 3
   g Some of the events Titor predicted fail to materialise. 6

3 SPEAKING Work in pairs. Read the text and check your answers to exercise 2. Then discuss questions 1–3.

   1 Do you think the world in 2036 is likely to be as Titor described it? Why? / Why not?
   2 Do you agree with Titor's description of the world in 2000 and its people? Why? / Why not?
   3 Do you believe that John Titor really was a time traveller? Give reasons for your answer.

4 Read the text. For each question, choose the best answer (a–d). Use the first sentence or two of each paragraph to confirm where the information you need is located.

   1 John Titor's claims to be a time traveller were not immediately dismissed as a joke because
      a he posted so many messages.
      b he knew things only a time traveller could know.
      c he was happy to provide a lot of information.
      d he did not try to conceal his identity.
   2 In the future described by John Titor,
      a armed conflict no longer exists.
      b there is not enough food for everyone.
      c everyone keeps livestock.
      d people talk to their neighbours and help each other.
   3 When Titor offered to take volunteers with him, he warned that
      a it would be an uncomfortable journey.
      b they might become trapped in the year 1975.
      c people might not believe them.
      d it would not be possible to return to their own time.

   4 John Titor's comments about the IBM 5100 proved that
      a he could make accurate predictions about how computers would develop.
      b he had studied the history of computing.
      c he had worked for IBM at some point in his life.
      d he knew something about the IBM 5100 which few people knew.
   5 John Titor's predictions suggested that
      a there would be a decline in the popularity of sport.
      b a former US president would become president again.
      c more and more countries would develop nuclear weapons.
      d the world would be blighted by war and disease.
   6 Attempts to reveal the truth behind John Titor's story have resulted in
      a a computer scientist admitting that he wrote the messages.
      b two brothers being identified as possible perpetrators.
      c the closure of the John Titor Foundation.
      d a new theory about how time travel can change the future.

5 VOCABULARY Find the words and expressions below highlighted in the text. What part of speech are they? What do their meanings have in common?

alleged (adj) apparent (adj) likely on the face of it ostensibly
purported seemingly so-called supposed

6 Complete the sentences with an appropriate word or phrase from exercise 5. More than one answer is possible.

   1 The drawings _____ showed a time machine.
   2 He is _____ to have been a soldier.
   3 _____, John Titor appeared out of nowhere.
   4 Titor's comments about divergent timelines are consistent with the theory of a _____ 'multiverse'.
   5 Perhaps the story of John Titor shows people's _____ desire to believe in time travel.

CRITICAL ANALYSIS

7 Read the definition of a cliché below. Then explain the six underlined clichés in the text in your own words.

> **cliché** /ˈkliːʃeɪ/ (noun) a figurative phrase which is so widely used and familiar that it no longer seems figurative.

8 Work in pairs. Can you think of any clichés in your own language? What do they mean? Where are they used?

➡ **Vocabulary Builder** Figurative expressions: *day*: page 129

9 SPEAKING Work in pairs. Discuss the question below.

If you could travel backwards and forwards in time, which other times would you visit? Give reasons for your choices.

JOHN TITOR, TIME TRAVELLER

1 Posted by John Titor on 27-01-2001 12.45 p.m.: 'Greetings. I am a time traveller from the year 2036. I am on my way home after getting an IBM 5100 computer system from the year 1975.' This is the message that appeared on an internet forum in January 2001. Just a joke, you might assume, or a hoax. But more posts followed, and there was something about John Titor and his messages
5 that made people <u>sit up and take notice</u>. Perhaps it was the amount of detail he went into when describing where he had come from. Or maybe it was his apparent willingness to answer questions about – and even post photographs of – his time-travelling equipment, the so-called 'temporal displacement unit'.

2 Over the next few months, John Titor regularly joined internet discussions and answered
10 questions. The insights that he gave into the era he claimed to have come from were tantalising. He described a world in which globalisation had been halted because of wars and civil unrest. Now people lived in small, <u>close-knit</u> communities. Food was grown locally, and people spent time reading and chatting face-to-face – although the internet still existed. He even revealed how the people of 2001 would be judged by those living in 2036, and it wasn't flattering. 'This time period,' he wrote,
15 referring to the year 2000, 'is looked at as being full of lazy, self-centred sheep.'

3 Even though Titor claimed not to care whether people believed his story or not, he started to gather an increasing number of followers on the internet. At one point, he even suggested that a few volunteers could go with him on his travels through time. The plan was first to go back in time to 1975. The volunteers could either choose to stay in that year or accompany him on the next leg of the
20 journey – forwards to 2036. He warned that the physical experience of time travel was not pleasant: travellers have to put up with hot, airless conditions and uncomfortable G-forces.

4 One fascinating detail in John Titor's messages convinced many people that he was telling the truth. When he was asked why he needed an IBM 5100 computer, he explained that this computer had a feature that few people knew about: the ability to run very old programming languages. This
25 feature would allow scientists in 2036 to 'clean up' some very old computer systems that modern programmers could no longer understand. Amazingly, an engineer who helped design the IBM 5100 confirmed that the computer did indeed have this feature, and that, for commercial reasons, it had not been made public. If John Titor was a hoaxer, he was seemingly very well informed.

5 The messages continued to appear for several months and some of them purported to contain
30 information about what the near future <u>held in store</u>. They talked of a major civil war in the USA which would lead to the 2004 Olympic Games being cancelled. They referred to a small-scale nuclear conflict between Russia and the USA, as well as a serious epidemic that would <u>spread like wildfire</u> across the Western world. And they described the American president in 2005 as being like Abraham Lincoln.

6 But the trouble with predictions is that they have a habit of not coming true. The year 2004
35 came and went and the Olympic Games were not cancelled. Russia and the USA did not go to war and George Bush did not seem much like Abraham Lincoln. The attention given to John Titor and his messages began to wane, as did interest in the John Titor Foundation, a commercial enterprise that sold books and merchandise related to the supposed time traveller.

7 A few years later, several attempts were made to find out who was behind the John Titor
40 messages. A website called Hoax Hunter carried out an investigation and named two brothers as the likely culprits: Larry Haber and John Rick Haber. A separate investigation by a private detective also identified John Rick Haber as the man behind the messages, claiming that his knowledge of computer science would have allowed him to make them convincing. It was also revealed that Larry Haber was the CEO of the John Titor Foundation, so on the face of it he stood to make money out of the alleged
45 hoax.

8 It seems like an <u>open-and-shut case</u>. However, for people who believe that John Titor truly is a time traveller, there was a <u>get-out clause</u>. In some of his messages, Titor explained that by travelling back in time, he had altered the future. What is more, the longer he stayed in the 'wrong' time, the greater the divergence would become. So the reason why his predictions were ostensibly incorrect
50 was that our world was following a different 'timeline' owing to his interference. In other words, perhaps the fact that there was no Second Civil War in the USA in 2004 is mainly thanks to John Titor and his travels through time.

Collaborative task

I can discuss and reach an agreement about holidays.

1 SPEAKING Work in pairs. Decide which type of holiday from the list below you would enjoy most and least. Then discuss your choices and reasons. Do you have similar opinions?

Types of holiday beach holiday Caribbean cruise city break road trip safari sightseeing tour skiing trip spa holiday trekking holiday villa holiday

2 SPEAKING Work in pairs. Complete the phrases with the verbs below. Then decide which type(s) of holiday from exercise 1 would allow you to do each activity.

admire get away hit lounge put sample take take in try

On holiday
1 _____ the local cuisine
2 _____ the scenery
3 _____ your hand at water sports
4 _____ a dip in the sea
5 _____ a film or show
6 _____ the slopes
7 _____ your feet up
8 _____ from it all
9 _____ by the pool

3 SPEAKING Work in pairs. Decide how important the factors below would be if you were choosing a holiday. Try to agree an order from 1–6.

a minimising the environmental impact
b experiencing another culture
c improving your foreign-language skills
d being physically active
e meeting people of similar age and/or interests
f recharging your batteries

4 🎧 **2.25** Listen to a boy and girl discussing what type of holiday to choose. What do they decide and what are their main reasons?

> **Speaking Strategy**
> In a discussion, you may need to help the conversation move forwards by eliciting your partner's opinions on particular points. Try to ask open questions rather than closed questions. An open question allows your partner to voice opinions; a closed question just requires a yes/no or other simple answer.

5 KEY PHRASES Read the Speaking Strategy. Then look at the phrases below and decide which are open questions and which are closed.

Eliciting a response
What do you think of the idea that … ?
What's your view of … ?
Don't you agree that … ?
Would it be fair to say that … ?
Why do / don't you like the idea of … ?
Would you prefer to … ?
What do you like / dislike about … ?

6 🎧 **2.25** Listen again. Which phrases from exercise 5 do you hear? Who uses more of them, the boy or the girl? Why?

7 SPEAKING Work in pairs. Find out what your partner thinks about a–f below using open and closed questions from exercise 5.

a all-inclusive resorts
b eco-tourism
c working holidays
d budget airlines
e adults only resorts
f Airbnb and similar services

> Don't you agree that all-inclusive resorts prevent people from experiencing the local culture?

> What's your view of eco-tourism?

8 SPEAKING Work in pairs. Read the task below. Have you experienced any of these trips abroad? Which one do you think would be the:

cheapest? most interesting? most worthwhile?

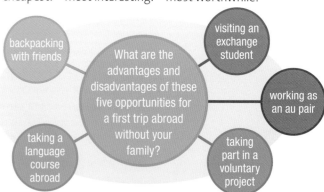

backpacking with friends

visiting an exchange student

What are the advantages and disadvantages of these five opportunities for a first trip abroad without your family?

working as an au pair

taking a language course abroad

taking part in a voluntary project

9 SPEAKING Work in pairs. Do the task in exercise 8. Use the phrases below to avoid repeating 'advantage' and 'disadvantage' too many times. Try to include phrases from exercise 5 in your discussion.

Revision advantages and disadvantages
For me, the main benefit / drawback would be …
Personally, … would be a real plus / minus.
I think … would be a bonus.
The upside / downside would be …
There are pros and cons.

10 SPEAKING Work in pairs. Now agree which one of the five trips abroad in the task is the most appropriate for a teenager.

Writing
Letter of complaint
I can write a letter of complaint.

1 **SPEAKING** Work in pairs. Look at the words below and say what kind of travel they are most likely to apply to (road, rail, air or sea). Which problems have you experienced?

Travel problems cancellations collision congestion delays diversions gridlock industrial action lost luggage mechanical fault overcrowding a pile-up a puncture road works a security alert tailbacks turbulence

2 Read the task and the letter below. How many of the problems from exercise 1 does it mention?

You recently missed a flight because of a problem with your bus to the airport. Write a letter of complaint to the bus company explaining what happened and demanding action.

Dear Sir or Madam,

I am writing to express my dissatisfaction with the service I received from your bus company on 14 August this year, which resulted in my missing a flight from Heathrow Airport.

The problems I experienced were a direct result of your company's failure to provide me with accurate travel information. I had booked a seat on the 06.40 bus from Oxford to Heathrow and arrived at the bus station in good time. When our bus failed to arrive, I and several other passengers sought to discover the cause of the delay by various means: we made enquiries with the staff at the bus station, we consulted your website and we attempted to contact your helpline. However, it was not until 07.30 that we were informed that the bus had been cancelled and that no further service would be available until 08.40. By this time, it was too late for me to make alternative travel arrangements, with the result that I arrived at Heathrow twenty minutes after boarding had closed for my flight.

I understand that a collision on the motorway had caused severe tailbacks and delayed the arrival of several buses. Whilst I appreciate that certain events may be beyond the control of your company, I can see no reason why passengers cannot be kept fully informed of the situation. In this instance, had I known that the delays were so severe, I would have endeavoured to reach the airport by other means.

I fully expect your company to offer compensation, since it was their mismanagement of the situation that prevented my reaching the airport on time. I would very much appreciate your giving this matter your immediate attention. Should you wish to speak to me in person, I can be contacted on the number below.

Yours faithfully,

Mr CF Chapman

3 In which paragraph of the letter (1–4) does the writer:

a give a detailed account of the events?
b clearly state what he expects to happen next?
c summarise his reason for writing?
d provide more information about why he is complaining?

Writing Strategy

To make the language of a letter appropriately formal, we often use:

• *should* + subject + base form instead of *if* + subject + present simple in first conditional sentences:
Should you wish to complain, call this number.

• a possessive adjective instead of an object pronoun in verb patterns that include a gerund:
I understand your wanting to complain.

• a variety of higher-level vocabulary instead of simple verbs like *go, try, do*, etc.
We proceeded to the check-in area and attempted to find the correct desk.

4 Read the Writing Strategy. Then find in the letter:

1 an example of a first conditional sentence with *should*.
2 two examples of a possessive adjective with a gerund.
3 three more formal synonyms for *try*.
4 a more formal way of writing *If I had known* …

5 Use the words below to replace the less formal words in the sentences.

boarded declined departed developed endeavoured experienced located purchased required withdrew

1 When the ticket inspector <u>went away</u>, I then <u>found</u> my ticket.
2 Before the train <u>left</u>, I <u>tried</u> to find a seat.
3 More passengers <u>got on</u> the train and <u>needed</u> seats.
4 Some passengers <u>bought</u> an upgrade to first class but I <u>said no</u>.
5 We <u>had</u> problems when our train <u>got</u> a mechanical fault.

6 Read the task below. Then plan your letter using your answers to exercise 3 to help you.

You recently missed an important event because of a problem with your train. Write a letter of complaint to the train company explaining what happened and demanding action.

7 Write your letter (220–260 words) using your plan from exercise 6. Remember to include formal language from the Writing Strategy.

CHECK YOUR WORK
Have you …
• written 220–260 words?
• used appropriately formal language?
• checked your spelling and grammar?

Exam Skills Trainer

Reading

Strategy

The gapped-text task with missing paragraphs tests comprehension of the text's structure, coherence and global meaning. Read the gapped text first to gain an overall idea of the structure and meaning. To decide which paragraph fits in a gap, study the information and references before and after each gap. Think about what information is missing. Then read the paragraphs that have been removed to find the one that fits the gap grammatically and semantically.

1 Read the strategy above and the gapped text in exercise 2. Follow the instructions in the strategy to find the paragraph that fits gap 1. Which information in the text indicated the correct paragraph? What was the missing information you had to find?

2 Read the text. Match paragraphs A–F with gaps 1–6.

To infinity … and beyond!

The 1960s was an important time for NASA. In the space of a decade, not only did they succeed in sending one astronaut into space and another into orbit, but in 1969 they also achieved the first moon landing. The names Alan Shepard, John Glenn and Neil Armstrong went down in history as the pioneers of space exploration, but what about the researchers behind their missions? Who were they?

1 _____

Take Dorothy Vaughan, for example; by the age of nineteen, she already had a university degree in maths. The only reason she stopped studying was because her family needed money, so she became a teacher. She met her husband, they had six children together, and then an opportunity at Langley came up.

2 _____

Despite this apparent concession, the new employees were required to work separately from their white counterparts. Consequently, Dorothy was allocated to the segregated West Computing Area when she joined Langley. Here she was required to use the separate dining room and bathroom facilities along with the other 'non-whites'.

3 _____

During her years as head of department, Dorothy trained a number of brilliant women mathematicians. One such expert was Mary Jackson, a new recruit with two degrees in maths and physics, who was taken on in 1951. Two years later, Mary was asked to assist a senior engineer in his experiments, and made such an impression that her new boss suggested she become an engineer herself. For an African-American woman, however, that was easier said than done.

4 _____

Dorothy was also the point of contact for Katherine Johnson, who was hired in 1953. A child prodigy, Katherine graduated from high school at fourteen and from university at eighteen with degrees in mathematics and French. Recognising her talent, Dorothy assigned her to the Flight Research Division after only two weeks in West Area Computing.

5 _____

NASA's main aim at the time was to catch up in the Space Race with the Soviets, who had already sent a manned spacecraft into orbit around the Earth. In the equivalent NASA mission, Katherine's job was to double-check the flight calculations from the new IBM computers. Her accuracy reassured astronaut John Glenn that his flight would go well, and on 20 February 1962, he orbited the Earth not once, but three times.

6 _____

Of the three women mentioned, not one of them has become a household name. Yet without the contribution of hidden figures like Dorothy Vaughan, Mary Jackson and Katherine Johnson, the flights of Shepard, Glenn and Armstrong would never have been successful.

A After this success, she went on to play a vital role in further NASA missions, from the 1969 Apollo 11 flight to the moon to the Space Shuttle programme. She retired in 1986 after 33 years' service, and in 2015 was awarded the Presidential Medal of Freedom, the highest civilian honour in the USA.

B As a 'human computer', she was responsible for carrying out complex mathematical calculations for NASA's engineers. So impressed were her superiors that only five years later she was promoted, making her the first female African-American supervisor in the agency. She continued in this role until 1958, when she joined the Analysis and Computation Division (ACD) as a computer programmer, before retiring in 1971.

C Her first major assignment was with Project Mercury, NASA's first manned space flight programme. She was tasked with calculating the trajectory astronaut Alan Shepard's capsule would take once it was launched. The flight took place on 5 May 1961, and proceeded without incident, enabling her to move on to greater things.

D The year was 1943, and the USA was still embroiled in the Second World War. Two years earlier, President Roosevelt had passed a new law to fill the gap in the workforce left by the men who were fighting at the front. Executive Order 8802 prohibited racial, religious and ethnic discrimination in defence industries and in the government, which opened the door to African-American workers.

E Trainee engineers had to take classes in after-work courses held at Hampton High School, which was segregated. Undaunted by this setback, she applied to the City of Hampton for permission to take part in the programme, and it was granted. She completed the course, and in 1958 became NASA's first African-American female engineer.

F To answer that question, we need to go back in time to the west wing of NASA's Langley Research Center. In the 1940s and 50s, this is where much of the aeronautical research data was processed. At the time, the agency had no technology to carry out this function, so they relied on women 'computers'. The employees in this particular wing, apart from being women, had something else in common: they were all highly qualified African-Americans.

Exam Skills Trainer

Listening

3 Read the strategy above and the short extract. Identify three idioms in the extract. Which of the idioms indicates the correct answer to the question below?

M How's your German course going, Amelia?

F OK, I suppose. I'm more or less on top of the vocabulary and I seem to be getting somewhere with the grammar, but my mind goes blank every time I speak.

The woman has most difficulty with

A learning new words.

B constructing sentences.

C communicating face-to-face.

4 🎧 **2.26** You will hear two different extracts. For questions 1–4, choose the answer (A, B or C) which fits best according to what you hear.

Extract 1
You hear two students talking about some voluntary work the woman is planning on doing.

1 What is she most worried about?

A How she will get on with her colleagues.

B How she will adapt to the climate.

C How she will understand the locals.

2 As a result of the experience the woman will

A become more independent.

B learn more about a new culture.

C add to her specialist knowledge.

Extract 2
You hear two friends talking about a concert.

3 Why has the boy's friend let him down?

A He suddenly fell ill.

B He couldn't afford a ticket.

C He decided not to go.

4 The boy is a fan of the band because of

A the instruments they use.

B the visual display they put on.

C the sound they produce.

Use of English

5 Read the strategy. Find the mistakes in the sentences below.

1 The appearance of the leading actor at the film premiere delighting the audience. (DELIGHT)

2 Our flight experienced an expected delay, so the plane took off later than scheduled. (EXPECT)

6 Complete the text with the correct form of the words in brackets.

Travellers have ¹_____ (COUNT) different ways of getting from A to B these days. Say your point of origin is Sheffield in the north of England and your ²_____ (DESTINE) Essex in the south, in all ³_____ (PROBABLE) you would take the train. Not Jordon Cox. After researching the ⁴_____ (VARY) options online, the savvy blogger opted for a flight via Berlin, saving himself £8 in the process. ⁵_____ (ADMIT), this route took eight and a half hours longer than the train would have done. But the stopover ⁶_____ (ABLE) him to visit the centre of Berlin. Jordon's advice to other travellers is to be aware of the ⁷_____ (LOGIC) pricing policies and use your imagination when planning a trip. Often the advantages of flying via another country ⁸_____ (WEIGH) the disadvantages.

Speaking

7 Read the strategy. Work in pairs. Use the ideas in the strategy to discuss the prompts in order of importance for you.
Why might these factors be important to consider when planning a trip around a large foreign country?

• accommodation
• food
• insurance
• language
• transport

Decide which two factors might cause the greatest problems.

Writing

8 Read the strategy and task and write a letter of complaint (220–260 words). Include a variety of linking words in your letter.

You recently went on a dream holiday which did not live up to your expectations. Write a letter of complaint to the travel company you booked with, explaining what happened and demanding action.

8A Vocabulary
Cover-up and conspiracy
I can talk about cover-ups, privacy and journalism.

1 SPEAKING Work in pairs. Who is the celebrity in the photo? What do you think he is protesting about?

2 Read the text. What do you think of journalists who hack famous people's mobile phones?

HACKED OFF

British tabloid journalists don't exactly have a sterling reputation for honesty. Gossip columnists in particular are often accused of libel, and newspapers frequently pay out damages when they damage a celebrity's reputation.

BUT even so, the scandal involving the hacking by journalists of the phones of celebrities, politicians, sports stars and crime victims was truly shocking. The first revelations emerged in November 2005, when Clive Goodman, royal editor at the tabloid *News of the World*, wrote a story about a knee injury suffered by Prince William. The injury was not public knowledge, so the royal family quickly guessed that someone had hacked into the prince's voicemail to secure the scoop. Goodman and Glenn Mulcaire, a private investigator employed by the paper, were sent to prison after revealing that they had obtained special codes used by mobile network operators in order to listen in on several hundred messages. However, despite the prosecution and the public outcry, the newspaper insisted that it was not involved in any other phone hacking. In fact, it was just the tip of the iceberg. In 2009, the *Guardian* newspaper revealed that the *News of the World*'s parent company, News Group International, had quietly paid out more than £1 million to settle lawsuits that might reveal the use of phone hacks to obtain inside information about famous people. Despite accusations that the *Guardian* was merely conducting a smear campaign in order to damage a rival newspaper, the paper accurately reported in 2011 that the phones of more than 5,800 people – including celebrities such as actor Hugh Grant – had been hacked by Mulcaire. The *News of the World* also faced allegations that it hacked into a missing thirteen-year-old's phone messages, possibly hampering a police inquiry into her disappearance and murder. As a result of the exposé, international media mogul Rupert Murdoch shut down *News of the World* in 2011. A year later, he admitted that there had been a cover-up and issued a public apology.

Political scandal conspiracy conspiracy theory cover-up
exposé libel plot public outcry revelations scandal
slander smear campaign

3 **VOCABULARY** Find seven of the words above in the text.
Check the meaning of all the words. What is the difference
between *libel* and *slander*?

4 **VOCABULARY** Complete the collocations with the verbs
below. All the collocations are in the text in exercise 2.

be accused of damage emerge face hack into
hamper issue listen in obtain pay out secure settle

Journalism: 'dirty tricks'

1 _____ of libel
2 _____ damages
3 _____ someone's reputation
4 revelations _____
5 _____ someone's voicemail
6 _____ a scoop
7 _____ on a message
8 _____ a lawsuit
9 _____ inside information
10 _____ allegations of / that
11 _____ an inquiry
12 _____ a public apology

5 Look at the newspaper headline. What do you know about
the Watergate Affair, a famous cover-up? What do you
think happened?

6 **2.27** Read the questions below. Then listen to an
account of the Watergate Affair. Answer the questions.

1 Which political party did Nixon belong to?
2 Why did the men break in to the Watergate Building?
3 What evidence connected the burglars to the president?
4 How did the break-in affect Nixon's popularity with
American voters?
5 What did Nixon do to try to hide his involvement in the
break-in?
6 Why were the tapes significant?
7 Why did Nixon finally have no choice but to release the
tapes?
8 How did Nixon escape trial and prosecution following his
resignation?

7 **VOCABULARY** Match the verbs with the definitions. Use a
dictionary to help you.

Verbs that express agreement or approval (1)
accede to authorise concur with condone

1 accept behaviour that is morally wrong *condone*
2 give official permission for *authorise*
3 agree to something (after initial reluctance) *accede to*
4 agree with somebody *concur with*

Verbs that express agreement or approval (2)
acquiesce in assent to comply with endorse

5 to obey (a rule, an order, etc.) *comply with*
6 accept something even if you don't agree with it *acquiesce in*
7 say that you support something or someone ~~comply to~~ *endorse*
8 agree to a request, idea or suggestion *comply with*

8 **2.27** Listen again. Which verbs from exercise 7 are used
in the recording? To understand the context they're used
in, can you quote the exact wording?

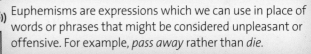

FLUENCY!
Euphemisms are expressions which we can use in place of
words or phrases that might be considered unpleasant or
offensive. For example, *pass away* rather than *die*.

9 Read the Fluency! box. Then find a phrase near the
beginning of the text in exercise 2 that means *are known
for telling lies*. Then complete the phrase below from the
listening that means *was being dishonest*.

He was being **efficient** / **economical** with the truth.

10 **VOCABULARY** Work in pairs. What do you think the
following euphemisms mean?

Euphemisms a frank exchange of views be expecting
economically disadvantaged ethnic cleansing
getting thin on top let (employees) go misinformation
pre-owned put on a few extra pounds rest room (US)

11 Replace the underlined phrases in the sentences with
euphemisms from exercise 10. Then write sentences that
include the other five euphemisms.

1 The army was accused of forcing people who did not share
their religion to leave the country.
2 We need more policies to help poor people in this country.
3 During the meeting the politicians had a massive argument
about the way forward.
4 The union accused the company of a campaign of lies.
5 I'm afraid we're going to have to sack a number of staff.

12 **SPEAKING** Work in pairs. Discuss the questions below.

1 Think of other examples of cover-ups. What were the
people trying to hide? Why? What happened in the end?
2 Why do politicians and businesses sometimes cover up the
truth about things that they have done wrong? Why does
it sometimes make matters worse for them?

➡ **Vocabulary Builder** Politics: compounds and collocations:
page 130

Emphatic forms

I can use a variety of structures to add emphasis.

1 SPEAKING Work in pairs. Do you know of any unexplained crimes? Describe one of them.

2 Read the text. What do you think happened to Ricky McCormick? Do you think anyone will ever crack the code?

LEARN THIS! Emphasis

There are a number of ways to add emphasis.

1 Cleft sentences with *it*, *what* and *all*.
I admire his courage. → *It's his courage that I admire.*
What I admire is his courage.
I just want some peace and quiet. → *All I want is some peace and quiet.*

2 Phrases such as *The problem / trouble / truth / fact / question is …*
The truth is I'm bored with my job.

3 *do / does / did* to emphasise an affirmative verb, especially for contrastive or emotive emphasis.
You do look nice in that hat.
I don't like his tie, but I do like his shirt.

4 *myself, herself*, etc. as emphasising pronouns.
I wrote to the Prime Minister himself.

5 Phrases that often indicate surprise or irritation.
What ever / on earth / in the world is the matter?
Goodness knows where my keys are. (= I don't know.)
I received no help whatsoever. (= No help at all.)

---

3 Read the Learn this! box. Find at least nine examples of emphasis in the text and match them to technique (1–5).

➜ **Grammar Builder 8.1** page 148

4 Use the correct tense and form of *do* to make the sentences more emphatic or to show a contrast.

1 Come in and do take off your coat.
  Do come in and take off your coat.
2 You've been late for school every day this week. Be on time today!
3 I don't much like listening to music on the radio, but I enjoy live music.
4 You've got an exam tomorrow. Go to bed early tonight.
5 I hate it when you raise your voice.
6 I didn't score a goal, but our team won, and that's what counts.
7 Stop talking, will you!
8 I didn't help with the housework but I did my homework.

5 Rewrite the sentences with *what* or *all* to give more emphasis.

1 I'd like to eat out this evening.
  What I'd like to do this evening is eat out.
2 His rudeness really irritated me.
3 I just want you to be happy.
4 His reluctance ever to apologise gets on my nerves.
5 I just need a few more minutes to finish this exercise.
6 You only need love.

On 30 June 1999, the body of Ricky McCormick was found in a cornfield in St Charles County, Missouri, 20 miles from his home. It was on 26 June that he'd last been seen, but no one had raised the alarm or reported him missing. There was no clue whatsoever to the cause of death, nor was there any clear evidence of a crime. What they did find on the body were two mysterious notes, covered in random letters and numbers. The FBI believed that they might hold the key to McCormick's death. The problem was, they could not decode them. All the FBI could do in the end was make the notes public, hoping that a member of the public might be able to make sense of them. It was assumed that an unbreakable code must be the product of a highly intelligent mind. But according to his family, McCormick wouldn't have been able to write the code himself since he was barely literate. One theory is that he was carrying a secret message between criminal gangs. He had a criminal record himself, and it is possible that someone wanted to kill him. What the FBI believe, however, is that McCormick wrote the notes himself. The fact is, we will probably never know how he met his end or what the mysterious message means.

6 Make the following sentences more emphatic, using techniques in the Learn this! box. You can sometimes emphasise more than one element of the sentence, or use more than one technique.

1 I saw the new Matt Damon film on Saturday.
  It was the new Matt Damon film that … It was on Saturday that … What I did on Saturday was …
2 Why did you do that?
3 My brother gave me this DVD, not my mum.
4 I don't like his attitude to women.
5 My brother married his childhood sweetheart in May.
6 I couldn't find a pen, but I found a pencil.
7 I met the American President!
8 The old woman was struggling with her luggage but she received no help from her fellow passengers.

7 SPEAKING Work in pairs. Complete these emphatic sentences with your own ideas. Then compare with your partner.

1 What I'd really like …
2 Why on earth … ?
3 What really annoys me …
4 All I want …
5 I don't particularly like … but I …

Listening
Spilling the beans
I can understand people gossiping.

I can't believe she would DO that!!

Really?

1 SPEAKING Discuss the questions in pairs.

1 What kinds of thing do people usually gossip about?
2 Why do you think people like to listen to gossip?
3 Do you think boys gossip more than girls, or the other way round? Why?
4 Do you like gossiping? What do you gossip about?
5 In what ways can gossip be harmful?

> **Listening Strategy**
>
> Notice how stress can affect the meaning of a sentence. Speakers stress certain words to indicate an alternative, make a contrast or to correct what someone has said.
>
> *'Have you been spreading rumours about me?'*
> *'I haven't. But Kate has.'*
> *'Did you walk round the hill?' 'No, we walked over it.'*

2 🎧 2.28 Read the Listening Strategy. Then listen to a question being repeated five times. Which piece of information is being emphasised each time? Match each question with a reply below.

a No, we played tennis. _____
b No, we played in the street. 1
c No, we watched it. _____
d No, we played on Sunday. _____
e No, I played with Harry. _____

3 🎧 2.29 Listen to six sentences. Which word is stressed in each sentence? Invent a follow-up sentence which makes sense of the stress pattern in the first sentence.

I bought my first TV in an electrical shop.

I bought my first TV in an electrical shop. I bought my second TV online.

4 🎧 2.30 Listen to two conversations and choose the correct answers.

Conversation 1: You hear two people talking about their friend Harry.

1 The girl is reluctant
   a to contact Kerry.
   b to believe the rumour about Harry.
   c to trust Ryan's word.
2 The boy is surprised that
   a Ellie hasn't heard the rumour about Harry.
   b everyone in the school hasn't heard the rumour.
   c Harry was seen with another girl.

Conversation 2: You hear two people talking about a job offer.

1 According to them both, Martha's current employers
   a have treated Martha badly.
   b will be embarrassed by Martha's departure.
   c will promote someone less qualified into Martha's position.
2 The man is telling the woman about Hannah
   a in order to save her embarrassment.
   b because her employers already know that she has been applying for jobs.
   c even though he was asked not to tell anyone else.

5 VOCABULARY Complete the idioms with the words below. Check the meaning of the idioms.

between breathe further hat hearsay let lips
quote rumour the latest tongue word

Idioms: secrets and gossip

1 Don't _____ on (to anyone).
2 If _____ gets out, ...
3 Don't _____ a word to ...
4 Keep it under your _____.
5 Don't _____ me (on that).
6 It won't go any _____.
7 It's just _____.
8 _____ has it (that) ...
9 _____ you and me, ...
10 Have you heard _____?
11 My _____ are sealed.
12 Bite my _____.

6 🎧 2.30 Listen again. Which idioms from exercise 5 did you hear?

7 Invent five false sentences that your partner can correct. Don't show them to your partner.

The Earth goes round the Sun once every two years.

8 SPEAKING Work in pairs. Read the false sentences to your partner. Your partner corrects the information using contrastive stress.

> No, the Earth goes round the Sun *once* every year.

whatever, whoever, whenever, wherever and however

I can use whatever, whoever, whenever, whichever, wherever *and* however.

1 **SPEAKING** Work in pairs. Which is more important in your opinion, love or money? Why?

2 Read the text. Why did Joe conceal his wealth?

3 Read the Learn this! box. Find all the examples of *whoever, whatever, wherever*, etc. in the text. Then match them with the uses below.

> **LEARN THIS!** *whoever, whichever, however*, etc.
>
> 1 We use *whatever, whoever, wherever*, etc. to mean 'it doesn't matter *what / who / where*, etc.'
> *I'll find my keys wherever they are.*
> *Whatever you decide, just let me know.*
> *I can go out with whoever I like.*
>
> 2 We can use *whoever, whatever*, and *whichever* to mean 'the person / thing / one that'.
> *Whoever gets home first can cook dinner for the others.*
> *Whichever team wins will go through to the final.*
>
> 3 We can use *however* with an adjective or adverb. After an adjective, we sometimes omit *it / the / she / they*, etc. + *be*.
> *However hard I try, I can never beat him at tennis.*
> *Try to answer every question, however difficult (it is).*

4 Complete the sentences with the words below.

however   however   whatever   whenever   wherever
whichever   whoever

1 _____ hard I tried, I couldn't work out the answer.
2 _____ you do, don't touch the grill. It's red hot!
3 _____ you go in Italy, you'll see wonderful buildings and ruins.
4 I'm free on Monday and Tuesday. Let's meet up on _____ day suits you best.
5 _____ phoned just now hung up without speaking.
6 I don't mind swimming in the sea, _____ cold it is.
7 _____ I visit London, I always go by train.

➔ **Grammar Builder 8.2** page 148

WHOEVER believes that love is more important than money will take heart from the story of Joe and Lisa Johnson. Lisa, a divorced single mum, was struggling to make ends meet when she met Joe in the café where she worked as a waitress. Joe, also divorced, used to come in for breakfast before work. The two got to know each other and Joe invited Lisa out on a date. Joe turned up in shabby clothes in a dirty, old car and took Lisa to a cheap restaurant. The two hit it off and continued dating. Whenever they went out in the early stages of their relationship, Lisa would offer to go halves on the meal or drinks, and Joe would accept. Under normal circumstances, that was to be expected, but Joe was hiding a big secret: he was a £10 million lottery winner. Whenever Lisa visited Joe's enormous house, he'd pretend it didn't belong to him and that he was house-sitting for a rich friend. Before taking Lisa to meet his family, he asked them whatever they did not to let Lisa know about his secret fortune. After dating for a few months, Joe proposed to Lisa and she accepted. Then, a week later, Joe revealed his big secret. At first Lisa was furious because it felt like a betrayal. But Joe explained that he'd hidden the truth from her because most of the women he'd dated before meeting her were only interested in his money. Lisa realised she could trust him and that she would have accepted his proposal however rich or poor he'd been. 'I can say with complete honesty that I fell in love with a man who I believed had nothing,' she said. Now, of course, she can buy pretty much whatever she wants, and go wherever she wants on holiday. Was Joe right to deceive Lisa, or should he have been honest from the outset? Whichever way you look at it, it is a story with a happy ending!

5 Rewrite the sentences in your notebook. Use *whatever, whoever, whenever*, etc.

1 I never tire of the Beatles, no matter how often I listen to their songs.
2 It doesn't matter which road you take, you'll arrive at about the same time.
3 It didn't matter how fast I ran, I just couldn't keep up with the other runners in the race.
4 I never get a good mobile signal at home – it doesn't matter where I put the phone.
5 Please come and see me any time you feel like it.
6 It doesn't matter who you ask, you'll get the same answer.
7 The charity is well worth supporting, so please make a donation, even if it's really small.
8 People say all sorts of things about politicians, but they do a difficult job.

6 **SPEAKING** Work in pairs. Complete the sentences with your own ideas. Then compare your ideas with your partner.

1 Whatever happens, …
2 Whoever you marry, …
3 Wherever I go for my next holiday, …
4 Whenever I speak English, …
5 However hard I try, …

Word Skills
Prefixes and suffixes
I can use a range of useful prefixes and suffixes.

1 SPEAKING Work in pairs. Have you heard of Wikileaks? What do you know about it?

2 Read the text and check your ideas. To what extent do you agree or disagree with the views of Zoe Brown and Jude Lee?

WIKILEAKS is an organisation that publishes secret information provided by anonymous sources. It has a website, hosted by a <u>Europe-based</u> internet provider, onto which it <u>uploads</u> the information it receives. The information is often sensitive and is leaked by employees of governments and organisations who feel that their employer is hiding information that should be in the public domain. Other secrets on the Wikileaks website are stolen by hackers who break into information systems. Governments and corporations have become much more <u>security-conscious</u>, and are determined to stamp out this type of <u>cybercrime</u>. But there's no <u>foolproof</u> way of keeping information safe. The hackers are only ever one step behind. Here's what two journalists think of Wikileaks.

ZOE BROWN Some people <u>downplay</u> the sensitivity of the information on the Wikileaks website, but some of the documents contain details that could harm national security and endanger lives. Wikileaks should take special care that it doesn't release the names of civilians who work for governments or international organisations.

JUDE LEE I think Wikileaks is doing a public service, and empowering ordinary people. If information is out in the open, we can hold governments and big corporations to account. Governments don't like it of course. It is alleged that there's been a <u>government-led cyberwar</u> against Wikileaks, but to no avail. How much of the information is <u>newsworthy</u> anyway? Probably not much. People <u>overestimate</u> the sensitivity and significance of the documents. Lots of them should be <u>declassified</u> anyway.

3 Read the Learn this! box. What does each prefix or suffix mean? Compare your ideas with a partner.

> **LEARN THIS!** Prefixes and suffixes
>
> New words are occasionally coined using these prefixes and suffixes. For example, *cyber* means *related to the internet* so the word *cybercrime* was coined to describe internet crime.
>
> | | |
> |---|---|
> | de- | debug, deforest |
> | down- | downsize, download |
> | over- | overbook, overwrite |
> | under- | undercover, underexposed |
> | up- | update, upgrade |
> | cyber- | cybercafé, cyberspace |
> | eco- | eco-friendly, eco-terrorism |
> | mono- | monorail, monolingual |
> | -free | fat-free, tax-free |
> | -proof | bullet-proof, future-proof |
> | -led | market-led, student-led |
> | -worthy | roadworthy, praiseworthy |
> | -based | London-based, class-based |
> | -conscious | health-conscious, safety-conscious |
> | -friendly | user-friendly, eco-friendly |
> | -phile/-phobe | Anglophile/phobe, technophile/phobe |

4 Find eleven examples of the prefixes and suffixes in the text.

5 Rewrite the sentences in your notebook. Replace the underlined words with words from the Learn this! box in the correct form. Make other changes as necessary.

1 Can you <u>give me the most recent information</u> about our finances?
   Can you update me on our finances?
2 The airline has <u>issued tickets to more customers than there are</u> seats on the flight. *over booked*
3 <u>There isn't enough light in</u> this photo. *underexposed*
4 I must <u>get rid of the viruses from</u> my computer. *debug*
5 Can you help me <u>move</u> these photos from the cloud to my computer? *download*
6 He <u>really hates using computers and other digital devices</u>.
7 They have <u>removed the trees from</u> vast areas of the Amazon basin. *deforest*
8 Is there a <u>coffee shop where they have computers</u> around here? *Cyber café*
9 We can take the bus or the <u>train that runs on one rail</u>. *mono rail*

6 Match each adjective (1–8) with a noun from below. Write a sentence for each combination.

campaign²   English speaker⁶ *monolingual*   instruction manual³   jacket⁴
lifestyle⁵   motor vehicle⁷   recipe¹   society⁸

1 fat-free   4 bullet-proof   7 roadworthy
2 student-led   5 health-conscious   8 class-based
3 user-friendly   6 monolingual

7 SPEAKING Work in pairs. Discuss this question: What information do governments have a right to keep secret?

➡➡ **Vocabulary Builder** Portmanteau words: page 130

Trade secrets

I can understand texts about trade secrets.

1 **SPEAKING** Work in pairs. Discuss this question: What do you think is the secret of the success of the fast-food and drinks in the photos?

2 Read the texts about four trade secrets. Match each to a headline below. There are two extra headlines.

1 Recipe is genuine, claims newspaper B
2 Company publishes secret recipe
3 Bid to sell trade secrets foiled by rival A
4 Secret recipe lost for ever
5 Long-forgotten lost recipe recovered C
6 List of original ingredients discovered D

> **Reading Strategy**
> With multiple-matching tasks consisting of several texts on the same topic, first identify the principal differences between the texts. This will help you to match sentences which contain detailed information with the texts.

3 Read the Reading Strategy. Then read the texts again. Which one of these statements is true? Explain why the other two are false.

1 All of the recipes were stolen. A
2 Attempts were made to sell each of the four recipes. D
3 All of the recipes date back at least 30 years. A B, C, D

4 Read sentences 1–6 below. Then match them with texts A–D.

1 A recipe was sold for thousands of dollars. D
2 The ingredients of this product have never been concealed. C
3 The recipe for this product is known by fewer than five employees of the company. A D
4 Three people hoped to make a lot of money from a recipe. A
5 A recipe was found in a book that belonged to a relative of the founder of the company. B
6 One company helped another company to find an old recipe. C

TRADE SECRETS

A Coke or Pepsi?
It would have been the most expensive bottle of soft drink in history. Joya
5 Williams, assistant to Coca-Cola's global brand director, was arrested for stealing a small bottle of a secret new product,
10 and attempting to sell it for £800,000 to Pepsi. The rivalry between Coke and the world's second-biggest cola maker has
15 long been regarded as among the most bitter in the business world. Williams wrote a note to Pepsi, saying, 'I have information that's all classified and extremely confidential, that only a handful of the top execs at my company have seen. I can even provide actual products and packaging of certain products, that no eye has seen, outside of
20 maybe five top execs.' But Williams catastrophically misjudged the rivals' present-day relationship. Pepsi reported her to her bosses, who called in the police. Undercover FBI officers posed as Pepsi executives and pretended to broker a deal which culminated in the arrest of Williams and two other employees who were also involved
25 in the attempted fraud. The public prosecutor praised Pepsi for doing the right thing: 'They did so because trade secrets are important to everybody in the business community. They realise that if their trade secrets are violated, they all suffer, the market suffers and the community suffers.'

30 **B It's finger-licking good!** The nephew of KFC founder Harland Sanders may have inadvertently revealed the secret recipe for one of the world's most widely eaten fast-food dishes. In 2016, *Chicago Tribune* journalist Jay Jones visited Kentucky to research an article about the Harland Sanders Café and Museum in the small town of
35 Corbin, formerly the service station where the Colonel first served his chicken to motorists in 1930. There the reporter met Sanders' nephew, 67-year-old Joe Ledington, with whom he leafed through an old scrapbook that had belonged to Claudia, the Colonel's second wife, who died in 1996. Inside was a copy of Ledington's aunt's will,
40 on the back of which was written a recipe for a fried-chicken spice blend made up of eleven herbs and spices. 'That is the original eleven herbs and spices that were supposed to be so secret,' Ledington told Jones. Contacted later to confirm the story, the Colonel's nephew was a little more cagey, telling the *Tribune* that he couldn't say 'for sure'
45 whether this was the mysterious recipe served today at some 20,000 locations in 123 countries. The newspaper cooked a batch according to the blend in the scrapbook and declared it 'the real deal', especially after they added monosodium glutamate, which KFC admitted is currently an ingredient in its chicken. When the *Tribune* piece was
50 published, the fast-food company issued a statement: 'Many people have made these claims over the years and no one has been accurate. This one isn't either.'

BIG MAC

C **Where's the sauce?** In 2002, the fast-food giant McDonald's was in trouble. Fred Turner, who had worked with Ray Kroc, the founder of McDonald's, was brought back from retirement to restore the company's fortunes. On his arrival, the then 71-year-old was shocked to discover that McDonald's had mislaid the recipe for the special Big Mac sauce. Luckily, Turner had a long memory. He remembered that a California supplier had helped to develop the sauce in the mid-1960s. Having been contacted by Turner, the supplier was able to find the recipe. The return of the special sauce marked a turn-around in McDonald's fortunes in the first decade of this century. But what goes into the sauce has never been a secret; it's the ratio of ingredients that remains a mystery. And in fact in 2016 McDonald's offered 4,000 bottles of Big Mac sauce for sale in Australia. The limited edition sold out in 15 minutes, and bottles were selling on auction websites for hundreds of dollars!

D **Is this the original Dr Pepper recipe?** In 2009, Bill Waters, a rare manuscripts collector from Oklahoma, stumbled upon an old tattered book while he was browsing in a store in the old Wild West town of Shamrock in Texas. He bought the dusty tome for $210, hoping to clean it up and sell it for a small profit on eBay. However, as he was leafing through the book, he came across a handwritten recipe for 'D. Peppers Pepsin Bitter'. The recipe seemed to come from the drug store in nearby Waco where the soft drink Dr Pepper was first served in 1885. 'I began feeling like I had discovered a national treasure,' said Mr Waters. Dr Pepper is made from a top-secret combination of 23 different ingredients and the exact combination is only made known to three senior employees of the firm at any one time. A spokesman for the company said that it bore little resemblance to the real Dr Pepper recipe and believed that the recipe was for a medicine rather than a soft drink. Waters put the book up for auction, hoping to sell it for $50,000 to $75,000, but it failed to reach the asking price. In the end, he sold it to Jack Weaver, an antique collector. Six years later, Weaver put the book up for sale again, believing that it should be where it is visible to other people, rather than in his own private collection. The book with the recipe sold for nearly $10,000, but it is not clear who bought it.

5 Read the texts again and answer the questions.

1 Why did Joya Williams's plan fail? *because Pepsi reported her to her boss*
2 In what way did Joe Ledington change his story about the KFC recipe? *he said it was unsure.*
3 Why did Fred Turner return to McDonald's after a long period away? *to rediscover the Big mac sauce*
4 Which recipe dated back over a century? *Dr. Pepper*
5 The makers of which two of the four products denied that the recipes were genuine? *KFC*

> **LEARN THIS!** **Avoiding repetition**
>
> When we mention something or someone for the second time in a text, we often describe it using different words.
> Manchester United bought Zlatan Ibrahimović in the summer. The 35-year-old will play in the number 10 shirt.

CRITICAL ANALYSIS

6 Read the Learn this! box. How are the following described on the second occasion when they are mentioned in the texts?

1 Pepsi (line 11)
2 *Chicago Tribune* journalist Jay Jones (line 33)
3 Claudia, the Colonel's second wife (line 38)
4 the *Tribune* (line 44)
5 KFC (line 48)
6 Fred Turner (line 54)
7 4,000 bottles of Big Mac sauce (line 65)
8 an old tattered book (line 70)
9 $50,000 to $75,000 (line 86)

7 **VOCABULARY** Complete the collocations with the words below. The collocations are all in the text.

a claim   a deal   a resemblance to   an article
the police

1 call in *the police*
2 broker *a deal*
3 research _____
4 make a resemblance → *a claim*
5 bear a claim → *a*

a mystery   a story   somebody's fortunes
the asking price

6 confirm _____   8 remain _____
7 restore _____   9 reach _____

8 **SPEAKING** Work in pairs. Discuss the questions.

1 Do you have a favourite food or drink that you'd like to know the recipe for?
2 Should manufacturers of food and drink be allowed to keep their recipes secret? Why? / Why not?
3 Do you think Pepsi did the right thing in reporting Joya Williams?

Discussion

I can agree, disagree, give an opinion and justify it.

1 SPEAKING Work in pairs. Discuss the meaning of the gestures in the photos. Are they the same in your country? Then read the quotation below. What does it mean? Is it good advice?

> 'If you tell the truth, you don't have to remember anything.' Mark Twain

2 KEY PHRASES Look at the phrases below for agreeing, disagreeing and giving opinions. Add them to the correct groups.

Agreeing
I couldn't agree more.
I'm of the same opinion.
That's a really good point.
1 _____
2 _____
3 _____

Adding an opinion
And I would add that …
As well as that, I'd say …
4 _____
5 _____
6 _____

Politely disagreeing
It isn't always the case (that …)
7 _____
8 _____
9 _____

Justifying your opinion
The principle justification for this point of view is …
10 _____
11 _____
12 _____

a And besides the argument we've just heard, …
b The reason I say that is …
c That's not necessarily true.
d The main reason for believing this is (that) …
e I think we'll have to agree to disagree.
f I was going to make the same point myself.
g I would concur with that.
h I'm not so sure about that.
i To give you just one example, …
j I'm with you 100% on that.
k It's also the case that …
l Not only that, but …

Speaking Strategy

In a discussion, listen carefully to the other participant(s) and, while they are speaking, work out your own opinion on the point under discussion. When it is your turn to speak, be prepared to pick up on points they have made, and either agree with them and reinforce them, or disagree with them and give your own opinion.

3 SPEAKING Work in pairs. Read the Speaking Strategy. Then discuss the three questions below. Try to include phrases from exercise 2.

1 Do you think lying is ever justified?
2 Some people say that we become more honest as we grow older. What do you think?
3 Is it possible to tell when someone is being dishonest? How?

4 🎧 **3.02** Listen to two students and the examiner discussing the questions in exercise 3. How do their opinions differ from yours on each of the three questions?

5 🎧 **3.03** Listen to each of the discourse markers below being used in context. Check that you understand the meaning by translating the discourse markers into your language.

Discourse markers anyway as a matter of fact besides by and large even so if anything incidentally mind you to be honest

6 🎧 **3.02** Listen again to the discussion. Which discourse markers do Joanna and Marco use?

7 SPEAKING Work in pairs or small groups. Read the six questions carefully and choose four of them to discuss together.

1 What are some typical situations in which people are dishonest?
2 Have you ever told a 'white lie'?
3 Politicians are often accused of being dishonest. Do you think that's fair?
4 How do you feel when you know someone is being dishonest with you?
5 What kinds of problem are caused when friends are dishonest with each other?
6 Why are people sometimes tempted to lie?

8 SPEAKING Work in the same pairs or groups, taking turns to start. Use phrases for agreeing and disagreeing and discourse markers.

Student A: Answer a question from exercise 7, justifying your opinion.
Student B (and Student C): Agree or disagree with student A, justifying your opinion.

8H Writing
Discursive essay
I can write a discursive essay using a variety of sources.

1 **SPEAKING** Work in pairs. Think of two pros and two cons of internet censorship. Compare your ideas with another pair.

2 Read the task and the essay. Are any of the ideas you discussed mentioned in the task or essay?

Your class has had a discussion about the possible effects of internet censorship. You have made the notes below about the possible effects of internet censorship:
1 combatting crime
2 government surveillance
3 freedom of expression

Some opinions expressed in the discussion:
'It helps to reduce identity theft and other fraud.'
'The authorities can spy on us.'
'It stops people from learning the truth.'

Write an essay discussing TWO of the possible effects in your notes. You should explain which effect is more important, giving reasons in support of your answer. You may, if you wish, make use of the opinions expressed in the discussion, but you should use your own words as far as possible.

The control and policing of the internet has become a hot topic of debate in recent years. Censorship has affected what we can and can't see and do on the internet in a number of ways, some positive and some negative.

One of the main consequences of censorship has been a reduction in crime: it has helped to reduce identity theft and other fraud. This is due to the fact that websites run by fraudsters are often quickly removed or blocked by the internet providers that host them. Not only that, but websites involved in more serious crimes such as terrorism, people trafficking or child pornography are also targeted by the authorities and quickly taken down. Consequently, the world is in my view probably a safer place. On the one hand, this censorship has given rise to the feeling that people's freedom of expression is being limited in certain ways. It is important that we know what is really going on in the world. Certain governments, however, are using internet censorship not just to combat crime but also as an excuse to control the information that their citizens have access to and so paint themselves in a better light. As a result, people sometimes feel unable to believe what they read.

So, just to round off, I reckon the reduction in crime is the more important of the two effects that I've talked about here. Of course, freedom of expression is important – no doubt about it – but perhaps not at the expense of our safety and security.

Writing Strategy
When writing an essay, make sure you:
1 read the task carefully and include all the relevant information.
2 write in an appropriate style for the genre.
3 organise the text in an appropriate way, presenting ideas coherently, and linking sentences and paragraphs.
4 use a range of grammatical structures and vocabulary, and use them accurately.

3 Read the Writing Strategy. Then analyse the task and essay in exercise 2. How well has the writer followed each point of advice in the Strategy? How could you improve the essay so that it follows the advice in the Strategy?

4 **KEY PHRASES** Complete the phrases with the words below. Then find five of them in the essay in exercise 2.

~~consequences~~ ~~due~~ exacerbated ~~given~~ principal
~~reason~~ ~~result~~ ~~resulted~~ ~~state of affairs~~ the result

Causes and consequences
This situation / ¹ *State of affairs* has been brought about by …
This is ² *due* to … / This is ³ *consequences* of …
One ⁴ *principal* for … is… *reason* *the result*
The situation/problem has been ⁵ *exacerbated* by …
The ⁶ *Principal* cause of … is …
This has ⁷ *given* rise to …
One of the main ⁸ *reason* of … is …
This has ⁹ *resulted* in …
Consequently, … / As a ¹⁰ ~~result~~ , … / Hence, …
consequence

5 Now read the notes below and the task and write your essay (220–260 words).

Your class has had a discussion about freedom of information. You have made the notes below about the possible impact of freedom of information:
1 holding politicians to account
2 waste of time and money
3 endangering innocent people

Some opinions expressed in the discussion:
'We can find out what the government is really doing.'
'It costs the governments millions of pounds to answer lots of trivial requests for information.'
'Some information has to be kept secret in order to protect people.'

Write an essay discussing TWO of the effects in your notes. Explain which effect is more important, and say why. You may make use of the opinions expressed in the discussion, but you should use your own words as far as possible.

CHECK YOUR WORK
 Have you …
• written 220–260 words?
• followed the advice in the Writing Strategy?
• checked your grammar and spelling?

9 Endings

9A Vocabulary
End of the world
I can talk about potential threats to our planet.

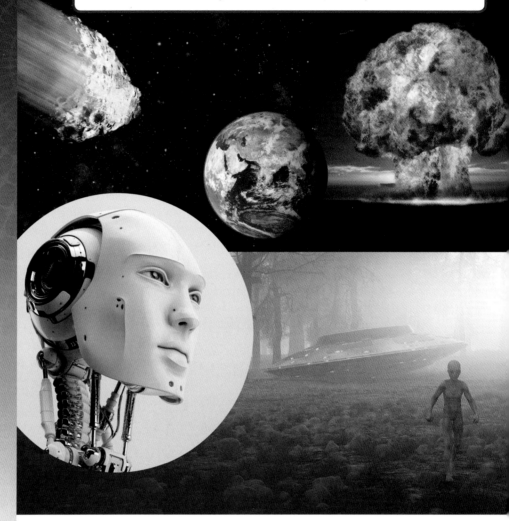

1 SPEAKING Work in pairs. What in your opinion is the biggest threat to the future of the human race? Why?

2 🎧3.04 VOCABULARY Complete the global threats with the words below. Then listen and say which global threat each person is talking about.

alien   asteroid   global   interplanetary   nuclear   pole   robot   supervolcanic

Global threats
1 *alien* invasion   2 *global* pandemic   3 *asteroid* collision
4 *robot* ascension   5 *pole* shift   6 *supervolcanic* eruption
7 *nuclear* impact   8 *interplanetary* holocaust

3 🎧3.04 SPEAKING Listen again. Which opinions do you agree or disagree with? Why?

4 VOCABULARY Match the verbs and phrases from the listening with the definitions.

Verbs and phrases for dramatic events   detonate   hurtle   overthrow   slam into   spell disaster   unleash   wipe out   wreak havoc

1 make a bomb or other device explode   *detonate*
2 cause confusion resulting in damage or trouble   *wreak havoc*
3 hit an object with a lot of force   *slam into*
4 destroy or remove something completely   *wipeout*
5 suddenly release a violent, uncontrollable force   *unleash.*
6 move very fast in a particular direction   *hurtle*
7 cause something bad to happen in the future   *spell disaster*
8 remove forcibly from power   *overthrow*

Luxury 'doomsday bunker' will allow 34 super rich families to survive the apocalypse

5 SPEAKING Work in pairs. Read the headline above and answer the questions.

1 What kind of people would you classify as 'super rich'?
2 What is 'the apocalypse' and which events do you think might cause it?

6 Read the article and check your answers in exercise 5.

As you read this, an American company called Vivos is building a global network of underground shelters to ensure that at least 6,000 of us survive the end of the world. The company considers that the Earth is facing all kinds of threats ranging from nuclear holocaust and a global pandemic to interplanetary collision or a sudden pole shift causing the globe's axis of rotation to suddenly change. According to Vivos, supervolcanic eruptions or an asteroid impact may be just around the corner, or perhaps we will be wiped out by an alien invasion or killer machines resulting from robot ascension.

Luckily for some, a few of these bunkers have already been completed, one of which is an extravagantly refurbished former military base in Rothenstein, Germany. Admission to the $1 billion building is not for everyone, however. Applications for a place are only being accepted from high-worth families who pass the selection process. Those who are successful have been instructed that, when disaster strikes, they should make their way to the nearest airport, where they will be picked up by helicopter and taken to the sumptuous shelter. Here they will be able to enjoy a year-long stay in their custom-made apartment while the rest of us are facing extinction.

7 SPEAKING Work in pairs. Discuss these questions.

1 Do you think the application and selection process is fair? Why? / Why not?
2 Would a place in the bunker be a good investment?
3 Do you think the bunker would offer protection from all global threats?
4 What problems would the people in the bunker face?

8 🎧 3.05 Listen to Justin and Lucy discussing the article in exercise 6. Answer the questions.

1 Where in Germany is the survival bunker located?
2 What do potential residents get for their money?
3 How are places in the bunker allocated?
4 What reason is given for the sudden interest in survival bunkers?
5 Who is more sceptical about the need for a bunker, Justin or Lucy?

> **FLUENCY!**
> A saying is an effective way of either giving advice or expressing an idea that is generally true.
> *Better late than never.* = It's better to do something late than not at all.
> Some sayings have two parts. In this case, we often only say the first part.
> *When in Rome ... (do as the Romans).* = Try to behave like the people around you when in a different place.

9 🎧 3.05 **VOCABULARY** Read the Fluency! box and complete the common sayings from the recording with the words below. Then listen again and check your answers.

birds   chickens   come   forewarned   ignorance   smoke   spoon   time

Common sayings
1 born with a silver _____ in your mouth
2 _____ of a feather flock together
3 first _____, first served
4 don't count your _____ before they are hatched
5 there's no _____ without fire
6 _____ is bliss
7 _____ is forearmed
8 only _____ will tell

10 Match the sentences with sayings in the Fluency! box and exercise 9.

1 We'll have to wait and see what happens. *only time will tell*
2 In most places in India, we ate with our fingers. *when in Rome*
3 Don't buy a new dress – you haven't been invited to their wedding yet. *don't count your chicken before they are hatch*
4 I'm glad you told me what they've been saying. *forewarned is forearm*
5 His dad's the Marquis of Bath. *born with a sliver spoon in your mouth*
6 I don't want to know the election results. *ignorance is bliss*
7 Craig is just like the rest of his friends: arrogant. *birds of a feather flock togethe*
8 Arrive early to avoid disappointment. *first come first serve*
9 Here's a present for your birthday last month. *Better late than never*
10 There might be some truth in that rumour about the sports centre closing. *there's no smoke without fire*

> **➡ Vocabulary Builder** Common sayings: page 130

11 SPEAKING Work in pairs. Answer the questions. Give reasons for your opinions.

1 Do you think we should take warnings about the end of the world seriously? Why? / Why not?
2 What if anything should governments do to safeguard their populations from global threats?
3 What do you think might happen to the world if humans as a species were wiped out?

9B Grammar

Ellipsis and substitution

I can use auxiliaries, modals, so and not … so to avoid repetition.

1 **SPEAKING** Work in pairs. Discuss this question: What problems do elderly people face in your country?

2 🎧 **3.06** Read and listen. Which words have been missed out, or are understood, following the highlighted phrases a–d in the dialogues?

1 **Vicky** I thought your grandma had retired, Beth?
 Beth ᵃShe has. But she still works at the charity shop.
 Vicky She must be over 70! Why does she do it?
 Beth Because ᵇshe wants to. It gets her out of the house.
 Vicky Isn't she fed up of working, though?
 Beth I don't suppose so, or she wouldn't do it!

2 **Owen** Matt, will you help me with my maths on Saturday?
 Matt ᶜI would if I could, but I'm going to the football with my grandpa.
 Owen Can't you tell him you'll go another day?
 Matt Why ᵈshould I? It's the highlight of his week!

LEARN THIS! Ellipsis: omitting verbs and verb phrases

- We can leave out a repeated main verb or verb phrase after an auxiliary or modal verb.
 'I didn't break the window!' 'Well, you may not have, but someone did!'
 'Did Jo call you?' 'He said he would, but I doubt he will.'

- We can leave out a repeated infinitive after verbs followed by *to* + infinitive.
 'Did you see the match on TV?' 'I was intending to but I forgot.'

---

3 🎧 **3.07** Read the Learn this! box. Complete the dialogue with seven of the words and phrases below. Then listen and check your answers.

can't does had to hasn't intend to love to meant to used to wasn't will won't 'd like to

Katie Rob, your grandma lives with you, doesn't she?
Rob She ¹_____, but now she's in a nursing home.
Katie Oh. She can't have been happy about moving out.
Rob She ²_____. She didn't really want to go, but in the end, she ³_____.
Katie Oh well. You'll just have to make sure you visit lots.
Rob I ⁴_____. In fact, I'm going after school. Do you want to come?
Katie I ⁵_____, but I ⁶_____. I've got hockey practice.
Rob Never mind. Maybe you can come another day.
Katie Don't worry, I ⁷_____.

→ Grammar Builder 9.1 page 149

LEARN THIS! Substitution: *so, not … so* and *not*

1 We can use *so* after *appear, assume, be afraid, guess, hope, imagine, seem, suppose* and *think* to avoid repeating a whole clause.
 'Is your mum at home?' 'I suppose so.' / 'It would seem so.'
 'Is your dad unwell?' 'I'm afraid so.'

2 We don't use *so* after *accept, admit, be sure* and *promise*.
 'Will Jo be here soon?' 'She promised she would.' ✓
 NOT *'She promised so.'* ✗

3 We use *it*, not *so*, after *doubt*.
 'Will Jo pass her driving tests?' 'I doubt it. / I don't doubt it.'

4 In negative replies we use *not* or *not … so* after *appear, believe, expect, imagine, seem, suppose, think. Not* is slightly more formal.
 I believe not. / I don't believe so.

5 We use *not* (NOT *not … so*), in negative replies after *assume, be afraid guess, hope, presume* and *suspect.*
 I guess not. ✓
 NOT *I don't guess not.* ✗

---

4 Read the Learn this! box and find a reply with *not … so* in the dialogue in exercise 2. How else could it be expressed?

5 Complete the responses to the sentences using the words in brackets and structures from the Learn this! box in exercise 4. Sometimes more than one answer is possible.

1 Will you be eating at home this evening? (we / think)
 We think so. / We don't think so. / We think not.
2 According to the forecast there's a storm approaching. (it / seem)
3 Do you think you've done enough revision? (I / guess)
4 Will Sam turn come to Sally's party? (I / imagine)
5 Do you think Harry will arrive soon? (I / be sure)
6 I think Chelsea will win the league. (I / doubt)
7 Is Lionne going to lend a hand? (he / promise)
8 Have you lost your smartphone? (I / hope)

6 **SPEAKING** Work in pairs. Take turns to ask and answer the questions below. Start your answer with a structure from the Learn this! box in exercise 4, before expanding it with your own opinion.

1 Can young people learn anything from elderly people?
2 Do we have as much of a duty to look after our elderly parents as we do to care for our own children?
3 Will you look after your parents when they get old?
4 Does the government help elderly people enough?
5 Should young people spend more time with elderly people?
6 Will there soon be more people over 50 than under 50 in your country?

Lost civilisations

I can use context to understand a text on lost civilisations.

1 **SPEAKING** Work in pairs. Discuss the questions.

1 Which civilisations do you think the photos represent?
2 Look at the factors that might cause the collapse of a civilisation. Number them 1–6 in order of probability.

Factors in the collapse of civilisation

climate change   corruption   economic collapse
foreign invasion   internal conflict   overpopulation

> **Listening Strategy**
>
> Read the rubric so that you are aware of the context of the task and read the questions so that you are aware of the information you require. This will help you work out exactly what you need to retrieve from the recording, and show you when the answer is coming up.

2 Read the Listening Strategy. Then look at the sentence below. What kind of information do you need to complete the sentence?

Both before and after their period of greatness, the majority of the Maya worked as _____.

3 🎧 **3.08** Now listen to some background information about the Mayan civilisation and complete the sentence in exercise 2. Which other options did you hear that might have completed the sentence? Why were they wrong?

4 🎧 **3.09** Listen to a talk by an archaeologist about the collapse of the Maya. Answer the questions.

1 Which of the factors in exercise 1 are mentioned as possible causes of the collapse of the Maya?
2 How did researchers create climate records for the distant past?
3 What two pieces of evidence coincided on two occasions, and led the researchers to believe their theory was correct?

5 Read the questions below so that you are aware of the information you require.

1 Archaeologists currently believe that _____ may have been responsible for the fall of the Maya.
2 Records from the area show that rainfall was _____ when the Maya civilisation was flourishing.
3 A period of drought began in _____ which caused part of the Maya civilisation to collapse.
4 At first sight, _____ cities, such as Chichén Itzá, appeared to have been unaffected by the droughts.
5 In a recent study, researchers looked at _____ to detect periods of prosperity and decline in these cities.
6 The study revealed that after AD 850, the number of new constructions fell by _____.
7 During the _____ century, the amount of construction fell once again.

6 🎧 **3.09** Listen again and complete the sentences in exercise 5 with a word or a short phrase.

7 **VOCABULARY** Complete the collocations from the listening with the verbs below.

enjoy   fall   give   play   put   spell   trigger   undermine

Verb + noun collocations
1 _____ the demise (of something)
2 _____ (somebody) an indication of something
3 _____ success
4 _____ a theory
5 _____ into decline
6 _____ something into perspective
7 _____ the end of / for something
8 _____ a role (in something)

8 Complete the paragraph with the collocations in exercise 7 in the correct form.

The first settlers from Polynesia landed on Easter Island around 1,200 years ago. The new culture, the Rapa Nui, [1]_____ and by 1550 AD numbered between 7,000 and 9,000. The people began to build massive stone statues called moai, all made at the same site and then transported across the island. First it was thought they were moved in an upright position, but recent computer simulations have [2]_____ this _____ by showing that they were transported horizontally on logs. At one point, moai formed an almost continuous line along the coast, [3]_____ of the power and influence of the Rapa Nui. Then something went wrong and the culture began to [4]_____.
The nation's obsession with its stone statues most definitely [5]_____ in this collapse. Deforestation has been identified as the chief factor that [6]_____, because of the huge number of trees that were felled, leading to erosion, crop failure and civil war. At its lowest level of population, the Rapa Nui numbered only 750. Later, slave traders from Peru came, taking away any healthy individuals, and then missionaries arrived, which [7]_____ for the Rapa Nui. Their story [8]_____ the effect poor management can have on the environment, and provides a valuable lesson for us to learn from.

➤➤ **Vocabulary Builder** Verb + noun collocations: page 130

9 **SPEAKING** Work in pairs. Discuss the questions.

1 What lessons can we learn from the collapse of civilisations such as the Maya and Rapa Nui?
2 What factors do you think contribute to a successful civilisation?

Advanced uses of the infinitive

I can use advanced uses of the infinitive.

1 SPEAKING Work in pairs. Answer the questions.

1 How would you define a minority language?
2 Which minority languages do you know of? Where are they spoken?

2 Read the article. What arguments does the writer use to support his opinion? Do you agree? Why?

WHY IT'S IMPORTANT TO SAVE DYING LANGUAGES

Languages develop over thousands of years ᵃonly to become extinct when the last speaker dies. Marie Smith Jones took the Eyak language of Alaska with her on her passing in 2008. But Eyak will not be ᵇthe last language to disappear this way. The loss of any of the 576 languages listed as critically endangered would be a tragedy for a number of reasons.

Firstly, a spoken language is ᶜthe only way to convey songs, stories and poems where there is no written system. If the language dies, so does the nation's entire oral tradition.

Secondly, each language has ᵈits own story to tell because of its unique reflection of human behaviour and emotion. 'Goodbye' in English, for example, expresses a finality that does not exist in the Cherokee 'I will see you again', although both expressions are used on parting.

Thirdly, languages contain vital facts about subjects like geography or mathematics. It is hard to believe that we could be ᵉso foolish as to allow this knowledge to disappear.

Finally, language is the one thing that makes us human. Yet we do ᶠnot do enough to protect the world's languages. Far more needs to be done – and fast – because each and every one of them is ᵍtoo precious to lose.

LEARN THIS! Advanced uses of the infinitive

We can use the infinitive:

1 after *only* to express a disappointing sequel. _a_

   We learned some Italian only to find they spoke English.

2 to replace a relative clause

   a after *the first, the second*, etc., *the last, the only* and some superlatives. _b_ _c_

   He was the first in the class to speak fluent French.

   b after nouns to show what is to be done with them. _d_

   I can't go out because I've got an essay to write.
   I need someone to practise my Italian with.

3 after *too* and *enough*. _f_ _g_

   Basque is too difficult a language to be mastered rapidly.
   You didn't study hard enough to pass the exam.

4 after *so* + adjective + *as*. _e_

   I'm not so fluent as to be able to hold a conversation.
   Would you be so kind as to test me on my grammar?

3 Read the Learn this! box. Match the highlighted phrases (a–g) in the article in exercise 2 to the rules (1–4).

→ Grammar Builder 9.2 page 150

4 USE OF ENGLISH Complete the second sentence so that it means the same as the first. Write no more than six words and include the word in brackets.

1 I studied Japanese for two years, so I was disappointed I couldn't understand people when I was in Tokyo. (find)
   I studied Japanese for two years _only to find_ that I couldn't understand people when I was in Tokyo.

2 In my experience of learning English, I can understand nobody better than the Scottish. (easiest)
   In my experience of learning English, the Scottish _are the easiest to understand._

3 Our teacher said, 'Can you read this newspaper article for homework, please?' (to)
   We've been given _an article to read_ for homework.

4 I need a book in which I can record new vocabulary. (to)
   I need a book _to record new vocabulary_

5 You'll need to learn more Spanish if you're travelling to South America alone. (enough)
   You don't know _enough Spanish to go_ to South America alone.

6 People think Steve is a native because his pronunciation is very accurate. (make)
   Steve's pronunciation is _so accurate as to make_ people think he's a native.

5 Complete the text. Write **three** words and include a verb from the list below in each gap.

~~discover~~ motivate ~~pass on~~ ~~speak~~ study ~~use~~

Joshua Hinson of the Chickasaw Nation was not concerned with speaking the language of his people until his first son was born. He then realised he had a culture ¹ _to pass on_ , but was unable to do so with the few Chickasaw words he knew. He decided to learn more, ² _only to discover_ that fewer than 100 members of his tribe were fluent in Chickasaw and they were all over 60. Hinson resolved to try to save his ancestral language. He decided not to write a grammar book because, for ordinary speakers, that would be ³ _too_ technical _to use_. Instead he tried to find a way to engage the young in his project, no mean feat considering they weren't so interested in Chickasaw ⁴ _as to study_ it outside school. He created a Chickasaw learning app that was attractive ⁵ _enough to motivate_ young people to want to use it. The app was an instant hit and now the future of Chickasaw looks brighter. The very ⁶ _last_ person _to speak_ only Chickasaw died in 2013, but thanks to Hinson, the language did not die with her.

6 SPEAKING Work in pairs. Answer the questions.

1 Which factors do you think can cause a language to die?
2 What measures can be taken to save a dying language?

Collocations with common verbs (*come, do, put* and *take*)

I can use collocations with common verbs to discuss spoilers.

1 SPEAKING Work in pairs. Read the definition of a spoiler. Why do you think spoilers are so frustrating?

> **spoiler** /'spɔɪlə(r)/ a remark or some information that gives away the ending of a book, film or TV series before you have seen it

2 🔊 **3.10** Listen to four speakers who have been victims of spoilers. For each speaker, answer the questions.

1 Which book, film or TV series was spoiled?
2 Who or what was the source of the spoiler?

3 VOCABULARY Complete the collocations below with *come, do, put* or *take*. Check the meaning of all of them.

1 come		3 do	
as a shock (to somebody)	✓	harm	✓
to an (untimely) end	✓	well	
2 put		**4** take	
one's foot in it		pleasure (in something)	✓
pressure on somebody/something	✓	it for granted	

4 🔊 **3.10** Complete these sentences from the listening with the correct form of the collocations in exercise 3. Then listen again and check your answers.

1 This _came_ _as_ quite _a shock_ to me ...
2 ... that particular character was the last person in the saga I was expecting to _do well_ .
3 He probably hadn't intended to _do_ any _harm_ ...
4 I guess he _came to an end_ that most people had already seen it.
5 ... the TV network that broadcasts the show really _put one's foot in_ it.
6 There were loads of complaints after that, which _put_ the channel _under_ a lot of _pressure_ to apologise.
7 ... the critic appeared to _take_ great _pleasure_ in revealing the true nature of this character ...
8 As far as I'm concerned, critics would _____ to keep quiet about plot details ...

5 Read the article about a teacher who uses spoilers in his classes. Answer the questions.

1 How does the teacher use the spoilers?
2 Why are they effective?
3 What do you think of this technique?

6 Find eight collocations with *come, do, put* or *take* in the article and add them to the chart in exercise 3.

7 USE OF ENGLISH Rewrite the sentences replacing the underlined words with the correct form of the collocations in exercise 3.

1 The Academy Awards have <u>been criticised</u> recently for being racist. _put under criticism_
2 Everybody at the table went quiet when Celia <u>said something embarrassing</u>. _put her foot in it_
3 My brother seems to <u>enjoy</u> spoiling all the TV series I start to watch. _take pleasure in_
4 Rob <u>tried as hard as he could</u> to study all the material before the exam, but he'd left it too late. _put pressure on himself_
5 If you've got a sore throat, making a drink with honey and lemon should <u>solve the problem</u>. _do you well / the trick_
6 I usually let my sister <u>be responsible for</u> the organisation of my birthday party. _took charge_
7 I was considering who to ask for help and <u>I thought of you</u>. _came to mind_
8 The film producers <u>tried to force</u> the director to cast an actor of their choice in the leading role.
9 Let's <u>actually try out</u> some of your new ideas. _get down to work_
10 You should <u>ignore</u> what you read in most tabloid newspapers. _n't take notice_

8 SPEAKING Work in pairs and answer the questions.

1 Have you ever been the victim of a spoiler?
a If so, without giving away too many details, what happened? How did you feel?
b If not, which book, film or TV series are you currently following that you wouldn't like to be spoiled? How would you feel if you came across a spoiler?

SPOILER ALERT: YOU'D BETTER BEHAVE!

On the subject of spoilers, the story of a certain maths teacher comes to mind. Teachers often come under fire for tolerating bad behaviour, but not this particular teacher. When faced with a noisy class, he found a novel way of putting a stop to the disruption. He took charge of the situation by issuing a dire threat to the students. He told them he had read _interweaving_ all the books in the Game of Thrones saga, and he would write the names of all the dead on the board if the students didn't behave. At first, the class took no notice of the warning and continued behaving as before. But then the teacher put his threat into practice and wrote up the first names. From then on, the warning did the trick, and the students got down to work in silence, doing their utmost to please the teacher. One of them wrote on social media later, 'My maths teacher is a genius!'

Reading
Grand finale
I can understand and react to an article contrasting the endings of books and films.

1 **SPEAKING** Work in pairs. In your opinion, which is it best to do first, read the book or see the film? Why?

2 Skim the text. What do all four film endings have in common?

> **Reading Strategy**
> In a multiple-matching task, the questions paraphrase the information given in the text. Read the question carefully and underline the key words and phrases. Then scan the text, watching out for paraphrases of the key words and phrases in the question.

3 Read the Reading Strategy and the question below. Underline the key words and phrases. Then scan the text to find the answer. How is the information paraphrased in the text?

Which section mentions ...
a film where the focus of the action has been swapped?

4 Match questions 1–9 with paragraphs A–D. Use the Reading Strategy to help you locate the correct answers.

Which section mentions ...
1 a group of characters whose fate is not clearly defined at the end of the book? A
2 an ending which features a last-minute rescue that didn't occur in the book? D
3 a film ending with a small sign that the protagonist will overcome an extremely negative experience? B
4 a film that radically changes the source of a life-saving solution? C
5 an ending to which a cruel twist has been added? A
6 a film that did not meet with the approval of the author? B
7 a situation which jolts people into a feeling of empathy? A
8 a character who meets his end in a completely different way than he does in the book? C
9 an ending that leaves more of an opening for a story to be continued in the film than it does in the book? D

5 Read the whole text again. Answer the questions in your own words.

1 The writer says the town 'becomes enveloped' in the mist. What image does this convey?
2 At the end of the film, Drayton is described as being 'crushed'. Explain his feelings in your own words.
3 Describe Forrest Gump's character, in your own words.
4 What grammatical mistake does the author have Forrest Gump make at the start of his next book? Why do you think he includes this mistake?
5 In the book *I Am Legend*, how many people are alive after the global pandemic? How do you know?
6 Why do the former vampires regard Robert Neville as a monster towards the end of the book?
7 Give examples of the 'thrills and spills' the first visitors to Jurassic Park may have experienced.
8 Why is the T-rex described as 'the star of the show' at the end of the film?

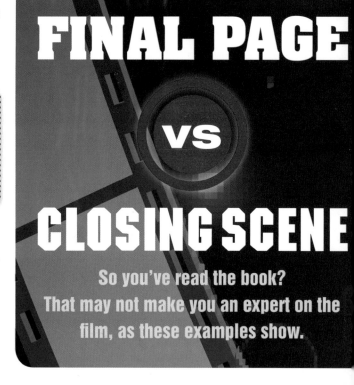

FINAL PAGE
VS
CLOSING SCENE

So you've read the book?
That may not make you an expert on the film, as these examples show.

CRITICAL ANALYSIS

In English, we can often choose between two verbs with the same or similar meaning: a phrasal verb, and a standard verb or verb phrase.
install = put up, conduct = carry out, ascertain = find out

6 **Look at the highlighted phrasal verbs in the text. Match them with their equivalents below.**

1 was released
2 raising
3 eat
4 diminishing
5 hidden
6 pass
7 starting
8 draw / present quickly
9 finds / discovers

7 **Find phrasal verbs in the text that could be replaced with the following standard equivalents.**

Text A
1 escaping from   2 killing *finishing off*
Text B
3 take care of *look after*
Text C
4 transform (sb) into   7 defending himself against
5 locating / hunting   8 conducts
6 hiding
Text D
9 be involved in

8 **SPEAKING** Work in pairs. Discuss the questions.

1 Do you think filmmakers who adapt a book should be obliged to be faithful to the original story? Why? / Why not?
2 What is your personal experience of seeing films after reading the book? How did the adaptation compare to the original?

A THE MIST

This Stephen King novella pushes scariness to the limit as it relates what happens in a small town when it
5 becomes enveloped in an eerie mist. The thick cloud hides huge insect-like creatures that threaten to *eat* gobble up anything and
10 everything that crosses their path, including a group of residents trapped in a local supermarket. Four survivors, led by David
15 Drayton, succeed in breaking out of the building to escape in Drayton's car. The rather ambiguous book ending leaves the group driving through the mist towards a city whose name they picked up through the static on the car radio. The end of the film, however, is more clear-cut – and far
20 bleaker. Drayton's vehicle eventually runs out of petrol, prompting him to pull out his pistol and kill his companions, including his son, Billy, so as not to leave them to the mercy of the monsters. With no bullet to use on himself, Drayton walks off into the mist … only to find the military
25 finishing off the last of the monsters. Crushed by the unnecessary killing, Drayton drops to his knees in despair, as did a large part of the audience when the film came out.

B FORREST GUMP

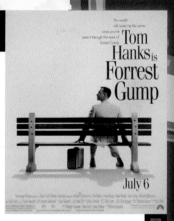

Author Winston Groom was far from pleased when he
30 saw Robert Zemeckis's film adaptation of his novel, which follows the kind-hearted but slow-witted title character through several
35 decades of his life. For one thing, the film makers had switched the two main plot threads, shifting the emphasis from the fantastic adventures of the protagonist
40 to his relationship with his childhood sweetheart, Jenny. As a result, the film's ending differs substantially from the original. The book concludes with Forrest setting up his own shrimp business in memory of his college friend Bubba. Jenny has married another man and they have
45 a child together, but she and Forrest remain friends. However, at the end of the film, Forrest looks after Jenny as she is dying. After the funeral, he is shown bringing up his and Jenny's child alone, the only glimmer of hope being that he appears to be doing a good job of it. Groom was so
50 disgusted with the changes made to his novel that he went on to write a sequel that began with the lines 'Don't never let nobody make a movie of your life's story.'

C I AM LEGEND

In Richard Matheson's 1954 novel, Robert Neville is the
55 sole survivor of a global pandemic, the effect of which is to turn its victims into vampires. He spends his days tracking down
60 inactive vampires to kill, and his nights holed up in his house, fighting off the vampires. Three years go by, and the attacks appear
65 to be dying down, but the lull is because the vampires have succeeded in building a new society and developing medication to combat the infection. Now, they regard Neville as he sees them: as a monster. At the end of the book, he
70 has been captured and is in a prison cell, awaiting execution for his crimes. However, in the movie Neville's initial predicament is improved by his knowledge that a survivors' camp exists for the 1% of the population who, like him, are immune to the disease. When he is not fighting for his life
75 – with zombies replacing vampires in the movie – Neville carries out medical research, and eventually comes up with an antidote. Later, he befriends two other survivors, to whom he entrusts the antidote, while he sacrifices himself to enable them to escape and make their way to the camp.

D JURASSIC PARK

80 Readers of Michael Crichton's best-selling novel will be familiar with the thrills and spills experienced by the first visitors to a dinosaur
85 park on the fictional island of Isla Nublar. In the book, the protagonists are caught up in a race for survival against the dinosaurs, and a race against time to stop a ship from the island reaching the mainland. Unbeknown to the captain, some small dinosaurs have
90 stowed away on the ship. After several run-ins with much larger versions of these creatures in the park, including a ferocious T-Rex, the group manages to contact the ship and stop it from docking in Costa Rica, and is then rescued by the Costa Rican military. As they leave the island, it is blown
95 to oblivion. In the 1993 blockbuster, however, director Steven Spielberg decided to leave the island intact, in all probability to allow for a sequel. Instead of blowing up the island, he had the T-Rex reappear to spice up the action during the final scene, during which the group faces an imminent
100 attack by some small but highly intelligent dinosaurs called velociraptors, which are on the point of bursting into the visitor centre, where the group is hiding. The visitors are saved in the nick of time by the T-Rex, whose actions ultimately turns it into the star of the show.

9G Speaking
Collaborative task
I can deal successfully with interruptions.

1 SPEAKING Work in pairs. Describe the photos. What different aspects of university life do they show? What are the benefits and drawbacks of going to university?

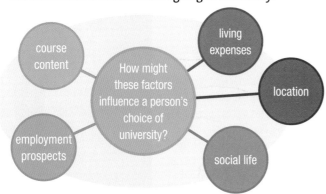

2 🎧 **3.11** Read the task above. Then listen to two students, Barbara and Sven, doing the task. Answer the questions.

1 Which factor(s) in the task do they discuss?
2 Which student tries to dominate the discussion?
3 What does the other student have to do in order to get the chance to speak?

Speaking Strategy

In a collaborative task, students are expected to share the interaction equally.

1 If the other student dominates the discussion, interrupt them politely to give your opinion.
2 If you are interrupted when you are speaking, you can choose to allow the interruption or to reject it politely.
3 If you reject the interruption, you need to go back to what you were saying.

3 KEY PHRASES Read the Speaking Strategy and complete the phrases with the words below.

ahead   butting   complete   continuing   could   go
interrupting   let   mind   saying   stop   think   want   was

Dealing with interruptions
Interrupting politely
Can I just ¹_____ you there for a moment?
Sorry for ²_____, but ...
Excuse me for ³_____ in, but ...
Before you ⁴_____ on, I'd just like to say ...
If I ⁵_____ just come in here, I think ...
Allowing an interruption
Sure. What do you ⁶_____?
That's OK. What did you ⁷_____ to say?
Yes, of course, go ⁸_____.
Rejecting an interruption
Please ⁹_____ me continue.
Can I ¹⁰_____ my train of thought?
Do you ¹¹_____ if I finish?
Continuing after an interruption
As I was ¹²_____, I think ...
¹³_____ where I left off ...
Where ¹⁴_____ I? Oh yes, ...

4 🎧 **3.11** Listen again to Barbara and Sven and tick the phrases in exercise 3 that you hear.

5 SPEAKING Work in pairs. Take turns to be A and B.

Student A: Choose an option from the text in exercise 2 that hasn't been mentioned. Speak about it for as long as you can. Try to politely reject Student B when he or she tries to interrupt and then try to continue with what you're saying.
Student B: Try to interrupt Student A in order to give your opinion on the topic.

Which two factors are the most important when choosing a university?

6 🎧 **3.12** Read the question above and look again at the factors in the task in exercise 2. Listen to two different students doing the task. Answer the questions.

1 What decision do the students come to?
2 Which student frequently uses the word 'important'?

7 🎧 **3.12** Listen again and tick the synonyms for *important* you hear.

Synonyms for *important*
critical _____   crucial _____   decisive _____   essential _____
fundamental _____   imperative _____   significant _____
vital _____

8 SPEAKING Work in pairs. Do you agree with the two students in exercise 6? Why? / Why not?

9 SPEAKING Work in pairs. Turn to page 151 and do the speaking task. Use the phrases for dealing with interruptions in exercise 3 and the synonyms for *important* in exercise 7.

Writing

A report

I can write a report.

1 SPEAKING Work in pairs. Imagine you had three months to spend in an English-speaking country to improve your language skills. Which country would you visit, where would you live and what would you do there? Why?

You have just finished a work programme in an English-speaking country. You had a full-time job in a fast-food restaurant and lived with a host family. The programme director has asked you to write a report in which you should evaluate the programme, explain which part of it was most useful, and recommend changes for future programmes.

2 Read the task above and the report. Does the report include any of your ideas from exercise 1?

LearnQuick work programme in Edinburgh

Introduction

The purpose of this report is to assess my recent participation in a LearnQuick scheme, identify the most valuable component of the programme and make recommendations for improvements to the project.

Assessment

In general, the LearnQuick programme lived up to my expectations. During my three-month stay, I gained an insight into Scottish culture, acquired a higher level of English and made a number of new friends. The downside of my placement was the long commute from my accommodation to my place of work, which was both time-consuming and expensive.

Most valuable component

While my job in a fast-food establishment brought me into contact with people of my own age, all of my co-workers were foreign and their English was much worse than mine, so I didn't speak much English. On the other hand, although I had very little in common with my host family, an elderly couple, they were always willing to converse. Therefore, weighing up the different factors, I would say that I benefited more from my host family than I did from my job.

Recommendations

As a result of my experience, I would like to suggest the following:

- Participants should be allocated accommodation near their workplace to avoid a long and expensive commute.
- Participants should be placed in a working environment where at least some of the employees speak English.
- Participants ought to be matched with a host family according to their age.

If these recommendations are carried out, they are likely to enhance the LearnQuick programme.

---

3 Read the Writing Strategy and look at the task in exercise 2. Underline the three elements to be included in the report. How are the elements paraphrased in the sub-headings to paragraphs 2, 3 and 4 in the report?

4 KEY PHRASES Complete four of the phrases with the words below. Then find the remaining phrases in the report and complete the missing words.

desired   edge   unlike   whole

Evaluating an experience / event
Broadly speaking, ... leaves a lot to be ¹_____
The ²_____ of my placement was ...
In general, ... lived up to my ³_____
On the ⁴_____, I gained a great deal / very little from ...
Comparing and contrasting different aspects
In terms of ... , ... definitely has / had the ⁵_____ over ...
The ... was superb, ⁶_____ the ... which was appalling.
⁷_____ the different factors, I would say ...

You have just finished a study programme in an English-speaking country. You studied English in the mornings and lived with other international students in a university hall of residence. The programme organiser has asked you to write a report, evaluating the programme, explaining which part of the programme was more useful, and recommending changes for future programmes.

5 Read the task above and prepare your report (220–260 words), following the advice in the Writing Strategy. Try to use some of the key phrases.

 CHECK YOUR WORK

Have you ...
- written 220–260 words?
- followed the advice in the Writing Strategy?
- included phrases for writing reports?
- checked the spelling and grammar?

5 Exam Skills Trainer

Reading

Strategy
The questions in the multiple-choice task may focus on opinion, tone, purpose, implication and main idea, as well as specific details in the text.

1 Read the strategy above and the questions in exercise 2. What does each of the questions focus on?

2 Read the text and choose the correct answers (A, B, C or D).

The secret of success

Walter Keane was a big name on the US art scene in the 1960s. Renowned for his melancholic paintings of big-eyed children, Keane postcards and prints sold by the million, and he was commissioned by Hollywood actors to paint their portraits. Yet behind this successful exterior, Walter concealed a terrible secret: it was his wife, Margaret, who was responsible for the paintings, not him.

There was a time when the couple had been in love. On their first meeting, at a San Francisco art fair in 1955, Walter had swept Margaret off her feet with his charm and they had married shortly after. All was well until the day Margaret accompanied Walter to a club, the Hungry i, where he had ostensibly been selling her paintings for her. She observed how he dealt with potential clients, turning on his charm to make a sale. When one of the clients enquired if she painted too, the truth suddenly dawned on her: Walter had been taking credit for her pictures.

Margaret could hardly contain her fury, but waited until they were home to confront Walter, demanding that he stop passing himself off as the artist of her work. But he managed to convince her that it was best for both of them if he continued selling the paintings under his name. He claimed that people would be more likely to buy them if they thought they were talking to the artist.

What she failed to realise was that in consenting to keep Walter's secret, Margaret had effectively signed her own prison sentence. Walter gradually began pressurising her to do more and more paintings for him. Soon he forbade her from having any friends and going out. It got to the stage that Margaret was painting for sixteen hours a day. Meanwhile, the children's eyes in her paintings became sadder and sadder.

Margaret endured this state of affairs for eight more years, and then she came up with a plan. She promised Walter she would continue painting secretly for him if he granted her a divorce. Aware that his marriage had been on the rocks for some time, Walter agreed. For five years Margaret kept her promise, but then suddenly decided it was time the truth be told. In October 1970, she finally let the cat out of the bag during a radio broadcast, announcing that Walter Keane was not the artist – the big-eyed paintings were hers.

Margaret's revelation produced a media storm. A 'paint-off' between the two Keanes was organised in San Francisco's Union Square, but Walter failed to turn up. In 1986, he had a second opportunity to prove his skill at a court case Margaret had brought against him for libel. At the trial, the judge ordered both Margaret and Walter to each create a big-eyed painting to determine who was the artist. Not surprisingly, Walter excused himself with a sore shoulder, while Margaret completed her painting in 53 minutes, and went on to win the case. She was

awarded $4 million in damages, of which she never saw a single penny, but more important to Margaret was the fact that the truth had been told.

1 The writer describes Walter Keane's success to illustrate
A the popularity of his paintings.
B the importance of his friends.
C the range of his output.
D the extent of his duplicity.

2 On her first visit to the Hungry i, Margaret Keane realised that Walter had been
A damaging her name.
B misleading buyers.
C denying her existence.
D selling her paintings.

3 How did Walter react to Margaret's demands?
A He became defensive and provoked a quarrel.
B He maintained he was a better painter than her.
C He talked her round to his way of thinking.
D He threatened her with legal action.

4 The writer suggests that Margaret's work reflected
A her desperation at her situation.
B her disappointment at her lack of fame.
C her disenchantment with her marriage.
D her disgust at her husband's behaviour.

5 Margaret's revelation was made
A in front of a camera.
B in writing.
C live on air.
D off the record.

6 Margaret took Walter to court in 1986
A to demonstrate her own talent in public.
B to put an end to his lies once and for all.
C to get her own back on him.
D to recuperate money that was rightfully hers.

Listening

Strategy
There are two different approaches to a multiple-matching task: attempting one task on each listening or attempting both tasks simultaneously, answering the easiest questions on the first listening and the more challenging ones on the second. You should identify the approach that works best for you.

3 Read the strategy above and the tasks in exercise 4. Which of the approaches do you think works best for you? Why?

4 🎧 **3.13** You will hear five short extracts in which people are talking about activities they did immediately after finishing school.

TASK ONE
For questions 1–5, choose from the list (A–H) each speaker's main reason for doing the activity.

Speaker 1 1 _____
Speaker 2 2 _____
Speaker 3 3 _____
Speaker 4 4 _____
Speaker 5 5 _____

A disconnect completely
B improve existing skills
C see something of the world
D keep somebody company
E make new friends
F prove someone wrong
G realise an ambition
H rise to a challenge

TASK TWO
For questions 6–10, choose from the list (A–H) what each person particularly enjoyed about the activity.

Speaker 1 6 _____
Speaker 2 7 _____
Speaker 3 8 _____
Speaker 4 9 _____
Speaker 5 10 _____

A being independent
B experiencing a different culture
C feeling valued
D finding their way around
E getting on well with companions
F having a flexible timetable
G sampling local food
H spending time outdoors

Use of English

Strategy
The missing words in an open-cloze text are often prepositions, especially from phrasal verbs. Use your knowledge of phrasal verbs and their particles to choose the correct word to fill the gap.

5 Read the strategy above. Complete the phrasal verbs in the sentences below with the correct words.

1 27 February 2017 has gone _____ in history as one of the most memorable nights at the Oscars.
2 Hugh Laurie's acting career was slow in taking _____; he didn't play Dr House until his 40s.

6 Complete the text with one word in each space.

And the winner isn't …

Only two people in the world know the secret ¹_____ the identity of each year's Oscar winners: the two accountants who count the votes and produce the envelopes to be handed ²_____ to the presenters on the big night. This system has its drawbacks, ³_____ the 89th Academy Award ceremony showed. ⁴_____ that occasion, veteran actor–presenters Warren Beatty and Faye Dunaway erroneously announced the musical romance *La La Land* to be the winner of the best film award. Not ⁵_____ the film's producers were making their acceptance speeches was the mistake discovered and rectified; the rightful winner was the drama *Moonlight*. Of course, the cast and crew of the winning film were overjoyed ⁶_____ the news, but the question remained as to how the mishap had occurred in the first place. It would appear that one of the two accountants had mixed ⁷_____ the envelopes he was holding, resulting in Warren Beatty being given the wrong one. Needless to say, the accountant in question will not be asked ⁸_____ to future Oscar ceremonies.

Speaking

Strategy
In the discussion you are expected to answer the questions promptly with a personal response. Use phrases to give you time to think if necessary.

7 Read the strategy above and complete the phrases for gaining time below with one word.

1 That's something I've never really _____ about, …
2 On reflection, I'd _____ …
3 Let me _____ about that for a moment …
4 That's a good _____ …

8 Answer the discussion questions below. Provide a prompt personal response and use the phrases for giving you time to think from exercise 7 if necessary.

1 What kind of behaviour can lead to the end of a friendship?
2 What's the best way to relax at the end of the day?
3 How do you feel when you reach the end of a good book?
4 What factors can cause a company to close down?
5 What will you do at the end of this school year?
6 At what age do you think childhood ends? Why?

Writing

Strategy
When you write an essay with notes and prompts to refer to in your answer, you can use the ideas and opinions in the notes, but you should paraphrase the actual words used.

9 Read the strategy above. Read the task in exercise 10 and write paraphrases for the words in bold.

10 Complete the task below.

Your class has had a discussion about what young people can learn from older people. You have made the notes below:

Areas where young people can learn from older people:
• money   • relationships   • work

Some opinions expressed in the discussion:
'You have to learn to **control your finances** when you live on your own.'
'Older people can tell **who's worth it**.'
'They've **been out** in the working world, so they know what it's like.'

Write an essay (220–260 words) discussing TWO of the areas in your notes. You should explain in which area young people could learn most from older people, giving reasons in support of your answer.

Culture
The legend of King Arthur
I can understand information about a legendary king.

1 SPEAKING Work in pairs. How much do you know about the legend of King Arthur? Complete the sentences with the words below.

Camelot   Excalibur   Guinevere   Lancelot   Merlin

1 _____ was the name of Arthur's castle.
2 Queen _____ was Arthur's wife.
3 Arthur's closest friend was called Sir _____.
4 As a boy, Arthur's teacher was a wizard called
   _____.
5 The name of Arthur's sword was _____.

2 Read the text below and find the answers to exercise 1.

3 Read the text carefully and answer the questions.

1 According to the text, what do nations often do in order to fill gaps in their early history?
2 Where does the name England come from?
3 How much of the story of Arthur's life is historically accurate, according to most experts?
4 In which book does Arthur's teacher Merlin first appear?
5 How does Arthur become king, according to a slightly later account of his life?

4 🎧 **3.14** Listen to an account of Arthur's life. Which of these events varies depending on which story you read? In what way does it change?

his birth   his marriage   his death

5 🎧 **3.14** Listen again. Number the events (a–h) in the correct order.

a Merlin creates the 'sword in the stone'. ___
b Arthur becomes king. ___
c Arthur is born. ___
d Arthur is badly wounded in a battle with Mordred. ___
e Uther Pendragon dies. ___
f Arthur pulls the sword from the stone. ___
g Arthur goes to live with Sir Ector and Kay. ___
h Arthur forms the Knights of the Round Table. ___

6 SPEAKING Work in pairs. Does your own country have any national heroes, legendary or real, who helped to create the nation? What stories are told about them?

King Arthur:
HISTORY OR MYTH?

The exact origins of most countries with a long history are lost in the mists of time. Their borders and even their national identities did not have neat beginnings but rather evolved
5 over long periods of time, continually shaped by invasions, migrations and tribal conflicts. But rather than accept these messy and incomplete histories, national pride seems to demand more heroic beginnings, so
10 legendary figures emerge to fill the historical gaps.

In the 5th century, Britain was emerging from nearly four hundred years of Roman rule, but already new settlers were arriving.
15 The Anglo-Saxons were Germanic tribes from Northern Europe who made their home in England (and gave the country its name). Historical records for this period are sketchy, but there were certainly conflicts between the
20 Anglo-Saxon settlers and the existing Britons.

King Arthur appears in several legends as a warrior king who united the Britons and bravely defended them against the Anglo-Saxon invaders. He is one of the best known
25 of all English kings and some of the details of his life – his home at Camelot, his wife Guinevere and his close ally Sir Lancelot – are probably more familiar to the British public than the biographical details of most
30 other monarchs. However, in the case of King Arthur, it is likely that none of these details are actually true. In fact, most historians believe that Arthur never existed.

Despite the lack of historical evidence for
35 his life – or perhaps because of it – Arthur has appeared in numerous poems, novels and paintings through the centuries, as well as a feature-length Disney animated film. Many of the characters and events of Arthur's
40 life are first mentioned in a book called

History of the Kings of Britain, written in the 12th century by Geoffrey of Monmouth. It describes how the wizard Merlin engineers Arthur's birth. It also refers to Arthur's sword
45 Excalibur, although the famous scene in which Arthur becomes king by pulling the sword from a large stone was added a few decades later by the French poet Robert de Boron.

The Sword in the Stone TH White

I can read and understand part of a novel about a legend.

1 SPEAKING Work in pairs. Discuss what qualities are needed in order to be the leader of a nation. Do you think your 'blood' (your ancestry) is important? Why? / Why not?

2 Read about TH White. Which author influenced White and which author did White influence?

TH White was a British author who was born in India in 1906 but educated in England. While studying English literature at Cambridge University, White wrote a thesis about a 15th-century version of the Arthurian legend by Thomas Malory. This later inspired him to write his own novels about the life of Arthur (or the Wart, as he is referred to when he is a boy) and his relationship with the wizard Merlin (or Merlyn). Merlin is in charge of Arthur's education and develops his physical and moral qualities by teaching him about the natural world and even transforming the boy into different creatures. The novels were a great success and have in turn provided inspiration for later writers, including JK Rowling, author of the Harry Potter novels.

3 Read the extract from *The Sword in the Stone*. What signs are there in the text that a magical event is being described? Think about what Arthur:

1 feels when he first touches the sword.
2 hears and notices around him.
3 sees (or imagines) as he tries to pull the sword out.
4 remembers about his education with Merlyn and how it comes back to him when he asks for help.

4 Explain in your own words the meaning of the highlighted phrases in the text.

5 🎧 **3.16** Listen to the next part of the story. In which two of these locations do the events take place? In what order?

the churchyard   Sir Ector's castle   the tournament

6 🎧 **3.16** Listen again and answer the questions. Some answers are implied rather than stated.

1 How does Kay react when he finds out the sword came from a stone? Why?
2 What lie does Kay tell his father after he has been given the sword?
3 Why does he later tell the truth, do you think?
4 Why does Sir Ector kneel down in front of Arthur?
5 How does Arthur feel when he sees Sir Ector and Kay kneeling in front of him?
6 At the end of the excerpt, why does Arthur wish that he had never seen the sword?

7 SPEAKING Work in pairs. Discuss the questions.

Why do you think stories that involve magic are popular? Do you personally enjoy them? Why? / Why not?

🎧 **3.15** 'How does one get hold of a sword?' wondered the Wart. 'Where can I steal one? Could I ¹waylay some knight and take his weapons by force? There must be some swordsmith or armorer in a great town like this, whose shop would still be open.'

5 He turned his horse and ²cantered off along the street. There was a quiet churchyard at the end of it, with a kind of square in front of the church door. In the middle of the square there was a heavy stone with an anvil on it, and a fine new sword was struck through the anvil.

10 'Well,' said the Wart, 'I suppose it's some sort of war memorial, but it will have to do.'

He tied his ³reins round a post, ⁴strode up the path, and took hold of the sword.

'This is extraordinary,' said the Wart. 'I feel queer when I have
15 hold of this sword, and I notice everything much more clearly. How clean the snow is! And is that music that I hear?'

It was music, and the light in the churchyard was so clear, without being dazzling, that you could have picked a pin out twenty yards away.

20 'Come, sword,' said the Wart.

He took hold of the sword with both hands, and ⁵strained against the stone, but nothing moved.

'It is well fixed,' said the Wart.

He took hold of it again and pulled with all his might. The music
25 played more and more excitedly, and the lights all about the churchyard glowed like jewels; but the sword still stuck.

'Oh, Merlyn,' cried the Wart, 'help me to get this sword.'

There was a kind of rushing noise, and a long chord played along with it. All along the churchyard there were hundreds of old
30 friends. They rose over the church wall all together, like ghosts of remembered days, and there were otters and nightingales and crows and hares and serpents and falcons and fishes and goats and dogs, and they all spoke solemnly in turn. Wart felt his power grow.

A bird sitting at the top of a tree cried out, 'Now then, Captain
35 Wart, I thought I once heard something about never letting go.'

'Don't work like a woodpecker,' urged an owl affectionately. 'Keep up a steady effort and you will have it yet.'

40 A snake, slipping easily along a wall, said, 'Now then, Wart, if you were once able to walk with three hundred ribs at once, surely you can coordinate a few
45 little muscles here and there?'

The Wart walked up to the great sword for the third time. He put out his right hand softly and drew it out as gently as from a
50 ⁶ scabbard.

GLOSSARY

1 **waylay (verb)** to attack or stop somebody
2 **canter (verb)** (of a horse) to travel quickly
3 **reins (noun)** the cords that a rider uses to guide a horse
4 **stride (verb)** to walk with long, confident steps. (past: strode)
5 **strain (verb)** to make a big effort without success
6 **scabbard (noun)** a holder for a sword

1 SPEAKING Work in pairs. Answer the questions.

1 Have you ever been to see a play at the theatre?
2 If so, describe the experience. If not, would you like to? Why? / Why not?

2 USE OF ENGLISH Read the text. Choose the best options (a–d) to complete the text.

1	a put on	b put up	c put in	d put over
2	a payment	b ticket	c price	d fee
3	a another	b an additional	c a bonus	d a surplus
4	a broad	b considerable	c extensive	d hefty
5	a invented	b occurred	c created	d came up with
6	a modelled	b copied	c imitated	d like
7	a a sudden	b an abrupt	c an instant	d a hasty
8	a jumped up	b sprang up	c came up	d built up
9	a like	b just	c much	d more
10	a reflect	b consider	c contemplate	d judge

THEATRE IN

Elizabethan England

IN the middle of the 16th century, during the first years of the reign of Queen
5 Elizabeth I, there were no purpose-built theatres in Britain. Companies of actors travelled around the country and ¹_____ plays in the yards of inns. These were enclosed areas surrounded by the inn
10 buildings. A stage was erected for the actors and people were charged a ²_____ to enter the yard and watch the play. They could pay ³_____ sum to watch from the balconies which often surrounded the inn yard. By the 1570s these theatrical productions were
15 becoming very popular and the producers of the plays were making ⁴_____ sums of money, especially in London. However, it was hard, tiring work for the actors, travelling around, carrying all the props and costumes with them, and erecting and dismantling the stage for
20 each performance. So an enterprising actor named James Burbage ⁵_____ the idea of building a permanent theatre. In 1576 he rented some land and built London's first theatre, aptly named 'The Theatre'. It was ⁶_____ on a classical Roman amphitheatre:
25 round, with a central open area, and with covered tiered seating and balconies for the audience. Burbage had to build his theatre outside the city walls because the Church and the city authorities considered theatres

3 Work in pairs. Read the text again. Then cover it and take turns to summarise the main points to your partner.

4 🎧 3.17 Listen to a historian talking about the Globe Theatre in London. Choose the correct answers.

1 The social status of actors and playwrights improved because
   A theatre was popular with the rich.
   B the church changed its views on the theatre.
   C Shakespeare joined a theatre company.
2 Burbage moved his theatre
   A because he'd found a better site for it.
   B following a disagreement.
   C with the agreement of the owner of the land.
3 The new Globe theatre
   A is built in exactly the same place as the old one.
   B looks exactly like the original.
   C is the result of careful research into the original.

5 🎧 3.17 Listen again and answer the questions. Some answers are implied rather than stated.

1 Where did Burbage get the materials to build the Globe theatre?
2 What happened to the first Globe theatre in 1613?
3 What happened to the Globe theatre in 1642?
4 Why are thatched roofs not permitted in London?

6 SPEAKING Work in pairs. In your own words, tell your partner three interesting facts that you have discovered about theatre in the time of Shakespeare.

to be immoral and dangerous. It was ⁷_____
30 success. Other companies of actors followed his example and a number of new permanent open-air theatres ⁸_____ around London.

A new form of entertainment had been born, and people flocked to the new theatres on Saturday afternoon
35 when the plays were put on, ⁹_____ in the way that people flocked to cinemas in the early 20th century. By 1600, there were half a dozen theatres just outside the city walls. Each could hold audiences of upwards of 3,000 people, and when we ¹⁰_____ that the
40 population of London was then approximately 200,000, it is estimated that on any Saturday afternoon an astonishing 20% of Londoners could be watching plays. It truly was the Golden Age of theatre.

As You Like It William Shakespeare
I can read and understand an extract from a Shakespeare play.

1 SPEAKING Work in pairs. Do the Shakespeare quiz.

Shakespeare Quiz

1 The line 'To be or not to be: that is the question.' comes from which play?
a *Romeo and Juliet*   **b** *Julius Caesar*   **c** *Hamlet*

2 In which century was Shakespeare born?
a 15th century   **b** 16th century   **c** 17th century

3 Where was Shakespeare born?
a London   **b** Stratford-upon-Avon   **c** Birmingham

4 Which English monarch reigned for most of Shakespeare's life?
a Elizabeth I   **b** Henry VIII   **c** James I

5 Shakespeare was a
a playwright   **b** playwright and actor
c playwright, actor and poet

6 Which of these plays are tragedies? Which are comedies?
Romeo and Juliet   *As You Like it*
A Midsummer Night's Dream   *Hamlet*

2 🎧 **3.18** Listen to part of a programme about the life of William Shakespeare. Check your answers to the quiz.

3 🎧 **3.18** Listen again. Answer the questions.

1 What are the main sources of information about Shakespeare's life?
2 What do we know about his education?
3 What do we know about his wife and circumstances of his wedding?
4 Why was it unusual to have small families at that time?
5 How did Shakespeare earn a living?
6 Why do some academics believe that Shakespeare didn't actually write the plays himself?

4 Read the extract from *As You Like It*. Answer the questions.

1 What does Shakespeare compare the world to?
2 What does Shakespeare compare people to?
3 How many 'ages of man' are there? What are they?

5 Read the extract again and match the numbered figures in the painting below with the 'ages of man' in the poem.

6 SPEAKING Work in pairs. Describe in your own words the characteristics of the seven ages.

> The first is a baby, crying and being sick. The second is …

7 SPEAKING Work in pairs. How many distinct stages would you divide a human life into? Describe them.

8 Make notes about the life and works of a playwright from your country.

9 SPEAKING Use your notes to present a biography of the playwright to the class. Speak for 1–2 minutes.

🎧 **3.19**

All the world's a stage,
And all the men and women merely [1]players;
They have their exits and their entrances;
And one man in his time plays many parts,
5 His acts being seven ages. At first the infant,
[2]Mewling and [3]puking in the nurse's arms;
Then the whining school-boy, with his [4]satchel
And shining morning face, creeping like snail
Unwillingly to school. And then the lover,
10 Sighing like a furnace, with a [5]woeful ballad
Made to his mistress' eyebrow. Then a soldier,
Full of strange [6]oaths and bearded like the [7]pard,
Jealous in honour, sudden and quick in quarrel,
Seeking the bubble reputation
15 Even in the cannon's mouth. And then the [8]justice,
In fair round [9]belly with good [10]capon lined,
With eyes severe and beard of formal cut,
Full of wise [11]saws and modern [12]instances;
And so he plays his part. The sixth age shifts
20 Into the [13]lean and [14]slippered [15]pantaloon,
With spectacles on nose and [16]pouch on side,
His youthful [17]hose, well [18]saved, a world too wide
For his shrunk [19]shank; and his big manly voice,
Turning again toward childish [20]treble, pipes
25 And whistles in his sound. Last scene of all,
That ends this strange eventful history,
Is second childishness and mere [21]oblivion;
[22]Sans teeth, sans eyes, sans taste, sans everything.

From *As You Like It* Act II scene vii

GLOSSARY
[1]actors   [2]crying   [3]being sick   [4]schoolbag   [5]pathetically bad
[6]swear words   [7]leopard   [8]judge   [9]stomach   [10]chicken   [11]proverbs
[12]examples   [13]thin   [14]wearing slippers   [15]old man   [16]small soft bag
[17]trousers   [18]looked after   [19]leg   [20]high voice   [21]unconsciousness
[22]without

The story of the sonnet

I can understand information about the sonnet.

1 SPEAKING Work in pairs. Which English-speaking poets do you know? What do you know about them or their poems?

2 USE OF ENGLISH Complete the text with the correct form of the word(s) in brackets.

3 Read the text. What similarities and differences are there between an Italian sonnet, the 16th-century English sonnet and a word sonnet?

All about the SONNET

Traditionally, a sonnet is a love poem of fourteen lines with a specific structure, regular line length and strict rhyme scheme. The sonnet is the most ¹_____ (wide / know) form of poetry in the English language. The first poem of its kind was
5 composed in Italy during the 13th century by a senior poet of the Sicilian school of poets, Giacomo da Lentini. At the time, poems tended to be extremely long, so this new and much shorter form was called a 'sonetto', Italian for 'a little sound or song'. The sonnet was later adopted by the great Italian
10 poet Francesco Petrarch, who made it famous in Italy and established the structure of the Italian sonnet: an eight-lined first stanza posing a problem, and a six-lined second stanza containing the ²_____ (resolve).

The sonnet reached England in this form during the
15 16th century, through Sir Thomas Wyatt's ³_____ (translate) of the works of Petrarch. Wyatt's contemporary, Henry Howard adapted the structure to suit the English language better. The new form was called the English sonnet and consisted of three four-lined stanzas and a final couplet.
20 The most famous practitioner of the poem was William Shakespeare, who published a collection of 154 English sonnets in 1609.

As the 17th century progressed, poets began to use the English sonnet to explore themes other than love. John Donne
25 turned to religion in his Holy Sonnets, while John Milton wrote about people and events. In the 18th century, interest in the sonnet waned, but there was a ⁴_____ (revive) at the start of the 19th century with the ⁵_____ (emerge) of the Romantic poets, such as William Wordsworth, who wrote
30 hundreds of sonnets. The first female sonneteers appeared at this point, most importantly Elizabeth Barrett Browning and Christina Rossetti.

By the turn of the century, poets were beginning to add new features to the sonnet, such as changing the rhyme
35 scheme. In 1928, WH Auden wrote one of the first unrhymed sonnets in English. The latest ⁶_____ (develop) is the 'word sonnet', a fourteen-line poem with only one word per line created by Canadian poet Seymour Mayne. Today, what passes for a sonnet would not be ⁷_____
40 (recognise) to the inventors of the form, but the fact that the poem is still being used is a reflection of its popularity and ⁸_____ (flexible).

4 Read the text again. Number the events 1–10 in chronological order.

a The fixed rhyme scheme was abandoned. _____
b The sonnet took off in Italy. _____
c The sonnet caught on in England for the first time. _____
d The fixed line length was abandoned. _____
e The first sonnet was composed. _____
f The first sonnets by female poets appeared. _____
g Petrarch's sonnets were translated into English. _____
h The sonnet expanded to include new themes. _____
i The sonnet fell into decline and then picked up again. _____
j The original Italian structure was abandoned in English. _____

5 🎧 **3.20** Identify the images in the photos. Then listen to a radio programme about five sonnets. Number the photos 1–5 in the order the images are mentioned.

6 🎧 **3.20** Listen again and match each of the five sonnets to a sentence (a–g). There are two extra sentences.

Which sonnet ...
a appears to contain a contradictory message? _____
b uses few words to convey a vivid image? _____
c is written in a somewhat melancholy tone? _____
d deals with a subject usually associated with a different genre? _____
e contains a particularly clever rhyme scheme? _____
f is a little exaggerated for modern readers? _____
g makes clever use of synonyms? _____

7 SPEAKING Work in pairs. Answer the questions.

1 Which of the sonnets in the radio programme did you like a) the most? b) the least? Why?
2 Choose one of the seasons and try to write a word sonnet about it.

Hour Carol Ann Duffy
I can read and understand a sonnet.

1 SPEAKING Work in pairs. Who is the most famous poet in your country? What do you think of their poems?

2 Read the text about the poet Carol Ann Duffy. Answer the questions.

  1 What events in her early life indicated she might grow up to be a poet?

  2 What is the poet laureate and what are his or her duties?

  3 In what ways is she different from previous poet laureates?

  4 What kinds of subjects does she deal with in her poems and what kind of language does she use?

Born in one of the poorer areas of Glasgow in 1955, Carol Ann Duffy is probably the best-known female poet working in Britain today. Her family moved to Stafford, England, when she was six, by which time she was
5 already a passionate reader. Duffy started writing poetry at the age of eleven, encouraged by her English teachers, and her first poems were published only four years later. After graduating in philosophy from the University of Liverpool in 1977, Duffy continued writing poems and became more
10 widely known when she won the 1983 National Poetry Competition. In 1996, she became a lecturer in poetry at Manchester Metropolitan University. In 2009 she was appointed poet laureate, the first woman and also the first Scot to have this prestigious role.
15   Dating back around four hundred years, the post of poet laureate is an honorary position appointed by the King or Queen on the advice of the Prime Minister. Originally held for life, the post has been limited to a period of ten years since 1999. The holder has no specific duties, but is
20 expected to write poems for significant national occasions, a requirement Duffy first fulfilled with her poem 'Rings' marking the 2011 wedding of Prince William and Catherine Middleton. Since her appointment, however, she has also written poems about less epic moments, such as the
25 cancellation of flights due to the eruption of an Icelandic volcano in 2010 and the exclusion of David Beckham from the England squad for the FIFA World Cup the same year.
   Duffy's versatility is one of the main reasons for her success. Her work blends fantasy with everyday life and her
30 poems are often tender, but tough; lyrical, but humorous; conventional, but unorthodox. Her use of familiar and conversational language makes them accessible to a wide variety of readers, which is why she is one of the most popular poet laureates there has ever been.

3 Read the poem *Hour*. Which conflict does it explore? Choose a, b or c.

  a love versus money
  b love versus time
  c time versus money

🎧 3.21

hour

Love's time's beggar, but even a single hour,
  bright as a dropped coin, makes love rich.
We find an hour together, spend it not on flowers
or wine, but the whole of the summer sky and a grass ditch.

For thousands of seconds we kiss; your hair
  like treasure on the ground; the ¹Midas light
turning your limbs to gold. Time slows, for here
we are millionaires, ²backhanding the night

so nothing dark will end our shining hour,
  no jewel hold a candle to the ³cuckoo spit
hung from the blade of grass at your ear,
  no chandelier or spotlight see you better lit

than here. Now. Time hates love, wants love poor,
  but love spins gold, gold, gold from straw.

GLOSSARY

1 Midas a mythical king whose touch turned things to gold
2 backhand give illegal payment in exchange for a favour
3 cuckoo spit foam produced by insect eggs left on long grass

4 What is the rhyme scheme of the poem?

  a ABBA CDDC EFFE GG   b ABAB CDCD EFEF GG

5 Read the poem again. Underline all the references to money or riches in the poem. Why are these images used?

  a To highlight that lovers need money to be able to spend time together.
  b To emphasise the value of time spent with a loved one.
  c To illustrate the different ways the rich and the poor spend time with a loved one.

6 SPEAKING Work in pairs. Answer the questions.

  1 Which verb plays with the two different meanings of the verb? (stanza 1)

  2 Which phrases illustrate how time passes more slowly when the lovers are together? (stanza 2)

  3 Which phrase illustrates the joy of spending time together? (stanza 3)

  4 Which phrase shows what triumphs in the end? (stanza 4)

7 SPEAKING What do you think of the poem? Give reasons.

Culture

The British in India

I can understand information about the British Empire.

1 SPEAKING Work in pairs. Try to answer these questions about India and its neighbouring countries.

1 Which country ruled India for large parts of the 18th, 19th and 20th centuries?
2 Can you name one famous Indian leader who helped the country gain independence?
3 In which decade of the 20th century did India become independent?
4 What religion are the majority of the Indian population?

2 Read the text opposite. Check your ideas from exercise 1.

3 Look at the map. Which period of history does it show? Choose a, b, c or d and explain why.

The map shows the Indian subcontinent:
a in the 17th century.
b between 1900 and 1947.
c between 1947 and 1971.
d after 1971.

4 Read the text again. Answer the questions.

1 What are the two official languages of India?
2 When were the first British trading posts in India established?
3 Who ruled the parts of the subcontinent over which Britain did not have direct control?
4 What was the approximate size of the British Empire at the start of the 20th century?
5 Which movement did Gandhi and Nehru lead?
6 Which of the three countries – India, Pakistan and Bangladesh – was the last to gain independence?

5 🎧 **3.22** Listen to a podcast about India from 1757 to 1857. Who effectively ruled the country during this period?

a the British government
b the British and French together
c a British company

6 🎧 **3.22** Listen again. Answer the questions.

1 Which other European countries were trading with India? What were they exporting?
2 What were the British trading in?
3 Why did the British first send ships to East Asia?
4 Why did the East India Company set up an army?
5 Who fought the British for control of India around 1750?
6 What was the result of the Indian Rebellion of 1857?

7 SPEAKING Work in pairs. Read the definition of 'colonialism'. Do you think colonialism can ever be a good thing? Why? / Why not?

> **colonialism** (noun) the practice of acquiring full or partial political control over another country, occupying it with settlers, and exploiting it economically. 🔍

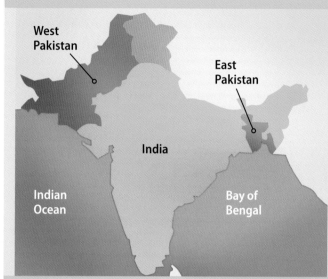

FROM EMPIRE TO INDEPENDENCE

The historical links between Britain and the Indian subcontinent are clear to see in both places today. In Britain, around five per cent of the population (three million people) have an Indian, Pakistani or Bangladeshi background, although many were born
5 in the UK. In India, English is used alongside Hindi as an official language and is the most widely spoken second language.

It was at the start of the 17th century that Britain first established trading posts in India. At that time, India was a collection of principalities rather than a unified country, and
10 by forming trade agreements with local rulers, British influence on the subcontinent spread rapidly. By the middle of the 19th century, large parts of modern-day India, Pakistan and Bangladesh were directly ruled by the British; other regions were still notionally ruled by princes but Britain had a great deal of indirect
15 control over these too. India was a key part of the British Empire, which by the start of the 20th century included approximately one quarter of the world's population.

British rule in India led to changes, some of which benefited the country: railways and canals were built, jungles were cleared
20 for farming, ports were developed and industries were created. Standards of living, even for the poorest Indians, undeniably rose during this period. But there was growing resentment among the Indian population towards their British rulers, who were exploiting the country's natural resources for their own gain, and plainly
25 considered British culture to be superior to local Indian traditions.

During the early decades of the 20th century, the desire to control their own destiny grew among the Indian population and their politicians. Leaders of the Independence Movement emerged – Gandhi, Nehru and others – and in 1947 the campaign
30 for independence finally triumphed. However, rather than becoming a single independent nation as many of their leaders wanted, the subcontinent was divided along religious lines. East and West Pakistan were created to provide homes for the Muslim population, while India itself remained a primarily Hindu nation, as
35 it is today. The eastern part of Pakistan became a separate country, Bangladesh, in 1971.

4 Literature

The Siege of Krishnapur JG Farrell

I can read and understand part of a novel about India.

1 **SPEAKING** Look at the photo of the British in India. Judging by appearances, would you say they are trying to follow local traditions or maintain their own? Give reasons.

2 Read about JG Farrell. What are his three best-known novels known as collectively? Order them according to a) publication date and b) the dates of the events they depict.

> **James Gordon Farrell** was born in Liverpool in 1935. Having graduated from Oxford University with a degree in French and Spanish, Farrell taught at a secondary school in France before becoming a full-time writer. He is best known for three novels which are collectively referred to as the Empire Trilogy. Although the novels have different plots, characters and locations, they are united by a common theme: a satirical look at the human consequences of British colonial rule.
>
> *The Siege of Krishnapur* was published in 1973. It is set in the fictional Indian town of Krishnapur during the Indian Rebellion of 1857. When the town comes under attack from an army of Indian soldiers, a group of British residents find themselves struggling to survive. Their self-image as a superior civilisation begins to look more and more ridiculous as their existence becomes squalid and precarious. The other two novels in the Empire Trilogy are *Troubles*, published in 1970 and set in Ireland during the Irish War of Independence (1919–21), and his 1978 novel *The Singapore Grip*, which depicts the 1942 Japanese invasion of South-East Asia during World War II.

3 Read the extract from *The Siege of Krishnapur*. Why do you think some of the lines are in brackets? Choose a, b or c.

  a To show that the speaker disagrees with what is said.
  b To show that the speaker is whispering the lines.
  c To show that the other characters do not let him speak.

4 Match the three characters (the Collector, the Magistrate and Fleury) with opinions a–c. Do you agree or disagree with the opinions? Explain why.

  a Civilisation is a negative influence which distances people from their true nature.
  b The local population has benefited greatly from being under British control.
  c British culture has had little or no effect on most of the local population.

5 🎧 **3.24** Listen to an earlier scene from the novel. What image does it portray of the British in India? Choose the best adjective from below or use your own words.

  courageous   innocent   ridiculous   stubborn   wise

6 🎧 **3.24** Listen again. Find at least three different pieces of evidence to support your answer to exercise 5.

7 **SPEAKING** Work in pairs. Find out what 'satire' means. Give examples of satirical books, films or TV programmes. Do you think satire can help to bring about change? Why? / Why not?

🎧 **3.23**

The Collector had been discoursing in an objective way on the perplexing question of why, after a hundred years of beneficial rule in Bengal, the natives should have taken it into their heads to return
5 to the anarchy of their ancestors. One or two mistakes, however serious, made by the military in their handling of religious matters, were surely no reason for rejecting a superior culture as a whole. 'After all, we're not ogres, even though we don't marry among the natives or adopt
10 their customs.'

'I must take issue with the expression "superior culture",' said Fleury; but neither of the older men paid any attention to him.

'The great majority of natives have yet to see the first
15 sign of our superior culture,' said the Magistrate. 'If they're lucky they may have seen some red-faced youth from Haileybury or Addiscombe riding by once or twice in their lives.'

('I say, "superior culture" is a very doubtful proposition,
20 but I think …')

'Come, come, Tom, think of the system of justice that the Company has brought to India. Even if there were nothing else …'

'This justice is a fiction! In the Krishnapur district we
25 have two magistrates for almost a million people. There are many districts where it's worse.'

('Look here, what I think …')

'Things are not yet perfect, of course,' sighed the Collector. 'All the same, I should go so far as to say that
30 in the long run a superior civilization such as ours is irresistible. By combining our advances in science and in morality we have so obviously found the best way of doing things, Truth cannot be resisted! Er, that's to say, not successfully,' the Collector added as a round shot
35 struck the corner of the roof and toppled one of the pillars of the veranda.

'What I think is this,' declared Fleury when the rubble had ceased to fall, determined at last to get his word in. 'It's wrong to talk of a "superior civilization" because
40 there isn't such a thing. *All* civilization is bad. It mars the noble and natural instincts of the heart. Civilization is decadence!'

'What rubbish!'

'I have seldom heard such gibberish,' agreed the
45 Collector, chortling as he got to his feet. 'By the way, what on earth are you dressed like that for?'

rican Civil War

nd a text about a famous civil war.

irs. Cover the text on the right and
d the text and check your answers.

N CIVIL WAR QUIZ

decade of the 19th century was the war fought?
40s **B** 1850s **C** 1860s

On what issue did the two sides disagree most fundamentally?
A slavery **B** the right to vote
C who should govern the country

3 Who was President during the war?
A Abraham Lincoln **B** Ulysses Grant **C** Theodore Roosevelt

4 What did the breakaway southern states call themselves?
A the Confederacy **B** the Union **C** the Southerners

5 Which side won the war?
A the North **B** the South **C** Neither

2 Read the text again. Answer the questions.

1 How did the economies of the North and South differ?
2 How did the South fear that the abolition of slavery would affect them?
3 What was the Kansas–Nebraska Act and what effect did it have?
4 What events convinced southerners that their whole way of life was under threat?

3 🎧 **3.25** Listen to a historian talking about the abolitionist John Brown. Put the events in the correct order.

a He started working in his father's tanning business. _____
b He spent two years raising money and support for the anti-slavery cause. _____
c He began training to go into the church. _____
d He was tried for murder and treason. _____
e His wife passed away and he got married again. _____
f He saw a black boy being beaten. _____
g He failed in his attempt to start a slave rebellion against slave owners. _____
h He was involved in the murder of pro-slavery men. _____
i He got married for the first time. _____

4 🎧 **3.25** Listen again. What evidence does Amy Weinberger give for these statements?

1 Brown had similar views on slavery to his father.
2 His own tanning business was reasonably successful at first.
3 He adopted militant tactics to oppose slavery.
4 He felt the killing of the pro-slavery supporters was justified.
5 People hold differing views on the morality of Brown's tactics.
6 His attack on the armoury in Virginia was a partial success.
7 His raid on the armoury spread a lot of fear in the South.

IN the mid-19th century, while the United States was experiencing an era of tremendous growth, a fundamental economic difference existed between the country's northern and southern regions. While in the North, manufacturing and industry
5 was well established, and agriculture was mostly limited to small-scale farms, the South's economy was based on a system of large-scale farming that depended on the labour of black slaves to grow certain crops, especially cotton and tobacco. Many people in the North wanted slavery abolished and did not
10 want it to become established in the new states that sprang up as Americans migrated westwards. This led many southerners to fear that the existence of slavery in America – and thus the backbone of their economy – was in danger.

In 1854, the US Congress passed the Kansas–Nebraska
15 Act, which essentially opened all new states to slavery by asserting that local democracy and an individual state's rights were more important than central government authority. Pro- and anti-slavery forces struggled violently in the mid-west state of Kansas, while opposition to the act in the North led
20 to the formation of the Republican Party. This was a new political party that opposed the establishment of slavery in the new states. Following a number of violent confrontations between supporters and opponents of slavery, more and more southerners became convinced that their northern neighbours
25 were determined to abolish slavery, on which they relied.

The election of the anti-slavery Republican Abraham Lincoln as president in 1860 was the final straw, and within three months seven southern states – South Carolina, Mississippi, Florida, Alabama, Georgia, Louisiana and Texas – had left the
30 United States and formed the Confederacy. Civil War broke out in the spring of 1861, and four more states – Virginia, Arkansas, Tennessee and North Carolina – joined the seven after the first shots of the war were fired. Four years of brutal conflict followed with historic battles at Gettysburg and
35 Vicksburg, among others. The War Between the States, as the Civil War was also known, pitted neighbour against neighbour and, in some cases, brother against brother. By the time it ended in the Confederate surrender in 1865, the Civil War had claimed the lives of 620,000 soldiers, with millions more
40 injured, and the population and territory of the South were left devastated.

5 **SPEAKING** Work in pairs. Discuss the question: Was John Brown justified in adopting the tactics he did in his attempt to end slavery?

5

Literature

Little Women Louisa May Alcott

I can read and understand extracts from a 19th-century American novel.

1 SPEAKING Work in pairs. How many female novelists can you name that write in English?

2 🎧 **4.02** Listen to a short biography of Louisa May Alcott. Complete the key facts below. Use up to three words in each gap.

FACTFILE: LOUISA MAY ALCOTT

- Born in 1832, she was the ¹_____ of four daughters.
- Her father established ²_____ which was not very successful.
- Forced to work to earn money for the family, she did not ³_____.
- She believed that women should have the right ⁴_____ and that ⁵_____ should be abolished.
- *Little Women* was partly based on her ⁶_____.
- *Little Women* was so popular that she wrote ⁷_____ to it.
- Alcott differed from the characters in her novel in that she ⁸_____.

3 Read the extract from *Little Women*. Answer the questions.

1 How would you describe the relationship between the four girls?
2 Who are they worried about? Why?
3 Whose idea was it not to exchange presents at Christmas? Why did he/she suggest this?
4 On what do they decide to spend what little money they have?
5 How did the girls come by money?
6 How do we know that the family used to be better off?
7 How are the King children different from the sisters?
8 What are the girls all doing as they chat to one another?

4 🎧 **4.04** Listen to the next part of the story. Answer the questions.

1 How do the girls change their plan for how to spend their money? What do they intend to buy?
2 Who arrives at their house? What news do they bring?

5 🎧 **4.04** Listen again. Choose the correct answers. Then give more information to support your choice.

1 The girls argue about
  a who is in charge.   b who should buy the slippers.
  c who should warm them by the fire.
2 Beth has
  a happy memories.   b mixed memories.
  c only hazy memories of former birthdays.
3 The girls think their mother looks
  a wonderful despite her old-fashioned clothes.   b more cheerful than usual.   c elegant, fashionable and noble.
4 Mrs March
  a gives the girls instructions.   b sits down with one of her daughters.   c helps prepare the evening meal.

🎧 **4.03**

'Christmas won't be Christmas without any presents,' grumbled Jo, lying on the rug.

'It's so dreadful to be poor!' sighed Meg, looking down at her old dress.

5 'I don't think it's fair for some girls to have plenty of pretty things, and other girls nothing at all,' added little Amy, with an injured sniff.

'We've got Father and Mother, and each other,' said Beth contentedly from her corner.

10 The four young faces on which the firelight shone brightened at the cheerful words, but darkened again as Jo said sadly, 'We haven't got Father, and shall not have him for a long time.' She didn't say 'perhaps never', but each silently added it, thinking of Father far away, where the

15 fighting was.

Nobody spoke for a minute; then Meg said in an altered tone, 'You know the reason Mother proposed not having any presents this Christmas was because it is going to be a hard winter for everyone; and she thinks we ought not to

20 spend money for pleasure, when our men are suffering so in the army. We can't do much, but we can make our little sacrifices, and ought to do it gladly. But I am afraid I don't.' And Meg shook her head, as she thought regretfully of all the pretty things she wanted.

25 'But I don't think the little we should spend would do any good. We've each got a dollar, and the army wouldn't be much helped by our giving that. I agree not to expect anything from Mother or you, but I do want to buy *Undine and Sintram* for myself. I've wanted it so long,' said Jo,

30 who was a bookworm.

'I planned to spend mine on new music,' said Beth, with a little sigh, which no one heard but the hearth brush and kettle holder.

'I shall get a nice box of Faber's drawing pencils. I really

35 need them,' said Amy decidedly.

'Mother didn't say anything about our money, and she won't wish us to give up everything. Let's each buy what we want, and have a little fun. I'm sure we work hard enough to earn it,' cried Jo.

40 'Don't you wish we had the money Papa lost when we were little, Jo? Dear me! How happy and good we'd be, if we had no worries!' said Meg, who could remember better times.

'You said the other day you thought we were a deal

45 happier than the King children, for they were fighting and fretting all the time, in spite of their money.'

'So I did, Beth. Well, I think we are. For though we do have to work, we make fun of ourselves, and are a pretty jolly set, as Jo would say.'

50 The four sisters sat knitting away in the twilight, while the December snow fell quietly without, and the fire crackled cheerfully within. It was a comfortable room, though the carpet was faded and the furniture very plain, for a good picture or two hung on the walls, books filled the

55 recesses, chrysanthemums and Christmas roses bloomed in the windows, and a pleasant atmosphere of home peace pervaded it.

6 SPEAKING Work in pairs. Did you enjoy the extracts from *Little Women*? Would you like to read the rest of the novel? Give reasons for your opinions.

The Industrial Revolution

I can understand information about the Industrial Revolution.

1 SPEAKING Work in pairs. Answer the questions.

1 When do you think the first factories were built?
2 What goods do you think they manufactured?

2 Read the text. Check your answers from exercise 1.

3 Read the text again. Match headings 1–5 with paragraphs A–E.

1 Machines take over manual work.
2 Carrying cargo to customers.
3 From farm to factory floor.
4 Other countries catch up.
5 Steel production and mining fuelled the growth of factories.

4 Answer the questions in your own words.

1 What demographic changes occurred at the start of the Industrial Revolution? Why?
2 Where and how were most fabrics manufactured until the 1750s?
3 What was life like for children in factories?
4 What other industries developed as a result of the new factories?
5 How were finished goods taken to their destination?

5 SPEAKING Work in pairs. What effect do you think the Industrial Revolution had on life in the cities?

6 🎧4.05 Listen to a podcast about life in the cities during the Industrial Revolution. Are the sentences true or false? Correct the false ones.

1 Workers left the countryside because immigration increased competition for farm jobs.
2 The population of Manchester doubled between 1771 and 1831.
3 Factory owners often built houses for their workers.
4 Travellers to London sometimes complained about the lack of visibility at midday.
5 By the beginning of the 20th century, electricity was being used to light the streets in British towns.

7 🎧4.05 Listen again and answer the questions.

1 Why did people leave the countryside during the industrial revolution?
2 Which was city was the first industrial city? And what was it nicknamed?
3 Which basic amenities were lacking in workers' houses?
4 What kind of jobs were available in London?
5 What could you hear on London's street corners?
6 What forms of pollution affected London at this time?

8 SPEAKING Work in pairs. What were the positive and negative effects of the Industrial Revolution? On balance, do you think it was good for society or not? Why?

The birth of the FACTORY SYSTEM

A During the second half of the 18th century, life in Britain changed dramatically with the start of the Industrial Revolution. This era marked the emergence of the factory system and the growth of cities, caused by the influx of workers from rural areas.

B The textile industry was the first to use modern production methods. Traditionally,
5 the manufacture of materials and garments had been a cottage industry, with individuals spinning cotton, weaving fabrics and making clothes in their own homes. All this changed with the invention of machines which made the process much less laborious for workers and far more cost-effective for textile merchants. The machines were installed in large industrial buildings, and operated by hundreds of employees,
10 including children, who were forced to work long hours in dangerous conditions for very little money.

C To support the new factories, the country needed metal to make the new machines and energy to power them. Innovations in the metal industry made cast iron easier to produce and led to the first inexpensive process for mass-producing steel. Both iron
15 and steel became essential materials, both for manufacturing tools and machines and for making vehicles to transport finished goods to the markets. As for energy, the first textile machines were powered by water until the invention of the steam engine, which soon took over in textile mills and was also used in heavy industry. The engines were powered by coal obtained from mines in Scotland, the north of England and Wales.

20 **D** Products from the new factories were exported all over the world, but for this to happen, the country first needed to improve its transport network. Some new roads were constructed, but by far the most effective way of transporting goods was by canal. By 1815, over 2,000 miles of canal were being used to carry thousands of tonnes of raw materials and manufactured goods to the ports. In the early 19th century, steam-
25 powered ships were developed to carry the goods across the Atlantic, and the steam locomotive was also coming into use. By 1850, Britain had more than 6,000 miles of railway tracks used by cargo trains and passenger trains alike.

E Britain was the birthplace of the Industrial Revolution, but it wasn't long before industrialisation spread first to Belgium, then to France and Germany and later to much
30 of the rest of the world.

Great Expectations Charles Dickens

I can read and understand an extract from a 19th-century novel.

1 SPEAKING Work in pairs. How would you define a 'lady' and a 'gentleman'? Do you think this kind of person exists in society today? Why? / Why not?

2 🎧 **4.06** Listen to a radio programme about Charles Dickens and *Great Expectations*. Choose the right answers.

1 An important theme in *Great Expectations* is
  a factory life.
  b wealth and poverty.
2 At the beginning of the story, the main character, Pip, is
  a living with his parents.
  b living with a close relative.
3 When he's older, Pip expects to
  a work in his brother-in-law's business.
  b move to London and become a gentleman.
4 When Dickens was a child, he spent three months
  a in a factory.
  b in prison.
5 Both Dickens and Pip moved
  a from the city to the country.
  b from the country to the city.

3 Read the extract from *Great Expectations*. Find evidence in the text for the following statements.

1 Miss Havisham wants Estella to become a lady.
2 Estella looks down on Pip.
3 Miss Haversham secretly wishes Pip ill.
4 Estella's attitude to Pip changes Pip view of himself.
5 Pip is reluctant to reveal how he feels about Estella.
6 Miss Haversham is manipulating both Pip and Estella.

4 SPEAKING Work in pairs. Discuss these questions.

1 What do you think of Miss Haversham's treatment of Pip and Estella?
2 What do you think of Estella's treatment of Pip?
3 Why do you think Miss Havisham might want Estella to 'break Pip's heart'?

GLOSSARY
1 signal with your hand for sb to move nearer
2 the feeling that sb isn't good enough to deserve your attention
3 a card game
4 beat him in the card game
5 the name of the picture card above the 10 and below the Queen in a pack of cards. 'Jack' is more informal than 'knave'.
6 rough

🎧 **4.07** *(Pip has just been taken to visit the wealthy spinster Miss Havisham for the first time. Her adopted daughter Estella has just entered the room.)*

Miss Havisham ¹beckoned her to come close, and
5 took up a jewel from the table, and tried its effect upon her fair young bosom and against her pretty hair. 'Your own, one day, my dear, and you will use it well. Let me see you play cards with this boy.'
  'With this boy! Why, he's a common labouring
10 boy!'
  I thought I overheard Miss Havisham answer – only it seemed so unlikely – 'Well! You can break his heart.'
  What do you play, boy?' asked Estella of myself
15 with the greatest ²disdain.
  'Nothing but ³beggar my neighbour, miss.'
  '⁴Beggar him,' said Miss Havisham to Estella. So we sat down to cards. […]
  'He calls the knaves, ⁵Jacks, this boy!' said
20 Estella, with disdain, before our first game was out. 'And what ⁶coarse hands he has. And what thick boots!'
  I had never thought of being ashamed of my hands before; but I began to consider them a very
25 indifferent pair. Her contempt was so strong, that it became infectious, and I caught it.
  She won the game, and I dealt. I misdealt, as was only natural, when I knew she was lying in wait

for me to do wrong; and she denounced me for a
30 stupid, clumsy labouring-boy.
  'You say nothing of her,' remarked Miss Havisham to me, as she looked on. 'She says many hard things of you, but you say nothing of her. What do you think of her?
35 'I don't like to say,' I stammered.
  'Tell me in my ear,' said Miss Havisham, bending down.
  'I think she is very proud,'
40 I replied in a whisper.
  'Anything else?'
  'I think she is very pretty.'
45 'Anything else?'
  'I think she is very insulting.'
(She was looking at me then with a
50 look of extreme aversion.)
  'Anything else?'
  'I think I should like to go home.'

Culture
Lewis and Clark
I can understand information about a famous expedition.

1 SPEAKING Work in pairs. Match the names below with an American a) mountain range, b) city, c) indigenous people, d) president and e) river.

Columbia   Jefferson   Rockies   Shoshone   St Louis

2 Read the text opposite. Which part of the continent did Lewis and Clark explore? Choose the area A, B or C on the map.

3 Read the text again. Are these sentences true or false? Correct the false ones.

1 The so-called 'Louisiana Purchase' represents almost half the area of the modern-day USA.
2 The existence of the Rocky Mountains was not generally known prior to the Lewis and Clark expedition.
3 The expedition did not expect to encounter Native American tribes during their journey.
4 The expedition did not continue through the winter months.
5 The entire expedition lasted about a year and four months.
6 Lewis and Clark achieved very little on their journey apart from reaching the Pacific.

4 🎧 4.08 Listen to the story of Sacagawea. For how much of the expedition did she remain with the Corps of Discovery?

5 🎧 4.08 Listen again. Complete the notes. Write one word in each gap.

1 When the explorers met Sacagawea, she was with her _____.
2 Sacagawea helped the explorers to find edible _____.
3 She also managed to retrieve important items from the _____.
4 At one point in the journey, Sacagawea was reunited with her _____.
5 After Sacagawea's death, William Clark took responsibility for her _____.

THE CORPS OF DISCOVERY

In 1803, two events occurred which had a significant effect on the history of the United States. Firstly, in what is referred to as the Louisiana Purchase, the US government bought a very large area of land from France, which almost
5 doubled the size of the nation. But an equally large area to the west remained unexplored. Americans knew that the Rocky Mountains lay between them and the distant Pacific, but there was no known route to the ocean. So in his second historically important act of that year, the US
10 President, Thomas Jefferson, commissioned a team of US army volunteers to undertake an expedition. Led by two officers, Meriwether Lewis and William Clark, their aim was to find a route westwards across the newly acquired territory and beyond to the Pacific. As well as claiming new lands for
15 the US, they were also expected to study the geography and wildlife of the area, while at the same time establishing trade links with local Native American tribes.

The Corps of Discovery, as it was known, set off from the city of St Louis on 14 May 1804, travelling north-west along
20 the Missouri River. By November they had travelled over 1,500 kilometres, mostly by boat but carrying their boats and supplies over land where necessary. They stopped and built Fort Mandan, in modern-day North Dakota, where they sheltered for the winter. In April 1805, they left the fort
25 and continued their journey westwards along the Columbia River, finally reaching the Pacific Ocean in November of that year. They had accomplished their mission! Having spent the winter near the Pacific, they then began their journey home, following a different route back to St Louis, which they
30 reached in September 1806.

The expedition was deemed a great success by Jefferson. As well as discovering a viable route to the Pacific Ocean, they made contact with more than twenty indigenous tribes, produced 140 maps of the area and discovered more than 200
35 plant and animal species previously unknown to European settlers. Lewis and Clark, however, did not become national celebrities until the 20th century, when there was a surge of interest in their expedition.

6 SPEAKING Discuss these questions with the class.

1 Do you think it was right for US explorers to claim land that was already inhabited by Native Americans?
2 Why do you think the explorers felt justified in claiming it? What does it tell you about their view of Native Americans?

On the Road Jack Kerouac

I can read and understand part of a novel about a road trip.

1 SPEAKING Work in pairs. What books and films can you think of that depict long journeys? Why are journeys a popular topic for writers? Think about:

characters plot settings metaphors

2 🎧 4.09 Listen to the radio interview about Jack Kerouac. What was the name of his first novel? How many novels did he write in total?

3 🎧 4.09 Listen again. Answer the questions.

1 What language did Kerouac speak at home?
2 When did Kerouac first move to New York?
3 When was *The Town and the City* published?
4 What experience in Kerouac's life formed the basis of *The Town and the City*?
5 What was unusual about the manuscript of *On the Road*?
6 How long after writing *On the Road* did Kerouac become famous?

4 Read the extract from *On the Road*. How successful is the first day of his journey? Justify your answer.

5 Find evidence in the extract that the narrator, Sal Paradise:

1 is looking forward to his journey.
2 regrets his choice of route.
3 has not dressed appropriately for his journey.
4 is going to try a different route next.

6 SPEAKING Work in pairs and discuss the questions.

1 If you could go on a long road-trip, where would you go? Why?
2 What could you learn from a trip of this kind?
3 What would the dangers be? How could you avoid them?

🎧 4.10 I'd been poring over maps of the United States in ¹Paterson for months, even reading books about the pioneers and savoring names like Platte and Cimarron and so on, and on the road-map was one long red line called Route 6 that
5 led from the tip of Cape Cod clear to Ely, Nevada, and there dipped down to Los Angeles. I'll just stay on all the way to Ely, I said to myself and confidently started. To get to 6 I had to go up to ²Bear Mountain.
    Filled with dreams of what I'd do in Chicago, in Denver, and
10 then finally in ³San Fran, I took the Seventh Avenue Subway to the end of the line at 242nd Street, and there took a ⁴trolley into ⁵Yonkers; in downtown Yonkers I transferred to an outgoing trolley and went to the city limits on the east bank of the Hudson River. If you drop a rose in the Hudson River at its
15 mysterious source in the Adirondacks, think of all the places it journeys as it goes to sea forever – think of that wonderful Hudson Valley. I started ⁶hitching up the thing.
    Five scattered rides took me to the desired Bear Mountain Bridge, where Route 6 arched in from New England. It
20 began to rain in torrents when I was let off there. It was mountainous. Route 6 came over the river, wound around a traffic circle, and disappeared into the wilderness. Not only was there no traffic but the rain came down in buckets and I had no shelter. I had to run under some pines to take cover;
25 this did no good; I began crying and swearing and ⁷socking myself on the head for being such a damn fool. I was forty miles north of New York; all the way up I'd been worried about the fact that on this, my big opening day, I was only moving north instead of the so-longed-for west. Now I was
30 stuck on my northermost hangup. I ran a quarter-mile to an abandoned cute English-style filling station and stood under

the dripping ⁸eaves. High up over my head the great hairy Bear Mountain sent down thunderclaps that put the fear of God in me. All I could see were smoky trees and dismal wilderness
35 rising to the skies. 'What the hell am I doing up here?'
    I cursed, I cried for Chicago. 'Even now they're all having a big time, they're doing this, I'm not there, when will I get there!' – and so on. Finally a car stopped at the empty filling station; the man and the two women in it wanted to
40 study a map. I stepped right up and gestured in the rain; they consulted; I looked like a maniac, of course, with my hair all wet, my shoes sopping. My shoes, damn fool that I am, were ⁹Mexican huaraches, plantlike sieves not fit for the rainy night of America and the raw road night. But the
45 people let me in and rode me back to ¹⁰Newburgh, which I accepted as a better alternative than being trapped in the Bear Mountain wilderness all night. 'Besides,' said the man, 'there's no traffic passes through 6. If you want to go to Chicago you'd be better going across the Holland Tunnel in
50 New York and head for Pittsburgh,' and I knew he was right. It was my dream that screwed up, the stupid hearthside idea that it would be wonderful to follow one great red line across America instead of trying various roads and routes.

GLOSSARY

¹Paterson, a city near New York ²Bear Mountain, the location of a road bridge that crosses the Hudson River north of New York ³San Francisco, a city in California ⁴trolley bus, an electric bus that is like a tram but without rails ⁵Yonkers, a city north of New York ⁶to ask drivers to stop and give you a lift ⁷(colloquial) to hit or punch ⁸the edges of a roof ⁹leather sandals ¹⁰Newburgh, a city north of Bear Mountain

8 Culture

The Cold War

I can understand a text and a speech about the Cold War.

1 SPEAKING Work in pairs. Look at the picture opposite and discuss these questions.

1 What was the Cold War?
2 Which two countries were the main participants?
3 What were its causes?
4 How did it endanger world peace?
5 When and why did it end?

2 USE OF ENGLISH Choose the best options (a–c) to complete the text.

1 a expressed   b remarked   c voiced
2 a attempt   b determination c struggle
3 a denouncing   b accusing   c blaming
4 a participated b occupied   c engaged
5 a supplied   b presented   c equipped
6 a enlarging   b building on   c building up
7 a commanded   b demanded   c necessitated
8 a setting off b dispatching   c launching
9 a tough   b strict   c hard
10 a intrude   b disturb   c intervene

3 Read the text and check your answers in exercise 1. Was any of the information new or surprising to you?

4 Work in pairs. Discuss and explain in your own words:

1 what Churchill meant by the phrase 'Iron Curtain'.
2 why the USA and USSR were allies in World War II.
3 why the USA and USSR mistrusted each other.
4 what a 'proxy war' is, and give an example of one.
5 the doctrine of 'Mutually Assured Destruction'.
6 how the powers competed outside the military sphere.
7 the policies of the two presidents in the 1980s.

5 🎧 4.11 Listen to a speech given in 1963 by President Kennedy. Where was he? Why was he giving the speech?

6 🎧 4.11 Listen again. Answer the questions.

1 Which ancient city does he compare to Berlin?
2 According to Kennedy, what effect does the wall have on ordinary people's lives?
3 What future political event does he tell Berliners to look forward to?
4 What lines does he repeat for rhetorical effect?

7 SPEAKING Work in pairs. Discuss the meaning of this quote from Kennedy's speech. Do you agree with it? Why? / Why not?

'Freedom is indivisible, and when one man is enslaved, all are not free.'

THE TERM COLD WAR' was coined by the writer George Orwell in an essay written in 1945, at the end of World War II. Shortly after that, Churchill famously [1]_____ that an 'Iron Curtain' had fallen across Europe, dividing the capitalist democracies in the west from the communist countries in the east.

OWN THE DVD BOX SET 5.8.12

It was the start of the Cold War, a [2]_____ between two global superpowers for global dominance that nearly brought the world to destruction. The Soviet Union (USSR) and the USA were allies in World War II, but had deeply mistrusted each other for decades. Their 'friendship' during the war was merely the result of their having a common enemy, Nazi Germany. Once Germany had been defeated, they resumed their rivalry, each [3]_____ the other's political and economic systems, and each believing the other wanted to destroy it. Though the two powers never [4]_____ each other directly in military combat (hence the term 'cold war'), there were 'proxy wars' throughout the 50s, 60s and 70s, with each power supporting a different side. For example, the USSR armed communist North Korea and North Vietnam, while the Americans fought with and [5]_____ arms to South Korea and South Vietnam.

The two superpowers also prepared themselves for an all-out war, and this led to an arms race, with each side [6]_____ enormous stockpiles of nuclear weapons. It was the doctrine of 'Mutually Assured Destruction' – with each side unwilling to use nuclear weapons for fear of massive retaliation – and it brought the world to the brink of nuclear war in 1962, when the USSR stationed nuclear missiles on Cuba, only 200 km from the US coast. The Americans [7]_____ their withdrawal, and after a tense stand-off the Soviets complied.

Aside from the arms race, the two powers also competed in a space race, with the USSR [8]_____ the first satellite and the first person into space, while the Americans were the first to land a man on the moon. In the 1970s, in an attempt to reduce the risk of war, the two sides signed treaties limiting their nuclear arsenals, but the deep ideological differences remained. In the 1980s, US President Reagan took an increasingly [9]_____ stance against the USSR, increasing spending on arms and backing anti-communist governments, especially in Central America.

Meanwhile, the USSR was suffering economically, and in an attempt to prevent it collapsing, President Gorbachev introduced the policies of *glasnost* (openness) and *perestroika* (economic reform). As a result, Soviet influence over the communist Eastern European states waned, and in 1989 they all replaced their governments with non-communist ones. Gorbachev refused to [10]_____ militarily. Then, in November 1989, the most visible symbol of the Cold War, the Berlin Wall, was torn down by the people and Germany was reunited. By 1991, the USSR itself had collapsed. The Cold War was over.

Literature

1984 George Orwell

I can read and understand extracts from a 20th-century novel.

1 **SPEAKING** Work in pairs. What is the difference between a utopian and a dystopian story or film? Can you think of any examples of either? Have you read or seen any? Did you enjoy them?

2 Read the extract from *Nineteen Eighty-Four*, by George Orwell. Is the novel utopian or dystopian? Find evidence in the text to support your answer.

3 Read the text again and answer the questions.

1 What is the purpose of the Big Brother posters?
2 Describe the 'telescreen'. What is its function?
3 What organisation or institution does Winston most fear? What is its role in society?
4 What aspects of life in Oceania are reminiscent of life in 20th-century totalitarian states?

4 🎧 **4.13** Listen to another extract from *Nineteen Eighty-Four*. Winston is talking to his colleague Syme, who is working on a dictionary of 'Newspeak', the official state language. What is the main aim of Newspeak? Choose a, b or c.

a To get rid of unnecessary words so that the language is much easier to learn.
b To make it impossible to think about certain things, because the words to describe them won't exist.
c To improve people's behaviour because they'll be able to express themselves more accurately.

5 🎧 **4.13** Listen again. Answer the questions.

1 What are the consequences of the new language for people like Winston?
2 What is the principal work of the people like Syme who work on the new dictionary?
3 What words will replace 'bad' and 'excellent'?
4 What does Syme predict will have happened by 2050?

6 **SPEAKING** Work in pairs. Discuss the meaning of Syme's words below. Do you think that language can affect thought to that extent?

'... the whole aim of Newspeak is to narrow the range of thought ... In the end we shall make thoughtcrime literally impossible, because there will be no words in which to express it.'

🎧 **4.12** *(Winston Smith has just entered the block of flats where he lives.)*

On each landing, opposite the lift-shaft, the poster with the enormous face gazed from the wall. It was one of those pictures which are so contrived that the eyes follow you about when you move. BIG BROTHER IS WATCHING YOU,
5 the caption beneath it ran.

Inside the flat a fruity voice was reading out a list of figures which had something to do with the production of pig-iron. The voice came from an ¹oblong metal plaque like a dulled mirror which formed part of the surface of the
10 right-hand wall. Winston turned a switch and the voice sank somewhat, though the words were still distinguishable. The instrument (the telescreen, it was called) could be dimmed, but there was no way of shutting it off completely. He moved over to the window: a smallish, frail figure, the meagreness
15 of his body merely emphasised by the blue overalls which were the uniform of the party. His hair was very fair, his face naturally sanguine, his skin roughened by ²coarse soap and blunt razor blades and the cold of the winter that had just ended.
20 Outside, even through the shut window-pane, the world looked cold. Down in the street little ³eddies of wind were ⁴whirling dust and torn paper into spirals, and though the sun was shining and the sky a ⁵harsh blue, there seemed to be no colour in anything, except the posters that were
25 plastered everywhere. The black-moustachio'd face gazed down from every commanding corner. There was one on the house-front immediately opposite. BIG BROTHER IS WATCHING YOU, the caption said, while the dark eyes looked deep into Winston's own. Down at street level
30 another poster, torn at one corner, flapped fitfully in the wind, alternately covering and uncovering the single word INGSOC. In the far distance a helicopter ⁶skimmed down between the roofs, hovered for an instant like a ⁷bluebottle and ⁸darted away again with a curving flight. It was the
35 police patrol, ⁹snooping into people's windows. The patrols did not matter, however. Only the Thought Police mattered.

Behind Winston's back the voice from the telescreen was still babbling¹⁰ away about pig-iron and the over fulfilment of the Ninth Three-Year Plan. The telescreen received and transmitted
40 simultaneously. Any sound that Winston made, above the level of a very low whisper, would be picked up by it, moreover, so long as he remained within the field of vision which the metal plaque commanded, he could be seen as well as heard. There was of course no way of knowing whether you were being watched at any given
45 moment. How often, or on what system, the Thought Police plugged in on any individual wire was guesswork. It was even conceivable that they watched everybody all the time. But at any rate they could plug in your wire whenever they wanted to. You had to live – did live, from habit that became instinct – in the assumption that every sound
50 you made was overheard, and, except in darkness, every movement scrutinised.

Winston kept his back turned to the telescreen. It was safer; though, as he well knew, even a back can be revealing. A kilometre away the Ministry of Truth, his place of work, towered vast and white
55 above the grimy landscape. This, he thought with a sort of vague distaste – this was London, chief city of Airstrip One, itself the third most populous of the provinces of Oceania.

GLOSSARY

¹rectangular ²rough and grainy ³swirls ⁴spinning
⁵unpleasantly bright ⁶flew close to ⁷a fly ⁸moved quickly ⁹spying
¹⁰speaking unclearly

Developments in science fiction

I can understand information about the history of science fiction.

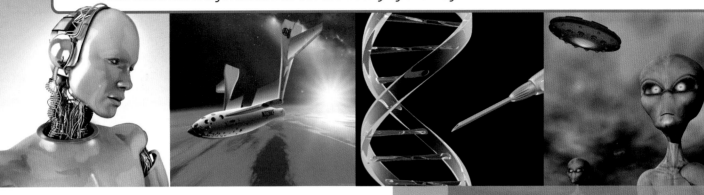

1 SPEAKING Work in pairs. Which science-fiction topic does each photo represent? Name a book or a film that features each of the topics.

2 Read about the early days of science fiction in literature. What is the significance of the dates below?

1864   1895   1896   1920   1926   1930   1932   1930s–1950s

3 Read the text again. Answer the questions in your own words.

1 Why is Mary Shelley's *Frankenstein* considered the first science fiction novel?

2 Which two authors are credited with writing the first science fiction novels?

3 Who or what made the genre popular in the USA?

4 Which word entered the English language from Czech? What does it mean?

5 How were dystopian novels regarded before *Brave New World*?

6 Where did science fiction flourish after the Golden Age of literature?

4 SPEAKING Work in pairs. What do you think is the appeal of science fiction?

5 🎧 **4.14** Listen to a podcast about science fiction in the cinema. Match 1–6 with the film titles below.

a *2001: A Space Odyssey*   d *Metropolis*
b *A Trip to the Moon*   e *Star Wars*
c *Forbidden Planet*   f *The Matrix*

Which science-fiction film …

1 was the first to be made? _____

2 was the first to feature an intelligent machine? _____

3 was the first to have a futuristic soundtrack? _____

4 gives an accurate description of an interplanetary voyage? _____

5 has been made into a famous brand? _____

6 is set in a dystopian virtual world? _____

6 🎧 **4.14** Listen again. Which three events in real life have influenced the evolution of the genre? In what way?

7 SPEAKING Work in pairs. Discuss the questions.

1 Have you read any of the books or seen any of the films in the lesson? If so, tell a partner. If not, which would you like to read or see? Why?

2 If you were making a science-fiction novel or film, what would it be about? Use ideas from the lesson or your own ideas.

STORIES have contained an element of fantasy since literature began, but it wasn't until the emergence of modern science during the 19th century that the genre we know today as science fiction was born. Arguably, the
5 first science-fiction novel ever written was Mary Shelley's *Frankenstein* in 1818, which featured a mad scientist dealing with advanced technology. However, the fathers of the genre are generally considered to be the French writer Jules Verne and HG Wells, who was British. In
10 *Journey to the Centre of the Earth* (1864), Verne used the technology of the day in a daring adventure, while Wells created a scientific device in *The Time Machine* (1895) to show Victorian society the error of its ways.

Thanks to Verne and Wells, the influence of science
15 fiction spread, not only throughout France and Britain, but also across the Atlantic to the US, where Edgar Allan Poe had already published *The Unparalleled Adventure of One Hans Pfaal* in 1835, a story about a flight to the moon in a balloon. Many other American authors began
20 to incorporate science and technology into their works, but the genre really took off in the US at the turn of the century with the birth of inexpensive fiction magazines known as 'the Pulps' in 1896. In 1926 the magazine *Amazing Stories* began, which was devoted exclusively to
25 works of science fiction and gave rise to the first sci-fi fans. Meanwhile, the genre had reached other countries, such as the former Czechoslovakia, where in 1920 the playwright Karel Čapek published *R.U.R.*, the first work about robots, introducing the word *robot*, Czech for
30 *slave* or *servant*, to the world's vocabulary. The early 20th century also saw the birth of the dystopian novel, stories about individuals trapped in repressive societies in the future with little hope of escape. These works were largely ignored by mainstream critics until Aldous Huxley
35 published *Brave New World* in 1932, an ironic portrait of an apparently happy society created by means of genetic engineering.

The middle of the 20th century saw the Golden Age of science fiction, with the publication of many classic
40 stories and the arrival in 1930 of a new magazine called *Astounding Science Fiction*. The 'big three' science-fiction writers at the time were the Americans Isaac Asimov and Robert A. Heinlein, and the British author Arthur C. Clarke, but there were also many others. By the end of
45 the 1950s, writers were moving on to new topics and this signified the end of the Golden Age of science fiction in literature. By then, however, the genre had begun to triumph in another area: the motion-picture industry.

9 Literature

Fahrenheit 451 Ray Bradbury

I can read and understand an extract from a 20th-century science-fiction novel.

1 **SPEAKING** Work in pairs. Which do you prefer, reading books or watching TV? Why?

2 **USE OF ENGLISH** Complete the information about Ray Bradbury and *Fahrenheit 451* with the correct prepositions.

Published in 1953, Ray Bradbury's award-winning novel *Fahrenheit 451* appeared during the Golden Age of science fiction. The title derives ¹_____ the temperature ²_____ which paper ignites. Set ³_____ a dystopian society, in which reading is illegal and 'firemen' burn any books that are found, using kerosene to set them alight, the story explores the fate ⁴_____ fireman Guy Montag.

The novel was written during the McCarthy era, a period ⁵_____ which the US government was actively pursuing any communist sympathisers in the country. Having witnessed the burning ⁶_____ books in Nazi Germany during the 1930s Bradbury was concerned that his own country might choose to adopt similarly repressive measures. At the same time, he saw the emergence of radio and television ⁷_____ a threat not only to reading, but also to society in general, as he believed that mass media could act ⁸_____ a distraction ⁹_____ much more important affairs.

3 🎧 **4.15** Listen to an extract from *Fahrenheit 451*. The firemen are acting on a tip-off about an old woman with a stash of books in her attic. Who starts the fire? Why?

4 🎧 **4.15** Listen again. Choose the correct answers.

1 Beatty says the books must be burned because they're
   a out of date.   b in a foreign language.
   c unrealistic.   d too academic.
2 Montag appears to be more ... than the other firemen.
   a persuasive   b dedicated to his job
   c advanced in years   d compassionate
3 Montag is carrying ... concealed inside his jacket.
   a a recording device b a stolen book
   c a secret camera   d a lethal weapon

5 **SPEAKING** Work in pairs. What do you think will happen to Montag if the object in his jacket is discovered?

6 Read a later extract. Check your answer in exercise 5. What is Beatty making Montag do?

7 Read the extract again. Answer the questions.

1 Which exchange in the dialogue is between Faber and Montag?
2 What do you discover about Montag's wife, Mildred, and the nature of their marriage?

8 **SPEAKING** Work in pairs. Discuss the questions.

1 Why do some governments and organisations consider books to be dangerous?
2 Do you think that the dystopian society portrayed in *Fahrenheit 451* could exist in real life? Why? / Why not?

🎧 **4.16** *The firemen are acting on another tip-off. Montag finds himself in front of his own house. This time, he is wearing a radio earpiece that enables him to speak to a friend, a man named Faber.*

5 Montag stood looking in now at this queer house, made strange by the hour of the night, by murmuring neighbour voices, by littered glass, and there on the floor, their covers torn off and spilled out like swan-feathers, the incredible books that looked so silly and really not worth bothering
10 with, for these were nothing but black ¹type and yellowed paper and ravelled binding.

Mildred, of course. She must have watched him hide the books in the garden and brought them back in. Mildred. Mildred.
15 'I want you to do this job all ²by your lonesome, Montag. Not with kerosene and a match, but ³piecework, with a flame-thrower. Your house, your clean-up.'

'Montag, can't you run, get away!'

'No!' cried Montag helplessly. '⁴The Hound! Because of
20 the Hound!'

Faber heard, and Beatty, thinking it was meant for him, heard. 'Yes, the Hound's somewhere about the neighbourhood, so don't try anything. Ready?'

'Ready.' Montag snapped the safety-catch on the flame-
25 thrower.

'Fire!'

A great nuzzling gout of flame leapt out to lap at the books and knock them against the wall. He stepped into the bedroom and fired twice and the twin beds went up in a
30 great simmering whisper, with more heat and passion and light than he would have supposed them to contain. He burnt the bedroom walls and the cosmetics chest because he wanted to change everything, the chairs, the tables, and in the dining-room the silverware and plastic dishes, everything
35 that showed that he had lived here in this empty house with a strange woman who would forget him tomorrow, who had gone and quite forgotten him already, listening to her ⁵Seashell radio pour in on her and in on her as she rode across town, alone. And as before, it was good to burn, he
40 felt himself gush out in the fire, snatch, rend, rip in half with flame, and put away the senseless problem. If there was no solution, well then now there was no problem, either. Fire was best for everything!

'When you're quite finished,' said Beatty behind him.
45 'You're under arrest.'

GLOSSARY

1 **type:** printed letters
2 **by your lonesome:** on your own
3 **piecework:** bit by bit
4 **The Hound:** a dog-like machine used to catch suspects
5 **Seashell radio:** a small radio that fits into the ear

V Vocabulary Builder

Introduction

IA Language terms

1 Match the underlined words with the terms below that describe them.

adjectival noun   cleft sentence   comment tag
defining relative clause   dependent preposition   ellipsis
gerund   non-defining relative clause   present participle
result clause   reduced relative clause
subordinating conjunction

1 You can stay at mine if necessary.
2 'I love learning new languages.' 'Do you?'
3 The rich should help the poor.
4 Kate's been working in the garden.
5 Our teacher is very strict on punctuality.
6 What I don't understand is why English spelling is so difficult.
7 The boy who sits next to me in class got full marks in the last test.
8 I'd have phoned you if I'd had time.
9 The boy over there, who recently joined our class, sits next to me in chemistry.
10 The man arrested last night is at the police station.
11 I speak Catalan though I don't speak Spanish.

2 Check the meaning of the terms which were less familiar to you and write example sentences.

IC Colloquial contractions

> **LEARN THIS!**
> In informal, spoken English we often use contracted forms of certain words and phrases. You might see them in text messages, song lyrics and as direct speech in fictional works. It would not be appropriate to use them in more formal kinds of written work.

3 Read the direct speech below. Write the full form of the underlined words.

1 'I'm driving into town. Wanna lift?'
   Do you want a lift?
2 'We met at a party last year. Dontcha remember?'
3 'I'm gonna order some food. Watcha want?'
4 'Gimme your phone. Mine ain't working.'
5 'Watcha doing?' 'Nothing. I'm kinda bored.'
6 'Where's Tyler?' 'Dunno. I ain't seen him.'
7 'Lemme help you with those bags.' 'Don't worry. They ain't heavy.'
8 'I ain't gonna do very well in my exams.' 'You gotta work harder!'
9 'This is hard! Aintcha gonna help me?'
10 'Look at this li'l kitten. Cute, innit?'

Unit 1

1C Science vocabulary: word families

1 Look at the word families below. Find a) seven words that refer to a field of study, and b) six words that refer to a person who studies, or works in, a particular field.

biology biological biologically (biologist) (microbiology) (microbiologist) (biotechnology)
gene (geneticist) genetic (genetics) genetically genetically modified (GM)
ecology ecologically (ecologist) eco-friendly ecosystem (ecotourism) (ecotourist) unecological
chemistry (chemist) (biochemist) (biochemistry) chemical weapons   chemical warfare

2 Complete the sentences with words and compounds from exercise 1.

1 The resort is popular with *eco tourists*, who are keen to leave as little impact on the environment as possible.
2 Some consumers are keen to avoid *genetically modified* ingredients when they buy food products.
3 Even a small rise in temperature can damage the coral reef's delicate _____.
4 Both countries have signed an agreement outlawing the use of *chemical weapons* in any conflict.
5 Cycling is more *eco-friendly* than driving.
6 Some twins come from the same egg and are therefore *genetically* identical.

1H Personality: phrases and idioms

3 Read the sentences. Match the underlined idioms with the definition (a–h) below.

a 1 Our next door neighbour is a real busybody. She's always looking over the fence to see what we're doing!
b 2 Bob is a creature of habit. He's very set in his ways. *b*
h 3 Luke has always worn his heart on his sleeve, so it was obvious how disappointed he was at his exam results.
d 4 My two sisters are down to earth people – but my brother thinks he's God's gift!
g 5 A lot of people find my uncle scary, but when you get to know him, you realise his bark is worse than his bite.
f
c 6 When she was younger, my sister was a real shrinking violet, but now she's the life and soul of the party.
e

a too interested in what other people are doing
b unwilling to change or to experience new things
c very shy and quiet
d to be realistic in your view of yourself and other things
e lively and entertaining when you're with other people
f to be less unpleasant or dangerous than you seem
g to have a very high opinion of yourself
h to show your feelings clearly

4 Choose four expressions from exercise 3 and use them to describe friends, relatives or well-known people.

My dad is very set in his ways. He has the same thing for breakfast every morning.

Vocabulary Builder

Unit 2

2C Compounds: journalism

1 Complete the compounds with the words below.

channel conference coverage freedom group news
poll press

1 pressure _____
2 opinion _____
3 breaking _____
4 gutter _____
5 news _____
6 press _____
7 press _____
8 media _____

2 Complete the sentences with the compounds in exercise 1. Use the plural form if necessary.

1 An _____ revealed that a majority of people are against the death penalty.
2 You'll find lots of sensational stories about people's private lives in the _____.
3 The Prime Minister's spokesperson held a _____ in which she briefed journalists.
4 There was a lot of _____ of the recent referendum – on TV, radio, online and in the papers.
5 We must defend _____ – it's essential in a democratic society.
6 Animal rights activists formed a _____ to try to get hunting banned.
7 There's some _____ on the BBC website – five people have been killed in a motorway accident.
8 Which _____ do you think is better, Sky News or BBC Worldwide?

2F Literary devices

3 Find examples of the literary devices below in the sentences. In two sentences there are two literary devices.

alliteration analogy assonance euphemism hyperbole
metaphor onomatopoeia personification simile

1 Just as our bodies need water, so an engine needs fuel.
2 We're as snug as a bug in a rug.
3 The snake hissed as it slithered away.
4 I'm absolutely starving. I could eat a horse.
5 Josie is the apple of her father's eye.
6 People are fed up with the EU, from Portugal to Poland, from Spain to Sweden.
7 The waves picked up the boat and hurled it against the rocks.
8 We had our faithful old dog put to sleep yesterday.

4 Check the meaning of the literary devices. Choose three of them and write examples of your own.

Simile – My hands were as cold as ice.

Unit 3

3A Love idioms

1 Read the text and match the highlighted idioms (1–8) with the meanings (a–h) below.

In Jane Austen's novel *Sense and Sensibility*, Marianne Dashwood has to choose between the loyal Colonel Brandon and the handsome John Willoughby. Brandon ¹has a soft spot for Marianne, but she falls for Willoughby, who ²sweeps her off her feet. The couple start seeing each other, and Marianne refuses to disguise the fact that she is ³head over heels in love with Willoughby. When Willoughby goes away, Marianne is unaware that their relationship is ⁴on the rocks until he ⁵dumps her for a woman with more money. Willoughby's rejection ⁶breaks Marianne's heart, and soon she falls gravely ill. She is visited by Willoughby, who attempts to ⁷patch things up between them, to no avail. On her recovery, Marianne turns to Brandon and before long they ⁸tie the knot and settle down happily together.

a improve the difficult relationship _____
b is deeply in love _____
c get married _____
d make her desperately unhappy _____
e in difficulties and likely to fail _____
f quickly makes her fall deeply in love with him _____
g likes _____
h end the relationship _____

2 Invent sentences using four of the idioms in exercise 1.

My brother has a soft spot for a girl in the year below him.

3C Business collocations

3 Match the verbs and nouns to make business collocations. Use a dictionary to help you.

1 attract	a a deal	6 hire	f an order
2 boost	b costs	7 launch	g a contract
3 break into	c investors	8 meet	h a product
4 close	d a market	9 place	i a deadline
5 cut	e confidence	10 sign	j employees

4 Complete the sentences with collocations from exercise 3. Use the correct form.

The company has ¹_____ many new _____ recently, including a new range of vacuum cleaners. This has enabled them to ²_____ new _____ , especially in the Far East. Thousands of ³_____ have been _____ by suppliers in these new markets, so the company's factories are working at full capacity, and hundreds of ⁴_____ have been _____ to meet the demand. Sales figures have been excellent and ⁵_____ has been _____ following disappointing results last year. Just a year ago, the company was in trouble, and had to dramatically ⁶_____ , closing two factories and laying off employees. The company hopes to ⁷_____ wealthy foreign _____ in order to raise money for further expansion.

V Vocabulary Builder

Unit 4

4F Speech verbs

> **LEARN THIS!**
> Speech verbs like *hiss, whine, snap*, etc. convey how the words are said. They can replace the verb *say* after direct speech but they cannot be used in reported speech.
> *'I want to go home,'* she snapped. ✔
> NOT ~~She snapped that she wanted to go home.~~ ✗

1 Match seven of the words below with the definitions.

blurt chant entreat hiss mouth nag retort scold
snap snivel squeal tease whine yell

1 _____ : tell somebody off for behaving badly
2 _____ : speak in a quick, loud, bad-tempered way
3 _____ : speak while crying with unhappiness
4 _____ : make fun of somebody in a light-hearted way
5 _____ : ask somebody to do something
6 _____ : say something in a slow, rhythmical way, often as a group
7 _____ : say something silently, by moving your lips

2 Choose the correct verb to complete the sentences.

1 'Let go of my arm,' she **hissed / blurted**, quietly but angrily.
2 'Help! They're stealing my bike!' she **snivelled / yelled**.
3 'You're lazy.' 'Not as lazy as you are!' **he retorted / entreated**.
4 'I'm cold and wet,' he **whined / chanted**. 'And my feet hurt.'
5 'Take your feet off the sofa!' his dad **teased / nagged**. 'And why aren't you doing your homework?'
6 'I've found you!' she **mouthed / squealed**, excitedly. 'Now it's my turn to hide!'

4H Formal and informal equivalents

3 Replace the underlined phrases with a more formal verb below in the correct form.

address advise conceive discard distribute ensure
prove seek submit yield

1 The new facilities have <u>turned out</u> to be very popular.
2 The local council should <u>do something about</u> these issues.
3 They have been forced to <u>look for</u> alternative solutions.
4 The army had to <u>give in</u> to demands to <u>give out</u> free drinking water.
5 The developers are obliged by law to <u>tell</u> local residents about their plans.
6 It's difficult to <u>think</u> of a more expensive project.
7 The charity sells old furniture that residents have <u>got rid of</u>.
8 <u>Make sure</u> that you <u>send in</u> your forms by next week.

4 Write sentences with five of the formal verbs from exercise 3.

Unit 5

5C Reporting verbs

1 Complete the reporting verbs. Use *a, e, i, o* and *u*.

1 __ dv __ s __
2 __ rg __ __
3 b __ __ st
4 cl __ __ m
5 c __ nc __ d __
6 __ nf __ rm
7 __ ns __ st
8 m __ nt __ __ n
9 pr __ p __ s __
10 qu __ st __ __ n
11 r __ v __ __ l

2 Match the reporting verbs in exercise 1 with the definitions.

1 tell someone about something, especially in an official way
2 talk with too much pride about something you have done or can do
3 admit that something is true
4 say that something is true even though you may not be sure, or others don't believe it
5 suggest to someone what you think they should do
6 give reasons why you think something is right or wrong, especially if you are trying to persuade somebody

3 **4.17** Listen to five people talking. Which reporting verb would you use to report what they are saying? Choose from 7–11 in exercise 1.

5F Intensifying adverbs

> **LEARN THIS!**
> • We often use *staggeringly, unbelievably, ridiculously, incredibly* when something is difficult to believe.
> • We often use *highly* with positive adjectives (e.g. *effective, intelligent*) and adjectives that describe probability (e.g. *unlikely*).
> • We use *utterly, totally, absolutely* and *completely* with extreme adjectives.
> • We often use *deeply, bitterly* and *desperately* with adjectives and verbs that describe feelings.
> • We often use *strongly* with verbs that are related to opinions and beliefs (*believe, feel, suggest, oppose*, etc.)

4 Read the Learn this! box. Then match the adverbs in A with the adjectives in B to make common collocations.

A absolutely bitterly deeply highly highly
ridiculously strongly
B expensive freezing probable regret successful
suggest touched

5 Which word does not collocate with the adverb?

1 **deeply:** believe moving religious
2 **ridiculously:** cheap easy impossible
3 **highly:** cold unusual unlikely
4 **strongly:** recommend believe care
5 **totally:** amazing large understand

6 Write sentences to illustrate five of the collocations in exercise 4.

Vocabulary Builder

Unit 6

6C Gender and language

> **LEARN THIS!**
> - Many words which refer to a 'man' that have a generic meaning have now been replaced by 'gender-neutral' words, e.g. *fire fighter* instead of *fireman*.
> - Other male/female pairs have been replaced by a single gender-neutral word, e.g. *chairperson* or *chair* for *chairman/chairwoman*.
> - Ms /məz/ is often preferred to Miss or Mrs.
> - *they* is often used instead of *he* or *she* and *their* is often used instead of *his* or *her*.

1 Read the Learn this! box. Then think of gender-neutral equivalents for the words below.

artists
actor / actress   air steward / air stewardess *cabin crew*
bartender
barman / barmaid   businessman / businesswoman *business person*
tors   *human, kind*
ner cleaning lady   mankind   policeman / policewoman *police officer*
worker   *salesperson*   *spokesperson*
al postman   salesman   spokesman / spokeswoman
waiter / waitress   wife / husband
server   *partners*

2 Rewrite the sentences so that they are more gender-neutral.

1 Harry's wife is an air stewardess.
2 Every salesman must hand in his report immediately.
3 Man and apes have a common ancestor.
4 Please address all complaints to Miss Elliott, the chairwoman of the local council.
5 A lot of actors and actresses struggle to find regular work.
6 Policemen spend far too much time filling in forms.
7 I've just employed a new cleaning lady.

6H Colloquial language and slang

> **LOOK OUT!**
> Slang expressions change over time. They are best avoided by learners, but it's useful to know what they mean if you hear them!

3 Match four of the expressions below with meanings a–d.

fam   go ape   lol   my bad   own somebody   shotgun (v)
sick   soz   yolo

a You only live once.
b claim something for yourself
c defeat someone in an argument
d 'laugh out loud' (expressing amusement)

4 Rewrite the sentences replacing the underlined words with the other five expressions in exercise 3.

1 <u>Sorry</u>. It was <u>my fault</u>.
2 My mum will <u>get really cross</u> if she finds out I stayed up all night.
3 The party was really <u>good</u>!
4 Call round when the <u>family</u> isn't around.

Unit 7

7A Phrasal verbs: travel

1 Match the phrasal verbs below with the definitions. Which verbs are transitive and which are intransitive?

break sth up   drop in on sb   drop sb off   get away
pass through (a place)   pull out   pull over   put sb up
see sb off

1 to move over to the side of the road and stop *pull over*
2 to move away from the side of the road and start driving *pull out*
3 to escape / spend some time in a different place *get away*
4 to leave a passenger in a particular place *drop sb off*
5 to say goodbye to somebody as they start a journey *see sb off*
6 to offer somebody a place to stay *put sb up*
7 to visit somebody (often unexpectedly) *drop in on sb*
8 to interrupt (a journey) *break sth up*
9 to go from one side of a town, region or country to the other on your way to another destination *pass through*

2 Complete the sentences with verbs from exercise 1 in the correct tense.

1 Our car starting making a strange noise, so we had to _____*pull*_____ _____*over*_____ to the side of the road.
2 I've been working so hard, I really need to _____*get*_____ _____*away*_____ for a few days. I think I'll spend a few days by the sea.
3 The taxi couldn't _____*drop*_____ us _____*off*_____ at the airport because of a security alert.
4 When I left for my gap year, my whole family stood on the doorstep to _____*see*_____ me _____*off*_____!
5 The bus _____*pulled*_____ _____*out*_____ suddenly onto the main road and collided with a cyclist.

7F Figurative expressions: *day*

3 Complete the sentences using the idioms below.

any day now   at the end of the day   day in day out
from day one   in this day and age   time to call it a day
the other day

1 If our team wins the league, I'll be overjoyed – but *at the end of the day* it's only a game.
2 I wouldn't say we're close friends, but when you sit next to somebody *from day one* you get to know them well.
3 Her uncle told her that girls don't become engineers – which is a terrible thing to say *in this day and age*
4 We've been revising for hours. Isn't it *time to call it a day*
5 I don't know when my pen-friend is coming to visit, but I should find out *any day now*
6 I heard a song on the radio *the other day* that reminded me of our holiday.
7 When the new managers took over the café, the food and service were better *day in day out*

4 Complete these sentences with your own ideas.

1 From day one, ...
2 It was as clear as day that ...
3 In this day and age,
4 At the end of the day,

V Vocabulary Builder

Unit 8

8A Politics: compounds and collocations

1 Complete the compounds and collocations.

champagne correctness hot spin	climb friends politics soapbox
¹_____ doctor	get on your ⁵_____
political ²_____	⁶_____ the greasy pole
³_____ socialist	have ⁷_____ in high
political ⁴_____	places
potato	play ⁸_____

2 Match the definitions with the compounds and collocations from exercise 1.

1 avoiding language and behaviour that may offend people
2 express strong opinions about a particular topic
3 overcome difficulties and reach the top of your profession
4 do or say something for political or personal reasons rather than out of principle

3 Complete the sentences with the other five compounds and collocations from exercise 1.

1 He's just a _____. He has left-wing views but has no idea what it's like to be hard up.
2 Joel only got the job because he _____.
3 Health care funding is a _____. It's incredibly difficult for any politician to deal with.
4 Government _____ have managed to sell some very unpopular policies to the electorate.

8E Portmanteau words

> **LEARN THIS!**
> A portmanteau word is created when parts of two words are combined, for example *motor* and *hotel* in *motel*.

4 For each portmanteau word, say what you think it means and which two words it is formed from.

banoffee biopic Brexit blog brunch chillax fanzine
glamping malware motel Oxbridge rom-com sitcom
smog skort spork staycation vlog webinar

5 Complete the sentences with words from exercise 4.

1 You need to stop stressing out and just _____ a bit!
2 We often lie in on Sundays and cook ourselves a big _____ at about 11.
3 Have you seen *The Social Network*? It's a _____ about Mark Zuckerberg.
4 52% of the UK population voted for _____, while 48% voted to remain in the EU.
5 My computer has got some nasty _____ in it.
6 The city is covered in _____ from all the factories.
7 You'll need a plastic mug, a bowl and a _____ for your camping trip.
8 Many of the brightest students apply to study at _____ when they leave school.

Unit 9

9A Common sayings

> **LEARN THIS!**
>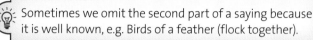
> Sometimes we omit the second part of a saying because it is well known, e.g. Birds of a feather (flock together).

1 Complete the sayings 1–8 with the phrases below. What do you think the sayings mean?

catches the worm   is worth two in the bush
makes Jack a dull boy   on the other side of the fence
saves nine   spoil the broth   there's a way
to make a world

1 My neighbour's favourite pastime is trainspotting. It takes all sorts _____.
2 If I were you, I'd accept that job you've been offered. A bird in the hand _____.
3 We all had a say in decorating our flat, but the end result looked terrible. Two many cooks _____.
4 You ought to come out tonight, you know. All work and no play _____.
5 Let's fix the door before it gets any worse. A stitch in time _____.
6 There's a sale tomorrow, so I'm going to queue up outside the store before it opens. The early bird _____.
7 I'm determined to go Interrailing even if I can't afford it. Where there's a will _____.
8 Don't be so sure you'd be happier living in a big city. The grass is always greener _____.

9C Verb + noun collocations

2 Complete the text with the correct form of the verbs below.

combat deal depose exacerbate face grind sack
swell

THE FALL OF THE WESTERN ROMAN EMPIRE

Stretching from the Atlantic Ocean in the west to the River Euphrates in the east, the Roman Empire ¹_____ a nightmare in administration and logistics. When expansion ²_____ to a halt in the 2nd century, the supply of slaves and war treasures dried up, leading to a labour deficit and severe economic crisis. Government corruption and political instability ³_____ the problem, as did the decision in the late 3rd century to split the empire in two. East and west failed to work together to ⁴_____ the threat posed by the Goths. Unable to recruit enough Roman soldiers, the military turned to these foreigners to ⁵_____ the ranks of the army, which was a recipe for disaster. After killing the Eastern emperor during an uprising in AD 378, the Goths went on to ⁶_____ the city of Rome in AD 410. However, the Western Roman Empire ⁷_____ its deathblow in AD 476 when the Emperor Romulus Augustus ⁸_____, making him the last Roman ruler to govern from Italy.

Introduction

I.1 Past simple and present perfect

Past simple

We use the past simple:

- for specific single or repeated actions or events in the past.
  Dan went climbing every weekend last summer.
- to give further information following a present perfect question or statement.
  'Have you been skiing this year?' 'Yes, I went in January.'

Present perfect and present perfect continuous

We use the present perfect:

- continuous for something which has been happening repeatedly in the very recent past.
  I've been going to gym a lot recently.
- simple when something has happened on several occasions over a period of time and may happen again.
  I've been to the gym three times already this week.
- continuous with *for* or *since* to say how long an action has been in progress.
  I've been learning English since I was five.
- simple or continuous with *for* or *since* with certain verbs, e.g. *live, teach, learn, hope, expect, look, sleep, snow, rain, stay, study,* etc.
  I've lived in London since I was little.
  My dad has been teaching English for years.
- simple with *for* or *since* if the verb is one which is not commonly used in continuous tenses.
  I've loved Chinese food since I went to Beijing.
- simple for a recent action that is now complete.
  I've just finished my homework.
- continuous for a recent action that is ongoing.
  Jamie has been seeing Kate for over two years now. I bet they end up getting married.
- simple in future time clauses with *when, as soon as, until, before,* etc. (The present simple is also often possible.)
  We'll go out as soon as we've finished the washing up.

1 Complete the sentences with the correct past simple or present perfect form of the verbs in brackets.

1 Fran _____ keen on her chemistry teacher at first, but she has since come to really like him. (not be)
2 Lots of people _____ recently that I set up a Facebook account, but I really don't want to. (suggest)
3 Since 1875, when Matthew Webb first _____ across the English Channel, thousands of people _____ to emulate his feat. (swim, attempt)
4 My brother _____ that car since he _____ school ten years ago. (have, leave)
5 How many times _____ you _____ at your mobile phone today? (look)

2 Complete each pair of sentences with one of the verbs below. Use the present perfect simple in one sentence and the present perfect continuous in the other.

disappear read stay stop swim

1 a I _____ all of Agatha Christie's crime stories.
  b I _____ a fantastic book about famous explorers. You can read it after me.
2 a Millie _____ at a friend's house while she looks for a place of her own.
  b I _____ at this campsite on two occasions.
3 a For several months now handbags and coats _____ from the office during the lunch break.
  b I'm sure I left my phone on the table, but it _____!
4 a Now it _____ raining, perhaps we can go to the beach.
  b The police _____ motorists to ask them about the accident.
5 a I _____ in the sea and now my hands are blue with cold!
  b Lucy _____ two kilometres today in the swimming pool.

I.2 Past tenses

Past continuous

We use the past continuous for:

- an action that was in progress at a particular moment in the past or when an interruption happened. (We use the past simple for the interruption.)
  At 8 p.m. yesterday evening, we were having dinner.
  I was getting ready for bed when the phone rang.
- setting the scene.
  It was raining hard. Pedestrians were hurrying along the pavement or sheltering in shop fronts.
- showing that an action is repeated or continuous.
  I was practising the guitar every day but I wasn't getting any better.
  She was singing out of tune and I was trying not to laugh.

Note that we do not use the past continuous with verbs that are not used with continuous tenses (e.g. *believe, understand,* etc.).

Past perfect simple

We use the past perfect simple for:

- an event that happened before another event in the past.
  We arrived at 11.15 but the bus had already left.
- a situation that continued up to a certain point in the past.
  She retired last month. She'd worked at the school for ten years.
- wishes and regrets with expressions like *I wish ..., if only,* etc.
  I wish she hadn't told everyone my news.
  If only we'd arrived ten minutes earlier!

Past perfect continuous

We use the past perfect continuous:

- for an action that continued up to a certain point in the past **or** happened repeatedly up to that point.
  The announcement wasn't a surprise: everyone had been expecting it.
  I knew her well. We'd been going to the same dance class every week for years.

Grammar Builder and Reference

- to explain what led to a particular situation in the past.
  My shoes were muddy because I'd been playing football in the park.
- to say how long a situation had been in progress.
  He'd been trying to find a new job for months.
- for wishes and regrets with expressions like *I wish ...*, *if only*, etc.
  I wish you'd been listening.
  If only I hadn't been wearing sandals!

Note that we do not use the past perfect continuous with verbs that are not used with continuous tenses (e.g. *believe*, *understand*, etc.).

1 Choose the correct option to complete these sentences, a, b or both.

1 I turned the volume up as soon as my parents _____ the room.
   a left **b** had left
2 Kyle couldn't go to the park with me because he _____ his homework yet.
   a didn't finish **b** hadn't finished
3 I wish I had my phone with me. If only I _____ it at home today!
   a didn't leave **b** hadn't left
4 By the time it _____ raining, it was too late to play basketball.
   a stopped **b** had stopped
5 First, we took the bike apart, then we _____ it.
   a cleaned **b** had cleaned
6 My brother missed a week of school because he _____ his arm.
   a broke **b** had broken
7 I enjoyed playing her at tennis, but I wish _____.
   a I won **b** I'd won

2 Complete the sentences with the correct past tense form of the verb in brackets. Sometimes more than one answer is possible.

1 I went back to the shop to look at the guitar again, but unfortunately it wasn't there – somebody _____ (buy) it.
2 As I opened the door, everyone _____ (become) silent, and I knew at once that they _____ (talk) about me.
3 It was 10 p.m., and although I _____ (write) for nearly an hour, I still _____ (not finish) the letter yet.
4 One of the glasses _____ (break) as I _____ (put) them back in the cupboard.
5 When I got home, I saw that Bess _____ (sit) on the front doorstep. I wish she _____ (tell) me she was there!
6 I _____ (take) off my football boots, _____ (clean) them and _____ (leave) them in the sun to dry.

3 Correct the mistakes. Some sentences do not have a mistake.

1 Before the summer, the team were training hard twice a week, but they weren't winning many matches.
2 Although I'd been watching the film for nearly an hour, I hadn't been understanding much of the plot.
3 It had snowed a lot overnight, but by the time we left the house, it didn't snow any longer.
4 As my mum was climbing out of the boat, she was falling into the river with a big splash.
5 If only I hadn't spent all my money on presents!
6 While she washed up, she accidentally broke a plate.
7 I didn't get a very good mark in my science test because I hadn't been finishing all the questions.
8 I loved football when I was at primary school. If I wasn't playing football, I was reading about it.

I.3 Articles

Indefinite article *a / an*

We use the indefinite article *a / an*:
- when we say what something is or what it is like.
  What's that? It's a mobile phone.
  My sister lives in a large country house.
- when we say what somebody's job is.
  My dad is a plumber.
- when we mention something for the first time.
  I've got a cat and a dog.
- when we mean 'any example of something'.
  We need to find a bank.
- to mean 'per' or for 'each'.
  I earn £100 a week.
  The car was travelling at 70 kilometres an hour.
- with names, to indicate that this is the first time we have become aware of that person.
  I've had a letter from a Mrs Joanna Black.

a / an* and *one

We can use either *one* or *a / an* when we are talking about an exact number, time, etc.
My guinea pig weighs nearly one kilo / a kilo.
I spent one week / a week in China.
Can you wait one minute / a minute?
We use *one* (but not *a / an*):
- when we need to emphasise the number.
  Do you want one biscuit or two?
- when we use it in expressions with *other* or *another*.
  We travelled from one town to another by bus.
  He passed the key from one hand to the other.
- when we are referring to a particular day, time, etc.
  We should go into town one day soon.
  One morning in July, he set off on a long bike ride.

Definite article *the*

We use the definite article *the*:
- when it is clear what we are talking about. This can be a) because we've already mentioned it, b) because there is only one of something, c) because it is clear from the situation.

Grammar Builder and Reference

a I've got a cat and a dog. The dog is called Buster.
b What time will the sun rise tomorrow morning?
c Let's go to the beach. (The beach that's near here.)

- with superlative forms.
  It's the largest hotel in the world.
- with adjectives, including nationality adjectives, to refer to everybody who has that characteristic.
  The French have a reputation for being good cooks.
  Only the rich can afford to fly first class.
- with the names of rivers, mountain ranges, deserts and seas.
  the Amazon, the Alps, the Gobi desert, the Mediterranean
- with a few countries (usually plural) and most groups of islands.
  the United Kingdom   the United States
  the Netherlands   the Czech Republic
  the Channel Islands
- with most large organisations.
  the United Nations   the European Union
  the Red Cross   the World Trade Organisation
- in various set phrases, for example:
  go to the theatre / cinema   listen to the radio / the news
  play the violin / the piano, etc.

Emphatic form of definite article
We use the stressed form of the (which rhymes with 'tea'):

- to indicate that we are referring to the best or primary example of something.
  For many years, Tuscany was the holiday destination for the British middle classes.
- with names, to indicate that we are talking about a famous person, not somebody else with the same name.
  My next door neighbour is called Katy Perry. She isn't the Katy Perry, of course!

Zero article
We don't use an article:

- with most countries, continents, languages, towns, lakes and mountains.
  I live in Berlin, in Germany. I speak German.
  Chicago is built on the shores of Lake Michigan.
  My cousin climbed Mount Everest.
- in various set phrases, often including a preposition, for example:
  watch television
  go to work / school   go home
  be in bed / hospital / prison
- with meals.
  have breakfast / lunch / dinner

Making generalisations
We normally use no article + plural or uncountable noun for generalisations, but we can also use the indefinite article + singular noun. We do not use the definite article in this kind of sentence.
Wide, straight roads are ideal for cyclists.
A wide, straight road is ideal for a cyclist. ✔
NOT ~~The wide, straight roads are ideal for the cyclists.~~ ✗

1 Choose the correct article.

1 There's **a** / **the** hotel on the corner of our road, and opposite **a** / **the** hotel is **a** / **the** three-storey house.
2 I'd like to get **a** / **the** dog, but my parents think it would be too much work. After all, **a** / **the** dog needs at least two walks **a** / **the** day.
3 We had **a** / **the** fantastic two-week holiday in **–** / **the** Canary Islands.
4 I go to **–** / **the** cinema quite often but I rarely watch **–** / **the** DVDs at home.
5 My cousin is **–** / **an** interpreter at **–** / **the** European Parliament in **–** / **the** Brussels.
6 For **–** / **the** homework, I had to write **an** / **the** essay on the history of **–** / **the** West Indies.

2 Complete the text with *a* / *an*, *the* or **–** (no article).

The idea that teenagers are destroying [1]_____ English language by using [2]_____ slang has been around since [3]_____ 1950s or earlier. Back then, English parents blamed teenagers in [4]_____ United States for spreading bad habits across [5]_____ Atlantic. These days, texts and instant messages are often seen as [6]_____ culprits. Teenagers have forgotten how to use [7]_____ English properly, people claim, because they use such [8]_____ informal style when they communicate with each other. But most linguists disagree, arguing that teenagers are enriching the language rather than destroying it. While [9]_____ teenager may use a great deal of slang and abbreviations with his or her peers, that same teenager would speak in [10]_____ very different way during [11]_____ job interview, for example. And although teenagers often don't use [12]_____ capital letters to start sentences in [13]_____ messages, they know they need to do it in a more formal piece of writing like [14]_____ essay.

I.4 Talking about the future

We use *will* + infinitive:

- for instant decisions, offers, promises, requests, refusals.
  'Can you ring Jo?' 'No time now. I'll text her later!'
  It's pouring down. I'll give you a lift home.
  I'll always love you.
- to talk about facts in the future and to make predictions.
  The sun will rise at 7.32 tomorrow.
  You'll never get the car into the garage. It's too wide.

We use *going to* + infinitive:

- for plans and intentions that we have already decided on before speaking.
  We've already booked our holiday. We're going to visit Rome.
- to make predictions about the future based on current evidence.
  It's nearly two and we haven't reached the stadium yet. We're going to miss the start of the match.

We use the present continuous to talk about personal arrangements we have already made.
I'm meeting Jason outside the cinema after work.

We use the present simple to talk about the timetables of future activities and events.

Our train gets in at 4.30 tomorrow.

1 Choose the sentence (a or b) which follows the first sentence better.

1 Fran can't come clubbing with us tonight.
   a She'll go to the cinema with Jeremy.
   b She's going to the cinema with Jeremy.
2 Harry has been saving half his salary every month.
   a He's going to buy a motorbike.
   b He'll buy a motorbike.
3 There's a live screening of an Ed Sheeran concert tonight.
   a It's starting at eight.
   b It starts at eight.
4 Darren is as white as a sheet.
   a I think he's going to be sick.
   b I think he'll be sick.
5 Why don't you go to the seaside for a few days?
   a The sea air is going to do you good.
   b The sea air will do you good.

2 Complete the dialogues with *will*, *going to*, the present simple or continuous. Use the verb in brackets.

1 A Shall we take the bus to town?
   B No, let's drive. It _____ a lot quicker. (be)
2 A What time do you have to be at the airport?
   B At about four. The plane _____ at 6.10. (depart)
3 A How about going for a walk after dinner?
   B Sorry, I can't. I _____ with Sam. (go out)
4 A Why have you bought an exercise bike?
   B Because I _____ and get fit. (try)
5 A Why are you taking your umbrella?
   B Because I can see that it _____. (rain)

Unit 1

1.1 Question forms

Subject and object questions

The following question words can be the subject or object of a question: *Who?*, *Which (one / ones)?* and *What?*

When the question word is the object, it is followed by an interrogative verb form.

Who do you know at this party? (I know everybody.)
What did you buy? (I bought a T-shirt.)

When the question includes a preposition, we use the object form. We usually put the preposition at the end.

Who did you talk to? (I talked to Sally.)

When the question word is the subject, it is followed by a normal, affirmative verb form.

Who lives in that house? (Justin lives in that house.)
Which car won the race? (The red car won the race.)

We only include the auxiliary (*do, does*, etc.) in a subject question for extra emphasis.

'I didn't break your phone.' 'Well who did break it then?'

Reply questions

We use reply questions to query a statement.

'She's Dutch.' 'Is she? I thought she was German.'

We use an affirmative reply question after an affirmative statement and a negative reply question after a negative statement.

'It's nine o'clock.' 'Is it? I should go home.'
'I'm not ready.' 'Aren't you? Well, hurry up!'

If the sentence includes a modal verb (*can, should, will, might*, etc.), we use it in the reply question.

'My sister can't skate.' 'Can't she?'
'I won't be late.' 'Won't you?'

If the sentence includes an auxiliary verb (*is/are, have, had*, etc.), we use it in the reply question.

'It's raining.' 'Is it?'
'I haven't finished yet.' 'Haven't you?'

If the sentence doesn't include an auxiliary verb, we use *do/does* (or *did*) in the reply question.

'This milk smells funny.' 'Does it?'
'I bought this shirt in New York.' 'Did you?'

We use *they* as the pronoun for *everyone / everybody* and *no one / nobody*. We use *it* as the pronoun for *everything* and *nothing*. Note that we use a negative reply question after *nobody* or *nothing* because the sense is negative, even if the verb form is affirmative.

'Nobody likes this song.' 'Don't they?'
'Everyone agreed with you.' 'Did they?'
'Everything's wet.' 'Is it?'
'Nothing really bothers me.' 'Doesn't it?'

Notice the word order when we use a full form of the negative in a reply question, compared with the short form.

'Maria wouldn't enjoy this film.' 'Wouldn't she?' / 'Would she not?'

Negative questions

We use negative questions to:
- ask for confirmation. The expected answer is yes.
  Doesn't your friend work in New York? (= I'm fairly sure your friend works in New York but I'd like you to confirm it.)
- express surprise.
  I love this film. Aren't you enjoying it? (= I'm surprised you aren't enjoying it.)

Notice the word order when we use a full form of the negative, compared with the short form.

Can't you hear that noise?
Can you not hear that noise?

Elliptical questions *Why (not)* ...?

We sometimes ask questions using *Why (not)* ...? with a base form rather than a finite verb.

The bus service into town is great. Why drive? (= What is the point of driving?)
Those T-shirts are really cheap. Why not buy two? (= Why don't you buy two?)

We sometimes ask questions using *Why* ...? without a verb at all.

Why all the noise? (= Why are you making so much noise?)

1 Write one object question and one subject question for each sentence. Write answers for both questions.

1 Jo sat next to the teacher.
   Who did Jo sit next to?   *The teacher.*
   Who sat next to the teacher? *Jo.*
2 At the party, his sister sang an Ed Sheeran song.
3 The bus drove into the wall.
4 Anita plays the violin.
5 Tyler listened to Molly's presentation.
6 Emily reads *The Economist* magazine every week.

2 Write reply questions for these statements in your notebook.

1 Nothing unusual happened last night.
   Didn't it?
2 Nobody can speak ten languages.
3 There weren't any humans when dinosaurs were alive.
4 Gorillas can't swim.
5 The population of the UK is growing.
6 Captain Scott died on his way home from the South Pole.

3 Rewrite the underlined sentences in your notebook to include negative questions.

1 I spoke to your brother about the party yesterday. <u>I'm surprised he didn't tell you.</u> *Didn't he tell you?*
2 Mr Wyatt is our English teacher this year. <u>I'm pretty sure he was your teacher last year.</u>
3 I remember the last time we went for a bike ride. <u>I think we got lost.</u>
4 The maths test isn't today. <u>I think it's on Tuesday.</u>
5 <u>I'm surprised you haven't heard.</u> I've been offered a place at university.
6 <u>I think you've been learning Spanish.</u> Why don't you say something to my Spanish pen-friend?

1.2 Habitual actions

Talking about habitual actions
To talk about habitual actions in the present, we can use:
- the present simple with an adverb of frequency.
  She often goes to work by bicycle.
- *will* with an adverb of frequency.
  He'll sometimes go to the park on the way home from school.

To talk about habitual actions in the past, we can use:
- the past simple with an adverb of frequency.
  I always had milk before bed when I was young.
- *used to* (negative: *didn't use to*). It often implies a contrast with the present.
  I used to have piano lessons. (I don't have them now.)
  The bus didn't use to stop on the High Street. (It stops there now.)
- *would* (short form: *'d*).
  Every summer, we'd go to the same hotel by the sea.

Note that we do not use *would* to talk about states, only habitual actions. For states, we use *used to*.
   I used to be very shy. ✓ NOT ~~I would be very shy.~~ ✗

We also use certain verbs and phrases to talk about habits. For example:

keep doing something	*tend to do something*
have a habit of doing	*have a tendency to do something*
be apt to do something	*be prone to do something*

Criticising habitual actions
To talk about annoying repeated behaviour, we use:
- the present / past continuous with the adverbs *always*, *constantly*, *continually* or *forever*.
  She's always complaining about her job.
  They were forever shouting at each other.
- *will* or *would* (emphatic form). We use *will* for the present and *would* for the past.
  She will stay up late watching TV, even when she needs to get up early the next morning.
  When I was at primary school, my mum would insist on giving me a goodbye kiss in front of all my friends.

1 Choose the correct option to complete the sentences.

1 My brother often _____ with his bedroom light on.
   a falls asleep   **b** is falling asleep
2 Her parents _____ about money a lot.
   a used to argue   **b** were forever arguing
3 My sister _____ her clothes on the bathroom floor.
   a will forever leave   **b** will leave
4 We _____ into trouble when we were kids.
   a would often get   **b** tend to get
5 On Sundays, the whole family _____ lunch together.
   a would have   **b** was having
6 At school, you _____ trying to make me laugh during lessons.
   a tended   **b** kept
7 My sister _____ very keen on horses when she was younger.
   a would be   **b** used to be
8 I loved seeing my grandfather when I was a child. He _____ us.
   a would often visit   **b** was always visiting

2 Rewrite the sentences in your notebook to include a different way of talking about habitual actions. Use the word in brackets.

1 You were always trying to read my diary when we were children. (would)
2 She'll often buy a coffee on her way to work. (habit)
3 He tends not to work late on Fridays. (won't)
4 My neighbours are forever playing loud music late at night. (keep)
5 After school, I would often meet friends in town. (used)
6 I didn't use to say anything in English classes. (wouldn't)
7 At weekends, my brother will spend hours playing computer games. (often)
8 Our dog had a habit of burying my footballs in the garden. (apt)

Grammar Builder and Reference

Unit 2

2.1 Conditionals

Second conditional
- We use the second conditional to talk about an imaginary situation or event and its result in the present or future.
- We form the second conditional with the past simple in the conditional *if* clause and *would* + bare infinitive in the result clause. It is also possible to put the *if* clause at the end of the sentence. Furthermore, *were* can be used instead of *was* in the conditional clause with *I, he* and *she*.

conditional clause	result clause
if + past simple	*would* + bare infinitive

If you lived in Madrid, you'd quickly learn Spanish.

Third conditional
- We use the third conditional to talk about the imaginary result of things that didn't happen in the past. It is often used to express criticism or regret.
- We form the third conditional with *if* + past perfect, *would have* + past participle. It is also possible to put the *if* clause at the end of the sentence.

conditional clause	result clause
if + past perfect	*would have* + past participle

If you had got up earlier, you wouldn't have missed the bus.

Mixed conditional
- We use mixed conditionals to talk about imaginary situations and events and their results in the present or past. They are a mixture of second and third conditionals.

conditional clause	result clause
if + past perfect	*would* + infinitive
if + past simple	*would have* + past participle

If you'd worn a coat, you wouldn't have a bad cold now.
If I owned a warm coat, I'd have worn it.

Inversion
In a more formal style in *if* clauses that contain the auxiliary verbs *should, were* or *had*, we can omit *if* and invert the subject and auxiliary verb.
Had I seen him, I would have told you. (If I had seen him, I would have told you.)

Alternatives to *if*
We can use *unless* instead of *if* ... *not* when we want to say we'll do the first thing if the second condition does not happen.
We'll have a barbeque unless it rains. (= if it doesn't rain)

We can sometimes use *so/as long as* or *provided that* instead of *if* in first conditional sentences.
We can watch the film as long as it's not too late.

In case introduces a possibility against which a precaution is needed.
Hold on to the handrail in case you slip.

We can use *what if* ...? or *supposing (that)* to ask somebody to imagine that something will happen or that something is true.
Supposing you fail the exam, what will you do?
What if you fail the exam?

1 Rewrite the sentences in your notebook with a first, second, third or a mixed conditional. Begin with the word in brackets.

1 Kate works in London. She spends a lot of time commuting. (If)
   If Kate didn't work in London, she wouldn't spend a lot of time commuting.
2 John hasn't applied to university. He'd get in if he did. (Were)
3 Harry didn't bring any water on the walk. He's really thirsty now. (If)
4 Joe spent all his money on phone apps. He's short of money now. (Joe)
5 I didn't know you hated pizza. I bought one for you. (If)
6 What will you do if you can't sell your house? (Supposing)
7 Sarah didn't lose her way. She arrived on time. (Had)
8 If they don't start winning matches, they will come bottom of the league. (Unless)

2 Complete the sentences with *unless, in case, supposing, what if, as long as,* or *provided that.* Sometimes more than one answer is possible.

1 _____ it rains tomorrow, what will you do?
2 Here's £5 _____ you need to buy lunch for yourself.
3 I'll assume he isn't coming to the party _____ he texts me to say he is.
4 _____ we can't stop global warning?
5 I'll lend you the money _____ you promise to pay me back.
6 Take your mobile with you _____ you need to get in touch.
7 I'll get to your house by about eleven _____ there aren't any major hold-ups on the roads.
8 You won't do very well in your exams _____ you put in a bit more effort.
9 _____ you're wondering why Liam is late, he missed his train.

2.2 Inversion of subject and verb (1)

Some adverbs can be used at the beginning of a sentence to add emphasis. The effect can also be to make the sentence sound more formal. In these cases the auxiliary verb is put before the subject. If there is no auxiliary verb, *do, does* or *did* is used.

Negative or near-negative adverbs (e.g. *never, not since, no longer, in no way, only, rarely, seldom,* etc.).
Never have I heard such a ridiculous thing! (= I've never heard such a ridiculous thing!)
Rarely did she write letters to her parents. (= She rarely wrote letters to her parents.)
- The adverbs *well* and *little*.
  Little did I know what would happen next. (= I little knew what would happen next.)

- *So* and *such* with *that* to express result.
  Such was his surprise that he fell off his chair.
  So embarrassed was he that he left the room.
- Adverbial expressions of place and movement (e.g. *in front of me, up, down, along, in, out, here, there*, etc.), especially when they are followed by intransitive verbs such as *come, sit, stand* or *walk*.
  Down the stairs he ran. (He ran down the stairs.)
  Words that describe certain noises, e.g. *bang, crash, pop*.
  Pop went the balloon. (The balloon went pop.)
  In conditional sentences with clauses that contain the auxiliary verbs *should, were* or *had*, we can omit *if* and invert the subject and auxiliary verb. (See 2.1 Conditionals: inversion).

1 Rewrite the sentences in your notebook with the underlined word(s) at the start of the sentence.

1 She was <u>so</u> upset that she burst into tears. *So upset was she, that she burst into tears.*
2 He'd <u>never</u> had such an adventure.
3 I've <u>rarely</u> heard a cuckoo in this part of the country.
4 I am <u>in no way</u> responsible for his bad behaviour.
5 My embarrassment was <u>such</u> that I blushed deeply.
6 We <u>little</u> realised the danger we were in.
7 The tree fell <u>down</u> with a great crash.
8 I realised you were there <u>only when</u> you spoke.

2.3 Inversion of subject and verb (2)

When placed at the start of the sentence, some adverbials require other changes in addition to the inversion of subject and verb.

- With *No sooner* ..., the main clause starts with *than*. (NB *No sooner ... than* is not used for future events.)
  No sooner did I see him than I realised we'd met before.
  (As soon as I saw him, I realised we'd met before.)
- We use *not only* ... *but also* ... to emphasise that two events have happened.
  Not only did his wife leave him, but he also lost his job!
  (He lost his job and his wife left him as well!)
- *Either* with a negative verb can change to *neither / nor* ... with an affirmative verb.
  I'm not hungry, nor am I thirsty. (I'm not hungry and I'm not thirsty either.)
- *Under any circumstances* with a negative verb can change to *under no circumstances* with an affirmative verb.
  Under no circumstances should you smoke. (You shouldn't smoke under any circumstances.)
- *Anywhere* with a negative verb can change to *nowhere* with an affirmative verb.
  Nowhere could we find a parking place. (We couldn't find a parking place anywhere.)
- *For one moment / second* with a negative verb can change to *not for one moment / second* with an affirmative verb.
  Not for one second did she hesitate. (She didn't hesitate for one second.)

- *Until* ... with a negative verb can change to *not until* ... with an affirmative verb.
  Not until he reached home did he stop running. (He didn't stop running until he reached home.)

1 Complete the second sentence so that the meaning is the same.

1 It was only when the smoke alarm went off that we realised the house was on fire.
  Not until *the smoke alarm went off did we realise that the house was on fire.*
2 As soon as Ben arrived, he started an argument.
  No sooner _____.
3 The manager couldn't find the keys to the safe anywhere.
  Nowhere _____.
4 We had no idea that grandad was so ill.
  Little _____.
5 Liam let me stay in his flat, and he let me use his car.
  Not only _____.
6 We only stopped working when it was too dark to see.
  Not until _____.

Unit 3

3.1 Reporting structures

We use direct speech to repeat the exact words that someone said. We use reported speech to report what someone has said but without using the exact words.
Anne said, 'It was an incredible concert. We had a fantastic time.'
Anne said they had really enjoyed the concert.

When we change direct speech to reported speech, we usually change the tense of the sentence, the pronouns and possessive adjectives from first and second person to third person, and the time expressions.
'I had an interview yesterday', said John.
John said he had had an interview the day before.

Reporting verbs
We can use a number of other reporting verbs to introduce reported statements apart from *say* and *tell*. These verbs are used with a variety of structures. A few verbs are used with more than one structure.

- verb + infinitive with *to*: *agree, ask, claim, offer, promise, refuse, threaten*
  She refused to see him.
- verb + object + infinitive with *to*: *advise, beg, dare, encourage, order, remind, urge, warn*
  He encouraged her to go out with her friends.
- verb + gerund: *admit, advise, deny, mention, recommend, regret, suggest*
  They mentioned seeing him at the party.
- verb + preposition + gerund: *admit to, apologise for, confess to, insist on*
  He confessed to loving another woman.
- verb + object + preposition + gerund: *accuse sb of, blame sb for, warn sb against*
  She accused him of being unfaithful.

Grammar Builder and Reference

- verb + *that* + *should* clause: *demand, propose, recommend, request, suggest*
  She demanded that he should leave immediately.
- verb + question word / *if* or *whether*: *ask, enquire, wonder*
  I wondered what she was thinking.

Formal reporting structures

The following reporting structures are more formal than the structures above.

- verb + perfect gerund (*having* + past participle)
  They mentioned having seen him at the party.
- verb + preposition + object pronoun (*me*) / possessive adjective (*my*) + gerund
  He confessed to his loving another woman.
- verb + present subjunctive (infinitive without *to*)
  She demanded that he leave immediately.

1 Compete the sentences with the correct form of the verb in brackets.

1 I apologised for _____ the day before. (not call)
2 He promised _____ fun of her again. (not make)
3 They blamed me for _____ the rumour. (spread)
4 She begged him _____ her. (forgive)
5 I enquired whether they _____ for lunch. (stay)
6 She insisted on _____ his parents. (meet)
7 They urged us _____ anyone. (not tell)
8 He regretted _____ himself to Hannah. (not introduce)

2 Choose the structure that cannot be used with the verbs.

1 She requested that _____ the truth.
   a he tell her   b he tells her   c he should tell her
2 I warned him _____ my photo on social media.
   a not posting   b not to post   c against posting
3 You asked _____ me.
   a to see   b seeing   c if you could see
4 He admitted _____ my e-reader.
   a losing   b to lose   c to having lost
5 He insisted on _____ her home.
   a accompanying   b his accompanying   c he accompany
6 We recommended _____ a lawyer.
   a seeing   b to see   c that he should see
7 They advised _____ early to avoid the crowds.
   a going   b us to go   c to go
8 She suggested _____ that evening.
   a to eat out   b eating out   c that we should eat out

3 Report the sentences using the verbs below.

accused advised dared insisted regretted requested
threatened wondered

1 'You've taken my headphones!'
   My sister accused me of taking her headphones.
2 'I'll tell your parents if you're late for school again.'
   Jack's teacher _____
3 'We're sorry we didn't go on the trip.'
   My friends _____.
4 'I must wear my new boots to the party.'
   Sandra _____.

5 'I wouldn't study political science if I were you.'
   My father _____.
6 'When will you be home?'
   Matt's mother _____.
7 'Would you follow me, please?'
   Our guide _____.
8 'I bet you aren't brave enough to do a bungee jump!'
   Katie's friends _____.

3.2 Comparative and superlative structures

Comparative and superlative adjectives and adverbs are formed with -er and -est or more / most and less / least unless they are irregular.

adjective / adverb	comparative	superlative
hard	harder	the hardest
stunning	more stunning	the most stunning
badly	worse	the worst

Some determiners also have comparative and superlative forms.
few fewer   the fewest (followed by a countable noun)
little less   the least (followed by an uncountable noun)
There are fewer people living in my village now than ten years ago.
I'd like to stay in the least expensive hotel we can find, if you don't mind.

Comparatives may be followed by a noun, a pronoun or a clause.
My mother's more absent-minded than my father.
I'm less resourceful than you.
The exam was more difficult than I had expected.

We can talk about a gradual change by repeating a comparative form.
The streets are becoming more and more dangerous for pedestrians.

We can use this comparative structure to show that two things change because they are connected.
The sooner we start, the earlier we'll finish.

We can use the following words to qualify comparatives: (so / very) much, far, a good deal, a lot, lots, even, slightly, a little, a bit, no.
She's slightly older than he is.

We can use the following words to qualify comparatives with *as ... as*: just, almost, nearly, nowhere near, nothing like.
We were just as gob-smacked as they were.

Advanced comparisons

We can use the following words to qualify superlatives: by far, easily, almost, nearly, practically.
She's by far the most interesting person I know.

We can use half, twice, three times, etc. before as ... as to make a comparison. We can use three times, etc. before a comparative, but not half or twice.
She married a man who was twice as old as her.
You can run three times faster than me.

We can leave comparisons with *as ... as* uncompleted to avoid repetition.
She's as fluent as me, but she isn't as accurate (as me).

Grammar Builder and Reference

as and like

Like is a preposition and it is used with a noun or a pronoun to describe similarities.

My brother's just like my dad. He isn't like me at all!

As is a conjunction and it is used before a clause to describe similarities.

He's a good player, as his father was when he was younger.

However, in informal speech *like* is also often used as a conjunction.

She doesn't dress like you do. She hasn't got your style.

In written English, when *as* is followed by an auxiliary or modal verb we often invert the word order.

He's a good player, as was his father when he was younger.

As is used to talk about a role or a function. In this case it operates in the same way as a preposition.

As your teacher, I recommend you work harder. (I'm your teacher.)

If we replace *as* with *like* in this sentence, it changes the meaning. *As* means 'I am your teacher' and *like* means 'I have the same opinion as your teacher.'

Like your teacher, I recommend you work harder. (I'm not your teacher, but I share the same opinion.)

1 Complete the sentences with a comparative or superlative form of the words in brackets.

1 The more you study, the _____ (good).
2 Friendship is one of the _____ (valuable) things in life.
3 The _____ (old) you get, the faster time seems to fly.
4 Crime is _____ (common) in the country than it is in big cities.
5 The _____ (fast) she speaks the _____ (intelligible) she becomes.
6 There seem to be _____ (few) shops on the High Street than there used to be.
7 Most people are at their _____ (low) when they come home from a holiday.
8 This has got to be the _____ (interesting) programme on TV. Can we change channels?

2 Choose the correct words.

1 The food was superb, **as / like** the service.
2 '**As / Like** your mother, I think you play too many games,' said his dad.
3 She's **slightly / practically** the most creative student in our class.
4 My family's **as / like** yours in some respects.
5 He's more hardworking than me, but he isn't **as / more** organised.
6 '**As / Like** your doctor, I recommend that you exercise more,' Dr Atkins said.
7 My new laptop works **twice / three** times faster than my old one.
8 There are **fewer / less** students in my class this year than there were last year.

3 Complete the second sentence so that it has the same meaning as the first. Use the word in brackets. Write between three and six words.

1 You weren't half as sociable in the past as you are today.
Today you're *twice as sociable as you used* to be. (used)
2 I do your accounts, so I'm advising you to cut down your expenses.
_____, I'm advising you to cut down your expenses. (accountant)
3 Nobody I know can swim anywhere near as well as my sister.
My sister is _____ I know. (far)
4 My cousin and my uncle are very similar – they're both passionate about football.
My cousin _____ – they're both passionate about football. (just)
5 The sequel is more entertaining than the first part, but the acting is worse.
The sequel is more entertaining than the first, but _____. (as)
6 Life is much harder in Africa than it is in Europe.
Life isn't _____ it is in Africa. (nearly)
7 Oscar's father set up his own business, and Oscar wants to do the same.
Oscar wants to set up his own business, _____ father before him. (his)
8 If you wait for something for a long time, you appreciate it more.
_____, the more you appreciate it. (the)

Unit 4

4.1 Compound future tenses

Future continuous

We form the future continuous with *will / won't + be + -ing* form.
I'll be playing basketball.

We use the future continuous to:
- talk about an action that will be in progress at a certain point in the future.
  This time tomorrow, I'll be taking my driving test.
- talk about a plan or arrangement which is definite (e.g. part of an itinerary).
  This afternoon, we'll be visiting the Houses of Parliament.
  This train will not be stopping at Birmingham.
- make polite enquiries in a formal situation.
  Will you be having breakfast at the hotel?
- speculate about something happening now.
  I'm sure Louis will be having a great time in the USA. He won't be worrying about his exams.

Note that we sometimes use the future continuous with the verbs *want* and *need*, which are not normally used in continuous tenses.

He'll be wanting dinner as soon as he gets home.
Will you be needing the car tomorrow?

Future perfect simple

We form the future perfect simple with *will / won't + have +* past participle.

I'll have finished by nine o'clock.

We use the future perfect simple to:

- say how long a situation will have existed by a certain point in the future.
  On 15 August, we'll have been married for five years.
- talk about a completed or uncompleted action in the future.
  I won't have finished this essay by the end of the lesson.
  This time next year, we'll have left school.
- speculate about a completed action in the present.
  Let's go outside. The rain will have stopped by now.
  Tyler is good at keeping secrets. He won't have told anyone.

Future perfect continuous

We form the future perfect continuous with *will / won't + have been + -ing* form.

I'll have been playing basketball.

We use the future perfect continuous to:

- say how long an action will have been in progress by a certain point in the future.
  This July, we'll have been living in this house for ten years.
- talk about a continuous action in the future that explains a particular situation.
  I won't feel like going out tomorrow night. I'll have been working all day.
- speculate about a continuous or repeated action that has continued up to the present.
  I doubt Harry has done his homework yet. He'll have been playing computer games all morning.

Compound future tenses: the passive

Note that we often use the future perfect simple in the passive but not the future continuous or future perfect continuous.

The email will already have been sent.
They'll be decorating our house tomorrow. / We'll be having our house decorated tomorrow. ✓
NOT ~~Our house will be being decorated tomorrow.~~ ✗
They'll have been making films for a hundred years. ✓
NOT ~~Films will have been being made for a hundred years.~~ ✗

1 Make predictions about your future. Use the prompts below and the future continuous or future perfect simple.

1 in ten years / live abroad
   In ten years, I'll be living abroad / I won't be living abroad.
2 at midnight tonight / sleep
3 this time next year / leave school
4 by the time I'm nineteen / pass my driving test
5 in five years / leave home
6 in ten years / get married
7 in fifteen years / still live in this town
8 by the age of forty / have more than ten different jobs
9 at fifty / see friends I made at school
10 in fifty years / still work

2 Complete the sentences with the future continuous or future perfect continuous.

1 I _____ (drive) to London tomorrow. Would you like a lift?
2 You can use my bike tomorrow, if you want. I _____ (not need) it.
3 Let's meet at the airport. I _____ (arrive) around midday.
4 My grandfather retires next year. He _____ (work) since the age of sixteen.
5 My new passport still hasn't arrived. By tomorrow, I _____ (wait) three months for it.
6 _____ you _____ (want) dinner at the hotel tomorrow evening?
7 Kyle has left the country and he _____ (not come) back again until the summer.
8 I think July is too soon to take your driving test. You _____ (not learn) for long enough.

3 Rewrite the sentences in your notebook using the future continuous, future perfect simple or future perfect continuous.

1 I expect Kyle is staying with his cousins.
   Kyle will be staying with his cousins.
2 I imagine the film has finished by now.
3 It's unlikely that they've started the match without me.
4 I guess his sister is working hard for her exams.
5 I expect they've been discussing the party for weeks.
6 It's probable that Becky is having weekly driving lessons.
7 I'm sure he bought his tickets online.
8 I doubt that my parents are worrying about me.
9 I expect he wants to spend the weekend with his friends.

4.2 Quantity

some, any and no

We can use *some* with plural and uncountable nouns:

- in affirmative sentences to mean 'a number of'.
  We've got some coffee and biscuits.
- in offers.
  Would you like some tea?
- to mean 'certain ones' in contrast with others. We give the word extra emphasis to convey this meaning.
  Some sharks attack humans but most sharks avoid them.

We can use *any* with plural and uncountable nouns:

- in negative sentences and questions.
  We haven't got any biscuits. Have we got any coffee?
- in affirmative sentences where the meaning is negative.
  I came out without any money.

We can use *any* before singular, plural or uncountable nouns in affirmative sentences to mean 'it doesn't matter which'.
Visitors from any country are welcome here.

We can use *no* (meaning *not any*) to be slightly more emphatic. Note that we use an affirmative verb with *no*.
There's no cheese in the fridge.

much, many, a lot of, etc.

We use these quantifiers with uncountable nouns to talk about a large quantity of something.

a lot of / lots of   loads of (colloquial)   much   a good deal of   a great deal of   a large amount of

We use these quantifiers with countable nouns to talk about a large number of something.

a lot of / lots of   loads of (colloquial)   many   a large number of

Note that in affirmative sentences, *much* and *many* are quite formal and sometimes unnatural. In spoken English, we would normally use *a lot of* instead.

I ate a lot of food at lunchtime. ✓

NOT I ate much food at lunchtime. ✗

(a) few and (a) little

We use *few / a few* with plural nouns and *little / a little* with uncountable nouns.

A few of the trees have already lost their leaves.

We've only got a little time.

We use *few / little* instead of *a few / a little* to emphasise the smallness of the number or quantity.

He has little money and few friends.

all, the whole and (a / one) half

We use *the whole* with singular countable nouns.

We redecorated the whole house.

We use *all* with uncountable nouns and plural nouns.

We redecorated all the rooms in the house.

Have we used up all the bread?

We use *half* with uncountable nouns and plural nouns.

We've only done about half the work.

About half the people here are from Iran.

Note that if we say *a half* or *one half* it must followed by *of*.

About a / one half of the people here are from Iran.

both, either and neither

We use *both, either* and *neither* to talk about two things. We use *both* with plural nouns.

Both hotels are cheap.

We use *either* and *neither* with singular countable nouns. *Either* means 'one or the other'. *Neither* means 'not one or the other'.

You can buy milk at either shop.

Neither shop is expensive.

Note that we use an affirmative (singular) verb with *neither*. After a negative verb, we use *either* to mean 'not one or the other'.

Neither film was very good.

I didn't like either film. ✓

NOT I didn't like neither film. ✗

Using quantifiers with of

Most quantifiers can be followed by:
- *of* + *the, his, my*, etc.
  most of the time   a few of my friends
- *of* + pronoun (*us, them, these*, etc.)
  several of these   all of us   many of them

However, *no* and *every* cannot be followed by *of*. Instead, we say *none of* and *every one of* (followed by a singular verb).

Every one of us needs to help.

None of the shops is open.

Note that with *all, half* and *both*, the word *of* is optional when followed by *the, his, my*, etc. However, when followed by a pronoun (*us, them, these*, etc.) it is not optional.

all of my friends / all my friends

half of the students / half the students

both of his sisters / both his sisters

BUT all of us ✓

NOT all us ✗

1 Choose the correct quantifier. If both are correct, choose both.

1 I read **all / the whole** book in one evening.
2 There are two take-aways in my town but I don't like **either / neither** of them.
3 I used to have several memory sticks, but I've lost **all of / all** them.
4 A **great deal of / large number of** people attended the opening night of the show.
5 You can use **either / neither** laptop, I don't mind.
6 I went out last night and met **a few / few** friends in a café.
7 I wish I could have spent **some / any** time exploring the city.
8 By midnight, **a half / half** the guests had left.
9 My grandmother gave £1,000 to **each / every** of her grandchildren.
10 **Several / Some** of my friends play indoor football at weekends.
11 The exam was difficult: I couldn't answer **all / the whole** the questions.
12 Luke refuses to let **any / either** of his parents come and watch him when he's in a show.

2 Correct the mistakes in the sentences.

1 I have two cousins but either my cousins live here.
2 No football boots mustn't be worn in this clubhouse.
3 On holiday, I spent at least a half my money on taxis.
4 She has six cats and every of them is black.
5 We planted fifty trees, but very few them survived.
6 I couldn't find the trainers I wanted in none of the sports shops in town.

Unit 5

5.1 Passive structures

We make passive forms with the verb *be* + the past participle.

	A general election ...
Present simple	is held every five years.
Present continuous	is being held at the moment.
Present perfect	has been held recently.
Past simple	was held last month.
Past continuous	was being held when the former Prime Minister died.
Past perfect	had been held twice in the previous year.
will	will be held soon.
be going to	is going to be held next month.
modal verb	must be held before the end of the year.

G Grammar Builder and Reference

The passive is used to talk about processes.
The tablets are manufactured in China and then imported into Europe.

The passive is used when we don't want to say or we can't say who performed the action.
The cars are all fitted with sat navs before they leave the factory.

The passive is used when it is obvious who performed the action.
The suspect has finally been arrested. (Only the police arrest people.)

The passive is also used to put the main focus at the beginning of the sentence. If we want to say who carried out the action, we introduce the person's name with the preposition *by*.
This window was broken by someone in this class, and I want to know who!

Passive gerunds and infinitives
Verbs that are followed by a gerund, infinitive or perfect infinitive can also be followed by a passive gerund, infinitive or perfect infinitive.
I hate people following me. – I hate being followed.
I don't want people to criticise me. – I don't want to be criticised.
They ought to have cleaned this room. – This room ought to have been cleaned.

Verbs with two objects
If an active verb has two objects, either can usually become the subject of the passive form. However, it is more common for the indirect object to become the subject of the passive form.
They awarded me a prize.
I was awarded a prize.
(Less common: A prize was awarded to me.)

When the direct object becomes the subject in the passive, the indirect objects usually require a preposition, normally *to* or *for*.
They showed me a photo.
A photo was shown to me.
They built us a house.
A house was built for us.

Common verbs that can have two objects are: *buy, cook, pass, sell, show, send, write, deny, offer, promise, leave, pay, tell, teach,* etc.

Passive structures with *believe, know, say,* etc.
We can use a passive construction with verbs like *believe, claim, consider, feel, know, say, regard* and *think*.
The family is considered (to be) extremely rich.

We can use passives with an introductory *it* and verbs like *believe, claim, feel, know, say* and *think* to talk about things in a general sense.
It is claimed that the journalist made up the story.

Passive structures with phrasal or prepositional verbs
Phrasal or prepositional verbs can be used in passive constructions. Take care to keep the particle or preposition.
They put the meeting off until tomorrow. – The meeting was put off until tomorrow.

Auxiliary passive
With verbs with two objects, we can also sometimes use a passive construction with *have*.
They awarded him two prizes. – He had two prizes awarded (to) him.
The following can also become the subject of the auxiliary passive:
1 The prepositional object of a verb
   They read a story to the children.
   The children had a story read to them.
2 A possessive (*their, Peter's*)
   They took away Clare's driving licence for a year.
   Clare had her driving licence taken away for a year.

NB This structure looks identical to causal *have*, but *have* here is being used in a passive not a causal, active sense. Compare these two sentences:
He had his hair cut.
(causal: he chose to have it cut)
He had his watch stolen.
(auxiliary passive: he was the passive victim)

1 Complete the sentences. Use a passive gerund, infinitive or perfect infinitive.

1 I don't like _____ (tell) what to do.
2 Please check your change as mistakes can't _____ (rectify) later.
3 It could _____ (paint) by Van Gogh. It certainly looks like his style.
4 My dad was upset at _____ (not offer) a promotion.
5 The train is very late. It must _____ (delay) because of bad weather.
6 I hate _____ (watch) while I'm working.

2 Rewrite the sentences in the passive, using the underlined words as the subject. Where both objects are underlined, rewrite the sentence twice.

1 I was given this book by my mum.
   This book was given to me by my mum.
2 A friend gave me this book.
3 How much were they paying you per hour?
4 We'll offer the prize to the student who writes the best essay.
5 They owe me quite a lot of money.
6 They have appointed her head teacher.
7 They are sending the tablet I ordered to me by courier.

3 Rewrite the sentences to include passive structures.

1 People think that United will win the match.
   It is thought that United will win the match.
2 It is believed Kate was at home last night.
   Kate _____.
3 People said that he was extremely dangerous.
   It _____.
4 It is known that dinosaurs became extinct 60 million years ago.
   Dinosaurs _____.

5 French wine is often said to be the best.
It _____.

6 It appears that they didn't invite Joe to their party.
Joe _____.

4 Complete the second sentence using the auxiliary passive.

1 The company paid for all their business expenses.
They had _____.

2 They have confiscated Liam's passport.
Liam _____.

3 Someone lent Owen a DVD about volcanoes.
Owen _____.

4 No one has ever explained the passive voice to me.
I _____.

5 They refunded the full cost of the holiday to us.
We _____.

6 Has anyone ever stolen your mobile?
Have you _____?

5.2 Uses of *it*

We can use *it* to introduce a gerund, infinitive or clause that is the subject of the sentence. It is more natural and less formal than putting the clause or infinitive first.

	More natural than
It was fun going to the cinema with you.	Going to the cinema with you was fun.
It would be stupid to do that.	To do that would be stupid.
It isn't important whose fault it is.	Whose fault it is isn't important.

We can add *of* + noun to say who or what the adjective refers to.
It was mean of the teacher to do that.

It can also stand for a clause or infinitive that is the object of a sentence.
I hate it when you won't speak to me.
I love it that he's so willing to help.
I'd appreciate it if you'd reply as soon as you can.
I don't find it easy to solve maths equations.
You can leave it to Ted to wash the car.
We owe it to him to give him the benefit of the doubt.

We use *it as* + noun / adjective + clause or infinitive with *see*, *take*, *regard*, *accept* and *view*.
I take it as read that you weren't involved.
I regard it as a compliment that I was included on the guest list.

1 Match 1–6 with a–f using the words below.

if   that   to   what   when   when

1–e   I love it when you sing to me.

1 I love it   a you're in a bad mood.
2 I'd appreciate it b you'd stop talking for a moment.
3 I find it easy   c he hasn't phoned for over a month.
4 She thinks it strange d learn new languages.
5 I don't like it   e you sing to me.
6 It isn't important   f the result is. It's taking part that counts.

2 Complete the sentences with the correct infinitive or *-ing* form of the verbs in brackets and the words below.

dangerous   important   nice   pointless   safe   use

1 It was *pointless doing* the homework. Our teacher didn't even mark it. (do)

2 It's _____ _____ so fast on narrow roads. (drive)

3 It's no _____ _____ to study maths if you don't actually enjoy the subject. (apply)

4 It's been _____ _____ to you. We must get together again soon. (talk)

5 It isn't _____ _____ off that beach. The currents are very strong. (swim)

6 It's _____ _____ your schoolwork on time. (hand in)

3 Rewrite the sentences with *it*.

1 I appreciate the fact that he always texts me when he's on the train.
I like *it that he texts me when he's on the train.*

2 To arrive any earlier would be silly.
It _____.

3 She should tell him the truth.
She owes _____.

4 Swearing like that was very rude of him.
It was _____.

5 We will load the dishwasher.
Leave _____.

6 To run two marathons in a week is very tough!
It _____.

Unit 6

6.1 Relative clauses and reduced relative clauses

	Defining relative clauses	Non-defining relative clauses
people	who / that	who
things	which / that	which
places	where	where
dates	when	when
possessive	whose	whose

Defining relative clauses

Defining relative clauses give essential information about the person, thing or place in the main clause. Without this information the sentence would be incomplete.
That's the flat that we want to buy.
I met the person who is going to take over the department.
I've bought you the book which I told you about.

We can omit the relative pronoun when it is the object of the defining relative clause.
That's the flat (that) we want to buy.
I've bought you the book (which) I told you about.

Grammar Builder and Reference

Non-defining relative clauses

Non-defining relative clauses give non-essential information about the person, thing or place in the main clause. This extra information must always go after or between commas.

The Queen, who was wearing a blue summer dress, opened the new hospital in Manchester.

My car, which I bought last year, is always breaking down.

We cannot omit non-defining relative pronouns from the sentence. Neither can we use the relative pronoun *that* in place of *which* or *who*.

Prepositions in relative clauses

If a relative clause includes a preposition we can often choose to put it at the beginning or the end of the clause. If it is used at the beginning of the clause it sounds more formal.

This is the church in which we got married.

When we put a preposition at the end of a relative clause, we usually use *that* or no relative pronoun.

This is the church (that) we got married in.

When we put a preposition at the beginning of a relative clause, we use *which* (not *that*) or *whom* (not *who*).

The people who I spoke to were really helpful.

The people to whom I spoke were really helpful.

We always put the preposition at the end of a phrasal verb.

I met the man who set up the company with my father.

In non-defining relative clauses we can use *of which* and *of whom* after numbers, quantifiers and superlatives. We do this when we want to add information about part of something or about an individual from a group already mentioned.

There are four members in the group, two of whom I know personally.

She has recorded more than fifty songs, many of which have become hits.

They've made a number of albums, the most famous of which is American Idiot.

Reduced relative clauses

We form reduced relative clauses by omitting the relative pronoun and auxiliary verb that forms the verb tense.

- A present participle replaces an active tense.
  A lot of the people (who were) sitting at the table were my relatives.
- A past participle replaces a passive tense.
  The buildings (which were) constructed in the seventies are ugly.
- A reduced non-defining relative clause is always written between commas.
  The new bus, gleaming in the sun, drove off towards its next stop.

1 Rewrite the relative clauses in your notebook in a more formal or informal style.

1 The armchair which my grandfather sits in is an antique.
   The armchair in which my grandfather sits is an antique.
2 The person she owes her life to is a paramedic.
3 This is the restaurant about which I told you.
4 My aunt, who I have always looked up to, is a brain surgeon.

5 Our village, which the River Avon flows through, often floods in the spring.
6 Their son, upon whom they pinned all their hopes, has just dropped out of college.
7 The boys he went camping with were old friends from school.
8 Elisa is the person with whom I am upset.

2 Rewrite the sentences in your notebook using a relative clause.

1 The rail strike has been cancelled. It was planned for tomorrow.
   The rail strike, which had been planned for tomorrow, has been cancelled.
2 I only watched the film until the adverts came on. I'd never heard of the film.
3 His cousins were at the party. I had met all of them before.
4 We went through the exam questions. I'd got three of them wrong.
5 I was introduced to the members of the team. The tallest was the captain.
6 She gave me her old jewellery. The most valuable piece was a ring.

3 Choose the correct word to complete the sentences.

1 Thousands of people are in the streets **demonstrated** / **demonstrating** against the austerity measures.
2 The mushrooms **fried** / **frying** in olive oil and garlic were delicious.
3 We only buy vegetables **grown** / **growing** locally.
4 There was a long line of taxis **waited** / **waiting** outside the airport when I arrived.
5 Her new novel, **based** / **basing** on a true story, is a best-seller.
6 My brother, **wore** / **wearing** a chef's hat, was in charge of the barbecue.

4 Complete the sentences with reduced relative clauses. Use the words below.

cover / in snow   hide / under the bed
live / on the coast   park / outside their house
protect / by a cover   stand / on top of the hill
start / at 4 p.m.   summon / at the last minute

1 The film *starting at 4 p.m.* won an Oscar last year.
2 Our garden, _____, looked like a picture postcard.
3 My tablet, _____, didn't break when I dropped it.
4 Many people _____ had to be evacuated.
5 There's a removal van _____.
6 The final witness, _____, gave valuable evidence in the trial.
7 The mansion _____ used to belong to a nobleman.
8 I found my little sister _____.

Grammar Builder and Reference

6.2 Modal verbs: speculation

Logical deductions about the present

We can use modal verbs to express different degrees of certainty, probability or possibility about situations and events in the present and in the future.

We use *will* and *won't* to talk about what we definitely know.
Is that the doorbell? That'll be Matt's friend. He said he'd be here around six.
There's no point in calling my parents. They won't be home yet.

We use *must* to talk about what we logically deduce is true.
It must be raining. I can see people carrying umbrellas.

We use *can't* to talk about what we logically deduce is not true.
It can't be raining. It never rains here in July.

We use *should (not)* to talk about what we expect to happen / be happening.
It should only take us five minutes to get there.
There isn't much traffic, so we shouldn't be late.

We use *may (not), might (not)* and *could* to talk about what we deduce is possible. We don't use *couldn't* to talk about possibility.
Ben may / might / could oversleep tomorrow morning.
He may not / might not hear his alarm.

We use *can* to talk about what is generally possible.
Doing exercise can be addictive, if you're not careful.

We can use:
- modal verb + infinitive.
  She's always buying new clothes. She must earn a lot of money.
- modal verb + continuous infinitive (*be + -ing*).
  He must be driving. He isn't answering his phone.

Logical deductions about the past

We can use the same modal verbs, except *can*, to express the same degrees of certainty, probability or possibility about situations and events in the past. We only use *can* in questions or with *hardly, only* or *never*, e.g. *Where can she have gone? I can only have seen you once before.*

We can use:
- modal verb + perfect infinitive (*have* + past participle).
  It's strange that he hasn't phoned. He might have lost his mobile.
  Where's John? He should have been here ages ago.
- modal verb + perfect continuous infinitive (*have been + -ing*).
  You can't have been sleeping. I heard you talking on the phone.
  Her light was on all night. She'll have been studying.
- modal verb + perfect passive infinitive (*have been* + past participle)
  I can't find my wallet. It must have been stolen.
  Police think the money may have been taken by one of the workers.

1 Complete the sentences using the modal verbs below.

can   can't be   'll be   may be   might not   must be
should   won't

1 I can't call my grandparents now – they'll be asleep. They always have a nap after lunch.
2 Can you hear that music? The neighbours _____ having a party.
3 We _____ arrive at six o'clock, if our train's on time.
4 It _____ get very hot in Rome in August.
5 You _____ studying – the PlayStation is on!
6 I don't think you should get Mum that skirt for her birthday. She _____ like it.
7 I'm not sure if I'll be at home tonight. I _____ going out.
8 His new film is awful. You _____ enjoy it.

2 Complete the second sentence in each pair so that it means the same as the first. Use the modal verbs below and up to four other words.

can't   could   may not   must   should   will

1 I expect they've heard the news by now.
  They should have heard the news by now.
2 I'm convinced someone has moved my glasses. I can't find them anywhere.
  Someone _____ my glasses. I can't find them anywhere.
3 There's a chance my sister isn't talking to me. I think I upset her yesterday.
  My sister _____ to me. I think I upset her yesterday.
4 It's possible Danny's got lost. He's got no sense of direction.
  Danny _____. He's got no sense of direction.
5 I know Tamara has been studying all night. She's got an important exam today.
  Tamara _____ all night. She's got an important exam today.
6 I'm sure my phone hasn't been stolen. I remember using it when I got home.
  My phone _____. I remember using it when I got home.

Unit 7

7.1 Modal verbs

Advice

To give advice or to say something is a good (or bad) idea, we can use:
- *should(n't)* or, less commonly, *ought to / ought not to*).
  You shouldn't leave money in your hotel room.
  You ought to phone the hotel to check your reservation.
- *be better off (not) + -ing* form.
  You'd be better off using your credit card.
- *had better (not)*. We only use it to talk about this moment, not for general advice or the past.
  You'd better ask before you use his phone. ✔
  NOT ~~Before you borrow somebody's phone, you'd better ask.~~ ✗

- *must / mustn't)* to be insistent but friendly. In this context, we often use it with the adverb *really*.

  It's a wonderful film. You really must go and see it.

When we are talking about the past, we use *should(n't) have* or, less commonly, *ought to have (ought not to have)*.

You shouldn't have stayed up so late. You're too tired to work!

Expectations and conclusions

To talk about things we expect to happen, we can use *should* or, less commonly, *ought to*.

The package should arrive before the weekend.
The torch ought to work now; I've put new batteries in it.

To talk about things we expected to happen in the past, we use *should have* or, less commonly, *ought to have*. Often, the implication is that it did not happen.

My alarm clock should have gone off at 7.30, but it didn't.

To talk about logical conclusions we are making, we can use:

- *must* + base form. This structure refers to the present; it cannot refer to the future.

  She goes on very expensive holidays. She must earn a lot.

- *must be* + *-ing* form. This structure refers to the present or the future, depending on the context.

  Dad isn't home yet. He must be working late. (PRESENT)
  We didn't have our maths test today. We must be doing it tomorrow. (FUTURE)

- *must have* + past participle, when we are referring to past actions.

  Clara already knew about the party. Somebody must have told her.

  Note that we do not use *mustn't* for a negative conclusion (i.e. something we deduce to be impossible); we use *can't*.

  You can't be tired. You've only been awake an hour!
  Sue isn't here. She can't have got my message.

Obligation and prohibition

To talk about rules and obligations, we can use:

- *must / mustn't* in formal language.

  Spectators must stand behind the white line.
  Passengers must not speak to the driver while the bus is moving.

- *have to* or *need to* in everyday language.

  We need to take our dictionaries to the next lesson.
  Do we have to dress smartly for the concert?

To say something is not necessary or not obligatory, we can use:

- *don't have to, needn't* or *don't need to* in the present.

  You don't have to give the magazine back. Keep it.
  You needn't reply / don't need to reply.

- *didn't need to* or *needn't have* when we talk about the past. We use *needn't have* for something that happened even though it was unnecessary.

  Food was provided. I needn't have brought a packed lunch.
  (= but I brought one anyway)
  Food was provided. I didn't need to bring a packed lunch.
  (= and I didn't bring one)

Combining modal verbs

Sometimes we combine modal verbs when we want to express, for example:

- a conclusion about an obligation.

  She must have had to run to get here so quickly.

- speculation about an obligation.

  We may have to show our passports at the airport.

1 Choose the correct modal verbs to complete the sentences.

1 Our taxi hasn't arrived, but it **must / should** be here any minute.

2 This train only takes two hours to get to Liverpool. It **must / should** be an express train.

3 It **mustn't / shouldn't** be difficult to find a good restaurant in this part of town.

4 We **mustn't / shouldn't** have turned left at the traffic lights. This is the wrong street!

5 Misha **must / should** have arrived hours ago. I wonder why she didn't.

6 I think you **must / should** go to hospital immediately.

2 Complete the sentences with the modal verbs below.

'd be better off   'd better   don't have to   didn't have to
must   must not   needn't have   shouldn't   shouldn't have

1 Important: baggage must not be left unattended.

2 We _____ travel tomorrow; the tickets are valid for a month.

3 You _____ book a return ticket, you know – two singles are cheaper.

4 You _____ get on this bus; it might be the last one.

5 We _____ got off the train here. It's the wrong station!

6 You really _____ visit us next time you're in London.

7 She _____ pay for accommodation in Sweden because she stayed with friends.

8 You _____ paid for my ticket, but it was very kind of you.

9 You _____ hiring a car when you arrive in New York.

3 Rewrite the sentences using modal verbs.

1 It isn't necessary to take cash with you when you travel.
   You don't have to take cash with you when you travel.

2 It probably won't be necessary to carry ID all the time.
   You shouldn't _____.

3 It would have been a good idea to buy a local SIM card for your phone.
   You should _____.

4 It isn't a good idea to keep in daily contact with your family back home.
   You ought _____.

5 It's essential to carry a credit card for emergencies when travelling abroad.
   You must _____.

Grammar Builder and Reference

6 Perhaps it was necessary for him to leave his passport at the hotel reception.
He may _____.

7 It's possible that it will be necessary for us to pay in advance for the taxi.
We might _____.

8 It's impossible that he had to pay his hotel bill in advance.
He can't _____.

7.2 Talking about ability

Present

To talk about ability in the present, we use *can* or *be able to*. We normally prefer *can*, rather than *be able to*, when:

- we're describing a current activity.
  I can smell burning.
  The boat is rocking too much. I can't walk straight!
- it means 'know how to'.
  Can you juggle?
  Don't go too near the lake. You can't swim!
- we're using a passive form.
  The wheels can be removed.
  The tickets can't be exchanged or refunded.

Past

To talk about ability in the past, we use *could, managed to* or *was / were able to*. We use *could / couldn't* to talk about general ability in the past (not a single occasion).
She could read before she was four years old.
I couldn't ride a bike until I was ten.

We can use the negative form *couldn't* to refer to something we were not able to do on a specific occasion.
I couldn't find a seat on the train.

However, when we need to use an affirmative form, we normally use *managed to* when we refer to a single occasion. We sometimes use *was / were able to* in this context, but we cannot use *could* (affirmative).
I managed to / was able to get home in time for dinner. ✓
NOT ~~I could get home in time for dinner.~~ ✗

Note: there are certain circumstances in which we use *could* to refer to a single occasion. We use it:

- with verbs connected with the senses (*see, hear*, etc.) or with thought (*understand, believe*, etc.).
  I could hear every word they were saying.
- if the sense is negative, even though the form is affirmative.
  Before I could stop him, he'd picked up my bag. (= I didn't stop him.)
  I could almost afford a first class ticket. (= I couldn't afford it.)

Talking about possibility: *can* and *could*

We also use *can* and *could* to talk about possibility. We use *could* to speculate and *can* for general statements.
Taxis can be expensive. Buses are usually cheaper. (general)
Let's get the bus. A taxi could be expensive. (speculation)

Note that we sometimes use *can* for speculation in questions.
What can the problem be?

In conditional sentences, we often use *could* in place of *would be able to*.
If you left now, you could catch the last bus home.

1 Complete the sentences with *can* or *could*.

1 Jordan isn't here. He _____ be at home.
2 Why don't you lend Maria your tent? She _____ need it when she's travelling.
3 If we lived nearer the sea, we _____ learn to surf.
4 Buses are often late, because they _____ get stuck in traffic.
5 The rainy season begins in November and _____ often last for three months or more.
6 Your new coat has been ordered. It _____ arrive tomorrow.

2 Rewrite the sentences in your notebook using *be able to*.

1 They managed to reach the campsite before nightfall.
  They were able to reach the campsite before nightfall.
2 We searched for our tickets but couldn't find them.
3 My cousin can speak four languages.
4 If you practised more, you could play this piece.
5 When can your sister pay me for her ticket?
6 I'll let you know if I can come to the meeting.
7 Most people can't type with their eyes closed.
8 Can you reach my coat?

3 Correct the mistakes in the dialogue.

Lucy Can I speak to you for a moment?
Alex Yes, sure. What's the matter?
Lucy Nothing's wrong. But I'm trying to get in touch with your friend Tom and I'm not able to remember his email address.
Alex I could give you his phone number, if you like.
Lucy Thanks! Then I'm able to text him. It's about his hoody.
Alex The one he left at your house?
Lucy Yes, that's right. I had a look for it and could find it in the end.
Alex Let's call him now. He can be in town at the moment. We might be able to meet up.
Lucy Good idea.
A few minutes later ...
Alex I couldn't get through on the phone. But I managed to send a text. He hasn't replied yet.
Lucy OK. Well, let's play table football while we're waiting.
Alex Do we have to? I'm not able to play very well.
Lucy Don't worry. I'll teach you.

G

Grammar Builder and Reference

Unit 8

8.1 Emphatic forms

We add emphasis to written English by using special structures.

Cleft sentences

We can use *It is / was … that …* to emphasise different parts of a sentence except the verb.

Harry lost his mobile yesterday.
It was Harry who lost his mobile.
It was his mobile that Harry lost.
It was yesterday that Harry lost his mobile.

We can use *what … is / was …* to emphasise the object of a sentence. When *what* refers to the predicate of the sentence, we use *do* or *did*.

Kate sold her flat.   What Kate sold was her flat.

If we use *what* to refer to the predicate of the sentence, we use auxiliary *do*.

Kate has sold her flat.   What Kate has done is sell her flat.

We can use *all … is / was …* to mean 'the only thing'.

I'd just like some strong coffee.
All I want is some strong coffee.
He just smiled and walked off.
All he did was smile and walk off.

After *want* and *would like* we have to add *for*.

I just want you to tell the truth.
All I want is for you to tell the truth.

Other structures

We can use phrases such as *the problem / trouble / truth / fact / fact of the matter / question is*.

The problem is, he never tidies his room.
The fact of the matter is, you can't trust many news websites.

We sometimes use the auxiliary verb *do* in front of an affirmative verb. It emphasises a contrast within the sentence or an emotion.

I'm not keen on apples, but I do love a nice juicy pear.
We really do enjoy watching back-to-back episodes of crime thrillers.

We use the pronouns *myself, himself, ourselves*, etc. to add emphasis. The pronoun is stressed in speech.

'Did your brother help you with your essay?' 'No, I wrote it all myself.'
They themselves admitted their lies.

Note the difference between *myself* (= me, not someone else) and *by myself* (= on my own, without help).

We use certain phrases to indicate surprise or irritation, e.g. *What ever, Where on earth, Why in the world, goodness knows, whatever / whatsoever*. They are often used in questions or negative statements.

Why ever did you say that?
What on earth are you doing?
Where in the world are my car keys?
Goodness knows how he'll pass his exams!
'What did he say?' 'Nothing whatsoever.'

Inversion

Some negative adverbs can be used at the beginning of a sentence to add emphasis. In these cases the auxiliary verb is put before the subject. (See Grammar Builder 2.2 on page 136.)

They had seldom experienced such bad weather.
Seldom had they experienced such bad weather.

We use phrases such as *Not only … but also, Neither … nor, not until* etc. to emphasise two negative events have happened. (See Grammar Builder 2.3 on page 137.)

Not only did it rain all day, but it was also freezing cold!

1 Rewrite the sentences in your notebook to emphasise the underlined words. Use *it* or *what*, or both if possible.

  1 I admire your courage.
    It's your courage that I admire.
    What I admire is your courage.
  2 <u>Tom</u> broke the window, not Michael.
  3 George <u>worked extremely hard</u>.
  4 I miss <u>my grandmother</u> the most.
  5 <u>His laziness</u> really irritates me.
  6 They need to create <u>more cycle lanes</u> to make it safer for cyclists.
  7 Kate takes after <u>her mother</u>, not her father.
  8 <u>Josh</u> found my keys under the sofa cushions.
  9 We need to build <u>more affordable homes</u>.
  10 It started to snow <u>when we left the house</u>.
  11 I love <u>the way she smiles at me</u>.

2 Complete the second sentence adding emphasis.

  1 I just turned on the light and the bulb went.
    All I did was turn on the light and the bulb went.
  2 I wasn't completely honest with you. That's the truth.
    The truth is _____.
  3 Why did he steal the money? That's what we need to find out.
    The question _____.
  4 That documentary taught me absolutely nothing!
    _____ whatsoever!
  5 We didn't pay for the meal. We paid for the drinks.
    We didn't pay for the meal, _____.
  6 I'm really, really bored, and that's a fact!
    The fact _____.

8.2 *whatever, whoever, whenever, whichever, wherever* and *however*

We use *whatever, whoever, wherever*, etc. to mean it doesn't matter *what / who / where*, etc. because the outcome will be the same. As these words are conjunctions, the clause containing them can come at the beginning or in the middle of a sentence.

I'll marry whoever I like, whatever my parents think.
Whatever he says, it won't make any difference.
The weather was terrible in Britain, wherever we went.

We can use *whoever, whatever*, and *whichever* (as pronouns) to mean the person / thing / one that.

Whoever gets home first can cook dinner for the others.
Whichever team wins will go through to the final.

Grammar Builder and Reference

Grammar Builder and Reference

We can use an adjective or adverb with *however* to mean it doesn't matter how. When we use *however* with an adjective we can sometimes omit the verb *be*.
However hard I try, I can never beat Josie at chess.
I want a bedroom of my own, however small (it is).
However famous he is, I still don't want to read his autobiography.

1 Complete the sentences. Use *however*, *whatever*, *whenever*, *wherever*, *whichever* and *whoever*.

1 *Whoever* told you that was lying.
2 Don't be late for your interview, _____ you do.
3 The museum is open seven days a week, so we can go on _____ day we like.
4 I don't think I'll ever be able to pay off my debts _____ much I earn!
5 This window leaks _____ it rains.
6 I'll find my mobile _____ I've left it.
7 Try to stay calm, _____ happens.
8 _____ he explained it to me, I still couldn't understand.
9 John moved to a village called Lympstone, _____ that is.
10 The rules are simple. _____ team scores the most goals wins.

2 Rewrite the sentences in your notebook using *however*, *whatever*, *whenever*, *wherever*, *whichever* or *whoever*.

1 You can ring and have a chat any time you feel like it.
You can ring and have a chat whenever you feel like it.
2 The person who lives in that house must be extremely wealthy.
3 No matter which route we take, it'll take us at least two hours to get to Oxford.
4 No matter where Cathy goes, her little sister follows her!
5 No matter what you give her, she won't like it.
6 It'll cost us at least £300 to get to the USA, no matter how we travel.
7 It doesn't matter how hard I try, my parents are never satisfied.

Unit 9

9.1 Ellipsis and substitution

Ellipsis
We can leave words out when the meaning is clear without them and also to avoid repetition.

We often leave out a repeated verb or verb phrase and just repeat the auxiliary or modal verb.
Everyone seems to like this music, but I don't (like this music).
'Can you help me?' 'Of course I can (help you).'

We often use a different auxiliary or modal verb.
'I think you should apologise.' 'I already have (apologised).'
I know you don't think you'll pass, but you might (pass).

We often use more than one auxiliary or modal.
If I could help you, I would, but I'm afraid I can't.
'Did you tell the teacher?' 'Perhaps I should have (told the teacher), but I didn't (tell the teacher).'

We can leave out a repeated infinitive after verbs followed by *to* + infinitive. This is known as a reduced infinitive.
I'd love to go to your party, but I'm afraid I won't be able to.
'You really upset me yesterday.' 'I'm really sorry. I didn't mean to (upset you yesterday).'

We can leave out a whole infinitive after *want* and *like* when these are used after the conjunctions *when*, *if*, *what* and *as*.
Come for lunch if you want.
Stay as long as you like.

In ellipsis, the pronunciation of *to* and the modal verb is strong.

Substitution
We often substitute a whole positive clause with *so* after verbs of thinking, e.g. *assume, believe, expect, guess, hope, imagine, presume, suppose, think*.
'Do you think we'll get there on time?' 'I hope so.'
'Are you going to be home for lunch?' 'I think so.'

With negative clauses, we use positive verb + *not* with *assume, guess, hope, presume*.
'Do you think the teacher would let me do the exam again?'
'I guess not.'
'Will the airline give us a refund?' 'I presume not.'

We usually use a negative verb + *so* with *believe, expect, imagine, think*.
'Do you think your team will win?' 'I don't expect so.'
'Will you be late tonight?' 'I don't imagine so.'

1 Cross out the words that can be omitted from the sentences because of ellipsis.

1 All my friends have seen that film but I haven't seen that film.
2 A Are your brother and his girlfriend getting married?
   B They hope to get married.
3 I really thought we would win the match, but we didn't win.
4 I'm sorry for shouting at you. I didn't mean to shout at you.
5 You can stay over at my house if you want to stay over at my house.
6 I could have popped in to see my grandma, but I didn't pop in and I should have popped in.
7 A When are you coming to see us?
   B I'll come when I can come.
8 You don't have to tell me if you don't want to tell me.

2 Complete the sentences with the correct form of a modal, an auxiliary or a verb + *to*.

1 She said she'd write when she *could*, but I know she *won't*.
2 Help yourself to whatever you _____.
3 I'm not really into hip-hop, but my friends _____.
4 My little sister slept through the storm, but nobody else _____.

5 I can't afford to go Interrailing with my friends, but I'd _____.

6 Oliver wears glasses now, but he didn't _____.

7 The new sushi bar's amazing! If you haven't tried it yet, you _____.

8 I didn't go out last night, although I'd finished my homework, so I _____.

3 Complete the responses using the verbs in brackets and substitution.

1 A Are you having lunch with your grandparents on Sunday?
  B I _____. We usually do. (expect)

2 A If your grandad's having an operation, he won't be going home for a while, will he?
  B I _____. It'll take him a few weeks to recover. (guess)

3 A Do you think your parents will move when they retire?
  B I _____. They're perfectly happy living where they are. (imagine)

4 A Do you suppose the government will lower the retirement age?
  B I _____. If anything, they'll make it higher! (believe)

5 A Will you be going to your cousin's wedding in Thailand?
  B I _____. It's too far away. (presume)

6 A Your great-grandmother's 100 this year, isn't she?
  B I _____. We're going to have a party for her. (believe)

9.2 Advanced uses of the infinitive

There are certain special cases where we always use the infinitive with *to*:

After *only* to express a disappointing sequel.
They ran to the station only to discover that the train had already left.

We can use the infinitive without *only* and without any idea of misfortune.
I returned home to learn that my mother had purchased a new car.

After *the first*, *the second*, etc., *the last*, *the only* and some superlatives to replace a relative clause.

The first, *the last*, etc. can be used either by themselves or followed by a noun or pronoun.
She was the first in the family to get a place at university.
He was the only student to pass the exam.
Basketball is one of the most exciting sports to watch.

After nouns and pronouns to show how they can be used or what is to be done with them.
I've got a lot of emails to write.
Would you like something to eat?
You'll need a folder to keep photocopies in.

We use *too* + adjective / adverb + infinitive.
That jacket is too expensive for me to buy.
She speaks too quickly to understand.

We use adjective / adverb + *enough* + infinitive.
Our house isn't big enough to hold a party in.
We didn't play well enough to win the match.

After *so* + adjective + *as*.
We were so late as to miss the whole of the first act of the play.
That film isn't so interesting as to watch it again.

1 Complete the sentences.

1 The doctor has given me some medicine _____ take for my cough.

2 My mother was _____ only person to remember my birthday this year.

3 I'm not so lucky _____ to be able to pass my exams without studying.

4 They bought a beautiful vase _____ to drop it as they were leaving the shop.

5 We arrived _____ late to get tickets for the concert. It was sold out.

6 He was the _____ athlete to finish the race. The other seven finished before him.

7 There weren't _____ people to go on the trip, so it was cancelled.

8 August is the _____ time to visit Athens, because it's too hot.

2 Complete the sentences with the words in brackets and the infinitive form of the verbs below. Write four words in each sentence.

apply arrive buy go leave lose see travel

1 You need to spend at least a week in Rome because there are so _____. (monuments)

2 I'm not _____ about the future as _____ any sleep over it. (worried)

3 He spent ages on the essay _____ at home when he went to school the next day. (only)

4 John's in bed with flu. He's _____ to the party. (ill)

5 I recommend going by train. It's _____ way _____ to the city centre. (best)

6 I was early, so I was _____ at the meeting. (first)

7 We're only just going to make it to the airport. We won't have _____ any souvenirs. (time)

8 She's _____ student _____ for an American university. No one else wants to study abroad. (only)

Unit 2

1 SPEAKING Work in pairs. Take turns to do the task.

Student A: Compare the photos and say what disadvantages people who can't read face in life.
Student B: Do you think that children read enough nowadays?

2 SPEAKING Work in pairs. Take turns to do the task.

Student A: Compare the photos and say which job is more difficult and why.
Student B: Whose job do you think is most under threat in the modern world?

Unit 3

1 SPEAKING Work in pairs. Read the task and follow the instructions. Remember you have about two minutes to discuss the options.

Here are some different ways in which friends communicate. Talk to each other about the advantages and disadvantages of communicating with friends in these different ways.

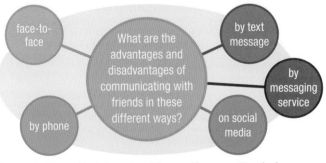

face-to-face

by text message

What are the advantages and disadvantages of communicating with friends in these different ways?

by messaging service

by phone

on social media

2 SPEAKING Work in pairs. Discuss the question below. Remember you have about one minute to reach an agreement.

Which of the methods of communication are likely to cause the greatest problems?

Unit 5

1 SPEAKING Work in pairs. Choose two photos and take turns to do each task.

Student A: Compare the photos. Say what skills these people might need to carry out their jobs, and what problems there might be recruiting people to do them.
Student B: Would you like to do either of these jobs? Why? / Why not? Which job is the most rewarding? Why?

Unit 9

1 SPEAKING Work in pairs. Read the task and follow the instructions. Remember you have about two minutes to discuss the options.

Here are some reasons why a person might choose to do voluntary work abroad. Talk together about how important these reasons are when choosing to do voluntary work abroad.

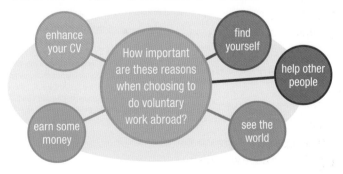

enhance your CV

find yourself

How important are these reasons when choosing to do voluntary work abroad?

help other people

earn some money

see the world

2 SPEAKING Work in pairs. Discuss the question below. Remember you have about one minute to reach an agreement.

Which two reasons are the least important when choosing to do voluntary work abroad?

OXFORD
UNIVERSITY PRESS

Great Clarendon Street, Oxford, OX2 6DP,
United Kingdom

Oxford University Press is a department of the
University of Oxford. It furthers the University's
objective of excellence in research, scholarship,
and education by publishing worldwide. Oxford
is a registered trade mark of Oxford University Press
in the UK and in certain other countries

© Oxford University Press 2017

The moral rights of the author have been asserted

First published in 2017

2021 2020 2019 2018

10 9 8 7 6 5 4 3 2

ISBN: 978 0 19 452051 5

Printed in China

This book is printed on paper from certified
and well-managed sources.

ACKNOWLEDGEMENTS

Back cover photograph: Oxford University Press building/
David Fisher

*The publisher would like to thank the following for their
permission to reproduce photographs*: 123RF pp.4 (girl
with stripy top/dolgachov), (Afro-Caribbean boy/Ian
Allenden), (fair haired girl/goodluz), 28 (young woman
studying/ammentorp), 37 (clownfish in an anemone/
divedog), 38 (two people running/Jacek Chabraszewski),
65 (cheetah/Bryan Busovicki), 75 (bike stand/nito500),
96 (bomb test/Warawoot Nanta), 99 (KuKulcan, Mexico/
Irina Schmidt), (Colosseum/Tomas Marek), (Easter
Island/Wasin Pummarin), 104 (university lecture hall/
kasto), 112 (countryside in snow/pixphoto); Alamy
Stock Photo pp.8 (painting/nuvolanevicata), 10 (couple
in a café/Mariusz Szczawinski), 14 (Walt Disney/
Glasshouse Images) 26 (*Woman in White*/Pictorial Press
Ltd), 34 (still from *Butch Cassidy and the Sundance Kid*/
Pictorial Press Ltd), 35 (Singh twins/Guy Bell), 49 (metal
head/Andrey Kuzmin), 56 (teenagers on Dartmoor/
Jonathon Short), 60 (fireman/Akhararat Wathanasing),
61 (nuclear missile launch/US Navy Photo), 65 (fighter
aircraft/David Gowans), 66 (Florence Welch/Geoffrey
Robinson), 68 (Clandon Park after fire/The National
Trust Photolibrary), 70 (Lincoln memorial/Eye
Ubiquitous), 82 (yoga/Dmitry Berkut), 87 (newspaper/
Granger Historical Picture Archive), 92 (Cola and Pepsi/
Lux Igitur), (KFC/RBflora), 93 (Dr Pepper/Newscast
Online Limited), (McDonalds/Fir Mamat), 103 (still from
I am Legend/Pictorial Press Ltd), (poster for *The Mist*/AF
archive), (poster for *Forrest Gump*/movies), (still from
Jurassic Park/Moviestore collection Ltd), 108 (historic
painting of three brothers/Igor Golovnov), (King Arthur/
Ivy Close Images), 116 (John Brown/Pictorial Press
Ltd), 119 (a scene from *Great Expectations*/Archivist);
Arnos Design Ltd pp.20 (book shelf/Dave Oakley);
Bridgeman Art Library pp.24 illustration (colour litho),
D'Achille, Gino (1935–2017)/Private Collection, 111 (*The
Seven Ages of Man*/William Mulready/V&A Museum);
Federal Bureau of Investigation [public domain], via
Wikimedia Commons p.88 (Ricky McCormick's note);
Folger Shakespeare Library p.110 (Yard Theatre);
Getty Images pp.9 (child at school/asiseeit), (kite/
Peter Cade), 12 (couple laughing/Flashpop), 15 (Oprah

Winfrey/Sunday Times), (Stephen Hawking/Dimitrios
Kambouris), 16 (meeting the bank manager/Peter
Dazeley), 22 (Gutenberg's press/Roger Viollet),
23 (camera lens/Vervitsiotis), 25 (Steven Spielberg/
Murray Close), 28 (reading newspapers on the train/
Image Source), (teenagers with a map/Yellow Dog
Productons), 28 (man doing DIY/Laurence Dutton),
30 (friends hanging out/franckreporter), 33 (Ben and
Jerry/Gareth Davies), 36 (oxpecker on a zebra/Richard
du Toit/Minden Pictures), 51 (skateboarder/Fran
Polito), 52 (coalition soldiers in Afghanistan/Jonathan
Saruk), 53 (Vietnam war/Keystone), 57 (demonstration/
Chung Sung Jun), 58 (blizzard/Kennan
Harvey), 60 (nightclub doorman/Mikael Vaisanen),
63 (man loading car/Blend Images – Terry Vine),
(woman in an office/Image Source/Dan Bannister),
65 (mountaineer on top of a mountain/AlexSava),
67 (Ferdinand Magellan/DEA/G.dagliorti), (Bessie
Coleman/Michael Ochs Archives), 71 (Martin Luther
King/AGP), 72 (child dressed as a pilot/andresr), (child
dressed as a doctor/Blue jean images), 75 (bicycle/
IlexImage), 78 (Arctic map/Dorlin Kindersley),
86 (Hugh Grant/Peter McDiarmid), 96 (alien/Matjaz
Slanic), 98 (playing guitar/Westend61), 104 (students
relaxing/Javier Larrea), 109 (King Arthur painting/
Print Collector), 112 (heart on misted window/Stefanie
Amm/EyeEm), 113 (clock/Bill Currie Photography),
116 (servants in India/Popperfoto), (US civil war/John
Parrot/Stocktrek Images), 118 (19th-century factory/
Time Life Pictures), 120 (statue of Sacagawea/Franz-
Marc Frei), 121 (Jack Kerouac/Fred W. McDarrah),
122 (Cold War/Charles Eshelman), 124 (space travel/
Detlev van Ravenswaay), (an alien/Mark Stevenson/
Stocktrek Images), 151 (Braille/Superstock), (book shop/
Matthias Ritzman), (librarian with books/Hill Street
Studios), (football referee/isitsharp), police officer/Peter
Dazeley), (ambulance driver/Caiaimage/Trevor Adeline);
Laurence Chandry and Geoffrey Getz p.42 (graph);
Jim McNeill p.78 (Arctic explorer); William Morris
[CC BY-SA 4.0 (http://creativecommons.org/licenses/
by-sa/4.0)], via Wikimedia Commons p.120 (Louisiana
purchase map USA); REX/Shutterstock pp.15 (Jay Z/
Startraks Photo), 29 (still from *Boyhood*/Ifc Prods./
Detour Filmproduction/Kobal), 52 (Taliban/Allauddin
Khan/AP), 54 (still from *Star Wars*/Lucasfilm/Bad Robot/
Walt Disney Studios/Kobal), 62 (traffic warden/REX/
Shutterstock), 64 (*Bucket List* film poster/Snap Stills),
101 (still from *Game of Thrones*/Helen Sloan/Hbo/Kobal);
Science Photo Library pp.11 (genetic engineering/
Richard Prideaux), 81 (warped clocks/Carol and Mike
Werner), 124 (robot/Victor Habbick Visions), (genetic
engineering/Laguna Design); Shutterstock pp.4 (boy in
white T-shirt/michaeljung), 5 (note pad/designer491),
8 (cloudy sky/prapann), 9 (carousel/Juriah Mosin),
14 (abstract pattern/vs148), 26 (background texture/
LanKS), 36 (bee on a flower/Jack Hong), 43 (exploding
world/Tund), 45 (computer tablet/Bloomicon),
46 (abstract pattern/agsandrew), 58 (free climbing/Greg
Epperson), (mountains/sabri deniz kizil), 60 (soldier/
NEstudio), 63 (bride and groom/Monkey Business
Images), 65 (kayaking/Mark Yuill), (scuba diving/Sergiy
Zavgorodny), 74 (learner driver/Monkey Business
Images), 75 (bike pump/kreatorex), 77 (passport/Maxx-
Studio), 91 (Wikileaks/IB Photography), 92 (background
swirl/Unscrew), 94 (woman with a long nose/pathdoc),
94 (fingers crossed/vectorfusionart), 96 (comet/
Alin Brotea), (robot/Ociacia), 100 (Earth with flags/
YadvigaGr), 102 (film texture/Vectomart), 109 (*Sword
in the Stone*/Fer Gregory), 110 (Globe Theatre/Kamira),
112 (red coral/Kristina Vackova), (secret agent/Stokkete),
(rubbish bag/Suphaksorn Thongwongboot), 113 (couple
in a field/seyomedo), 123 (eyes design/Who is Danny),
125 (burning book/Nils Z), 151 (children in class/
SpeedKingz), (Old Melbourne Gaol/ChameleonsEye);
SolarPix p.90 (Joe and Lisa Johnson); Superstock
p.68 (Clandon Park before fire/Stock Connection); The
Vivos Group p.97 (nuclear bunker).

Illustrations by: Phil Burrows pp.6, 7, 55, 69, 73, 89;
David Oakley p.114.

*The authors and publisher are grateful to those who have given
permission to reproduce the following extracts and adaptations
of copyright material:*

p.23 Adapted from '10 Most Courageous Undercover
Journalists' by Yvonne McArthur from http://www.
careernewsinsider.com. Reproduced by permission.
p.49 Adapted from 'Happy talk: How your language
shapes your brain and personality' by Megan Scudellari
from www.newscientist.com. © 2016 Reed Business

Information – UK. All rights reserved. Distributed by
Tribune Content Agency.
p.52 Extract from 'War in Afghanistan (2001–2014)',
https://en.wikipedia.org/wiki/War_in_Afghanistan.
The material is licensed under the Creative Commons
license https://creativecommons.org/licenses/by-sa/3.0/.
pp.58–9 Extract from *The White Spider* by Heinrich
Harrer. Reprinted by permission of HarperCollins
Publishers Ltd © 2005, Heinrich Harrer.
p.71 Adapted extract from 'Is Martin Luther King's
"I have a dream" the greatest speech in history?' by
Emma Mason, August 2013 © BBC History Magazine/
Immediate Media. Reproduced by permission.
p.87 Extract from 'Watergate Scandal', https://
en.wikipedia.org/wiki/Watergate_scandal. The material
is licensed under the Creative Commons license https://
creativecommons.org/licenses/by-sa/3.0/.
p.90 Adapted from 'How I fell for a secret millionaire
who only revealed his £10m fortune AFTER we became
engaged' by Amanda Cable, *Daily Mail*, 7 February 2009.
Reproduced by permission of Solo Syndication.
p.109 Extract from *The Once and Future King* by T. H.
White. Reprinted by permission of HarperCollins
Publishers Ltd © T. H. White 1939, 1940, 1958.
p.112 Extract from 'Sonnet', https://en.wikipedia.
org/wiki/Sonnet. The material is licensed under the
Creative Commons license https://creativecommons.
org/licenses/by-sa/3.0/.
p.113 Extract from 'Carol Ann Duffy', https://
en.wikipedia.org/wiki/Carol_Ann_Duffy. The material
is licensed under the Creative Commons license https://
creativecommons.org/licenses/by-sa/3.0/.
p.113 'Hour' from *Rapture* by Carol Ann Duffy.
Published by Picador, 2005. Copyright © Carol Ann
Duffy. Reproduced by permission of the author c/o
Rogers, Coleridge & White Ltd., 20 Powis Mews, London
W11 1JN.
p.115 Extract from *The Siege of Krishnapur* by J. G. Farrell,
published by Weidenfeld & Nicolson, 1973. Copyright
© J. G. Farrell. Reproduced by permission of the author's
Estate c/o Rogers, Coleridge & White Ltd., 20 Powis
Mews, London W11 1JN and The Orion Publishing
Group, London.
p.121 Excerpt from ON THE ROAD by Jack Kerouac.
Copyright © 1955, 1957, Jack Kerouac, used by
permission of The Wylie Agency (UK) Limited.
p.123 Extract from *Nineteen Eighty-Four* by George Orwell
(Penguin Books, 2004). Copyright © Eric Blair, 1949.
This edition copyright © The Estate of the late Sonia
Brownell Orwell, 1987. Reprinted by permission of Bill
Hamilton as the Literary Executor of the Estate of the
Late Sonia Brownell Orwell and Penguin Books Limited.
p.124 Extract from 'History of science fiction',
https://en.wikipedia.org/wiki/History_of_science_
fiction. The material is licensed under the Creative
Commons license https://creativecommons.org/
licenses/by-sa/3.0/.
p.124 Extract from 'History of science fiction films',
https://en.wikipedia.org/wiki/History_of_science_
fiction_films. The material is licensed under the
Creative Commons license https://creativecommons.
org/licenses/by-sa/3.0/.
p.125 Extract from 'Fahrenheit 451', https://
en.wikipedia.org/wiki/Fahrenheit_451. The material is
licensed under the Creative Commons license https://
creativecommons.org/licenses/by-sa/3.0/.
p.125 Extracts from *Fahrenheit 451* by Ray Bradbury,
copyright © 1951, 1953, 1967 by Ray Bradbury.
Copyright renewed 1979, 1981, 1995 by Ray Bradbury.
Reproduced by permission.

Sources:

Great Expectations by Charles Dickens
Little Women by Louisa May Alcott
Woman in White by Wilkie Collins
As You Like It by William Shakespeare
www.livescience.com
http://news.nationalgeographic.com
www.newscientist.com
www.history.com
www.bbc.com
www.poets.org
www.scottishpoetrylibrary.org.uk

*Although every effort has been made to trace and contact
copyright holders before publication, this has not been possible
in some cases. We apologize for any apparent infringement of
copyright and if notified, the publisher will be pleased to rectify
any errors or omissions at the earliest opportunity.*